library

P9-BTX-983

THE AMERICAN HENRY JAMES

The American

HENRY JAMES

BY *Quentin Anderson*

JOHN CALDER : LONDON 1958

813.4
J27Yand
1958

First published in Great Britain in 1958
by John Calder (publishers) Ltd,
17 Sackville Street, London, W1.
Copyright © 1957
By Rutgers, The State University, U.S.A.

PRINTED BY LITHOGRAPHY IN GREAT BRITAIN
BY JARROLD AND SONS LTD, NORWICH

FOR THEL

Acknowledgments

THE EXTRAORDINARY GROUP OF TEACHERS AND SCHOLARS under whom I was privileged to work at Columbia, at Harvard, and again at Columbia, makes rather too thunderous an index to my book. It includes Lionel Trilling, Jacques Barzun, F. O. Matthiessen, Perry Miller, and Dino Bigongiari. My colleagues and friends in the Department of English in Columbia College, Richard Chase, Andrew Chiappe, F. W. Dupee, Charles W. Everett, Joseph Mazzeo (now of Cornell), George Nobbe, John Thompson, Jr., Eugenio Villicana, and Robert C. Waddell, have given me much sympathetic attention and counsel. My friends, James Dinerman, Joan Doris, Elsa and James Grossman, James Gutmann, Diana Trilling, and Elzie Wechsler have in many ways helped, provoked, and encouraged me.

Among those especially concerned with Henry James and for whose generosity and discernment about James I have particular reason to be grateful are F. W. Dupee, Francis Fergusson, and F. R. Leavis (who gave me a hearing in *Scrutiny*). Mr. Fergusson had from the outset of my work seemed to me uniquely qualified to judge the thesis this book presents, and the discovery that he concurred with it was the realization of a cherished hope. I also wish to thank John Crowe Ransom and the late Philip Blair Rice for opening the columns of the *Kenyon Review* to my original article on James and his father, an act of considerable editorial boldness.

The chief of all these debts is that to Lionel Trilling, and since it is so largely the debt of friendship, inexpressible. But neither he nor the others I have named ought to be held responsible for what I have written.

Contents

Foreword

THE THESIS OF THIS BOOK WILL COME AS A SHOCK TO MANY
of Henry James's devoted readers. He was, after all, a
thinker, and he had a secret relation to a body of thought:
his father's combination of philosophy and psychology.

In spirit Henry James's father was an envoy from the
age of cosmic analogy—the unreconstructed pre-Cartesian
world in which symbols of human nature and destiny did
duty as instruments of investigation. Unlike Swedenborg
(from whom he got much of his impetus and most of his
ideas), he had no scientific interests or capabilities. Nor had
he any sense of the historical antecedents of his position.
This left him free to think in the mode of the Cambridge
Platonists and their predecessors. In his hands, universal
analogy was used to criticize the post-Cartesian world view,
and to proclaim a religion of consciousness. His anthropo-
centrism is thorough: Historical Christianity, nature, God
himself are all swallowed up in human consciousness. The
result is a characteristic mid-nineteenth century American
system, at once inclusive and parochial, quirky and cosmic.

What this meant to the novelist was that he did not have
to cobble up for himself a set of inclusive values and beliefs
about man and his destiny, as did Hawthorne and Melville.
He did not so much borrow as continue to employ a mode

of vision which had colored his childhood. That this was
both a great gain and, in certain directions, a crippling re-
striction will be apparent to the reader. James had, that is, a
past of a compelling and liberating order—so liberating indeed to his own genius that it is no wonder that recognition
of its restrictive elements has been long delayed.

The elder James had undertaken to detect our nascent
divinity in his neighbors and current events; Swedenborg
had talked with angels. The distinction ultimately appears
as that between *The Golden Bowl* and Blake's *Prophetic
Books*, for Blake had taken his Swedenborg straight. Neither
the elder nor the younger Henry James believed that any
power transcended the power of man's own mind and spirit.
Though it was a humanist's piety, it was a piety nonetheless,
and it involved assertions about the nature of man not
directly given in experience. The novelist could not sustain
himself without it, though he tried to do so at times. Nothing less would contain the range of his perceptions or supply
principles to order the very world in which he lived—a
world in which consciousness seemed the only datum.

So it comes about that emblems derived or borrowed
from his father's system of universal analogies must be identified for an understanding of *The Golden Bowl* and much
of James's earlier work. The bowl, the house of life, the
portrait, rivers, and the sea have an importance in his work
which quite transcends that ascribed to them by students
of James's imagery. These are not simply images but emblems representative of the principles which are thought to
order consciousness itself.

To establish this fact, one must juxtapose the elder
James's curious scheme with his son's works in such a way
that the reader is provided with a standard of relevance
which will enable him to participate in the process of judgment. Only a cumulation of such details can lead to conviction, because no evidence of relationship between analogical
systems is ever, in the scientific sense, conclusive. The reader

is invited to consider the evidence here presented and to form his own opinion. I suggest that he first of all recall what has seemed anomalous in James, for example, the conclusion of *The Portrait of a Lady*, the virtues attributed to Adam Verver, the over-intricate appearance of the later prose, James's insistence on the moral authority of Milly Theale. Then he may ask himself whether my thesis does not have the power to dissolve these very difficulties.

If, in the process of giving the novelist a father and a past, I have made him seem less imaginatively disposable or less a hero among artists, I shall plead that I have tried to make him rather more a man among the men of his own American time.

QUENTIN ANDERSON

New City, New York
September, 1955

THE AMERICAN HENRY JAMES

I The Bootstrap Myth

TWO GENERATIONS OF PASSIONATE AND INTELLIGENT READERS have made themselves at home in the works of Henry James. To take up any book of his is to be reminded of many good things that have been said about it and of James's own opinions and feelings about it; and, not infrequently, it is to recall particular hopes, beliefs, or theories which others have founded on it. But the impulse to make James's work the clinching exemplification of one's theory —about the artist, about art, of the prime importance of form, or of the prime importance of sensibility—seems, happily, to be lessening in force. F. W. Dupee, F. R. Leavis, R. P. Blackmur and others have contributed generously to an account of James which is less private, less interested (in the bad sense), and much more widely apprehensible than most of the earlier work. The good things that have been said have begun to fall into place as parts of a more ordered judgment; those who have opposing views are finding common terms in which to state their differences. In short, James now has a place in history.

This does not mean that history is about to conclude with James, but it does mean that those who write about him in the future will have to reckon with the historical figure now being described. This book is an attempt to place James as a moralist, a moralist of a particular sort, who emerged from a particular scene. The description it contains will not bring about a radical alteration in our general sense of his work; rather, it will clarify it, and make it more useful. In addition, it will give us a more coherent approach to just those novels which have proved hardest to treat: *The Sacred Fount, The Ambassadors, The Wings of the Dove*, and *The Golden Bowl*.

Henry James was a moral man in a simpler sense than we can easily imagine. We spend much time in the search for appropriate principles, and find few cases, whether in literature or in life, on which we can readily pronounce moral judgment. This was not true of James, who never had to hunt for canons of moral judgment, never felt obliged to derive his standards from an ideal of 'social responsibility' or a religion, and lived for over seventy years a life so steadily responsible, in both large and small matters, that we find it hard to conceive. In an age in which intellectual and moral leveling was the rule, he withstood the temptation to abandon the moral claims of literature: literature was the vessel and the exponent of the noblest qualities of life, of the qualities we seldom bluntly name, of courage, of justice, of charity, of personal honor, of that without which these things stagnate, the generous imagination.

When I consider what he finally achieved in the light of his paternal inheritance, I conclude that that inheritance was the necessary condition of his achievement; that it was precisely his father's view of the nature of man and of the human condition which freed him to become the artist we know. To understand how his father's beliefs and his own work are related is not easy. For example, the phrases he used to describe his most inclusive value are phrases most persons would nowadays blush to use, or would use in some Pickwickian sense: He was concerned with "the life of the soul," or "the life of the spirit"; he had what he found lacking in Flaubert: "faith in the power of the moral to offer a surface."[1]

Contemporary objection to such phrases is in one sense well founded; they seem too general to carry any precise intention or to denote particular instances either in conduct or art. Yet it is on just this question of how universal principles and particular forms are related that James's father proved most useful to him as an artist. James was free to use these phrases because he believed what his father had preached: that universals were to be found only in specific forms, such forms as the artist creates. The phrase last quoted exemplifies this neatly, for the "power of the moral" is felt by the artist who has faith that the sources of life shine through appearances, and it follows that James is pointing to the artist's capacity to give the moral life the form appropriate to it: the form of works of art. So assured was he that no one could connect his general moral intention with other men's commonplaces that James felt quite free to use such terms as "the life of the soul."

A passage on Flaubert, whom he greatly admired, suggests how far he was willing to go in applying a standard which might seem heavily moralistic to contemporary critics.

Let Flaubert always be cited as one of the devotees and even, when people are fond of the word, as one of the martyrs of the plastic idea; but let him be still more considerately presented as one of the most conspicuous of the faithless. For it was not that he went too far, it was on the contrary that he stopped too short. He hovered forever at the public door, in the outer court, the splendor of which very properly beguiled him, and in which he seems still to stand as upright as a sentinel and as shapely as a statue. But that

[1] *Essays in London and Elsewhere*, pp. 183, 156 (on Pierre Loti), 147 (on Flaubert). The phrase "life of the soul" is also employed, with reference to James's father, in *Notes of a Son and Brother*, p. 110. See also the discussion of *The Author of Beltraffio* in Chapter V, below.

immobility and even that erectness were paid too dear. The
shining arms were meant to carry further, the other doors
were meant to open. He should at least have listened at the
chamber of the soul. This would have floated him on a
deeper tide; above all it would have calmed his nerves.[2]

These sentences, from an essay published in 1893, point
to James's curious historical position on the question of
morals and art in the very decade of "art for art's sake"
and the symbolist movement. This innovator in fictional
technique was, even then, a moral anachronism, a product
of the American 1850's. The very conception of the house
of life containing the altar on which James laid his "shining
arms," of the sacred fount from which flowed the "deeper
tide," and of Flaubert's regrettable "erectness" he owed to
his father's resolution of a cultural situation far removed
from and quite incommensurate with those Flaubert had
encountered.

Here, on the question of the likeness of Flaubert's dedication to art—or Baudelaire's, or Verlaine's—to Henry
James's own, criticism has gone astray. Those who saw
society as massed against the artist were reacting to a grave
cultural crisis, announcing a division between the life of
the imagination and the preponderant powers of the century. James, however, was quite incapable of conceiving
of society as a set of alien powers arrayed against him or
against art. He never thought society in that degree "conscious" (and in this respect he may have been quite right).
Society might heave (as it does in *The Princess Casamassima*), but it was not as an entity truly going anywhere;
it might change, but if it did, the change would be due to
persons rather than blank forces, and it would represent a
good or a bad use of the creative imagination. James found
nothing else thinkable, and he was not hospitable to the
unthinkable. We must put quite aside the notion that
James was engaged, together with his European confréres,

[2] *Essays in London*, pp. 149–150. The figurative use of a house and
arms recurs in the essay "Criticism" in the same work, p. 265.

in preparing a stronghold from which the artist might carry on a warfare with *organized* philistinism.

During the last third of the century James was engaged in doing something so very different, so quintessentially American rather than European, that we have no terms in which to describe it. He was engaged in celebrating a triumph, the triumph of the vision of the moral life founded on personal freedom and unsupported by institutional props which the generation of his father and Emerson had elaborated. In this respect he was very nearly the contemporary of Hawthorne, Whitman, and Melville, each of whom, like himself, had worked out a version of tradition, a more or less complete apologetic, which, incorporated in their works, had served to define the very criteria by which they wished to be judged. [3] Far from being able to think of their relation to the morals and manners of their contemporaries as in danger of rupture, they had been forced to start with the premise that on their continent no such relationship had ever really existed. The triumph James celebrated was no less a triumph for being simply his own. He had found that his version of tradition worked at least for him, and in this measure had carried out his father's intentions.

In our eagerness to defend the artist against the pressures of the nineteenth century and our own we have associated James with a dilemma quite foreign to him. An altogether proper emphasis on his technique, on the discrete quality of his imaginative successes, on his effort to give each work its liberty by stamping it with his precise intention, [4] has been coupled with the erroneous assumption that he

[3] I have dealt with the question of American versions of tradition at greater length in the Introduction to *Henry James: Selected Short Stories*, ed. by Quentin Anderson, esp. pp. xv–xix.

[4] For one of James's declarations of principle on the "liberty of the subject," see *The Question of Our Speech, The Lesson of Balzac: Two Lectures*, p. 100. Also see "The Question of the Opportunities" (1898), reprinted in *Literary Opinion in America*, ed. by Morton Dauwen Zabel, p. 51.

was trying to cope with a threatening cultural situation in which, as a matter of fact, he was not involved. That his last visit to America and the coming of the World War seem to have led him to doubt the adequacy and efficacy of his beliefs would appear to confirm his peculiar insularity during the previous forty years.

Faithfulness to the demands of the given work was not, on the part of Henry James, a response to the ideal of art for art's sake, or an exacerbated reaction to the world's indifference; it was a principle derived from the value he attributed to human variety and spontaneity.[5] His commitment to these things was radical, was something that came out of the wells of his being, out of the past, and in particular out of the atmosphere and ideas of his father's generation. Yet some confusion on this point among James's readers has been inevitable. This confusion is due to James himself. He did not always qualify such phrases as "the illimitable alchemy of art,"[6] and his failure to do so, to state, when discussing his calling, what he took for granted as its basis, not infrequently leaves the reader up in the air.

There was of course a context in which he prized the variety and spontaneity which art served: the context was that of consciousness. This has been many times remarked, but not, I think, with sufficient emphasis on the truly metaphysical status which James grants consciousness. It is

---

[5] *Within the Rim and Other Essays, 1914–1915,* pp. 29–31, 90.

[6] The passage which concludes with this phrase helps to fill out the sense of my description of James's attitude toward morals and art: "Every out-and-out realist who provokes serious meditation may claim that he is a moralist; for that, after all, is the most that the moralist can do for us. They sow the seeds of virtue; they can hardly pretend to raise the crop. Excellence in this matter consists in the tale and the moral hanging well together, and this they are certainly more likely to do when there has been a definite intention—that intention of which artists who cultivate 'art for art' are usually so extremely mistrustful; exhibiting thereby, surely, a most injurious disbelief in the illimitable alchemy of art." (*French Poets and Novelists,* p. 256.)

very hard adequately to convey James's piety in this matter. F. R. Leavis has remarked on this point that to be conscious is simply the condition which makes art possible—or, one might say, makes possible the typing of this sentence. [7] But this won't do. Not only is it true that much that happens to our consciousness cannot be communicated to others; it is also true that many of the things we can communicate to one another cannot themselves be connected as parts of an inclusive system; and it is true as well that we never plumb the meaning of many things that are of the greatest immediate importance to each of us, for instance, our birth, our death, our filial or parental relationships. [8]

Art has many modes of acknowledging and suggesting these limitations, but the art of Henry James is wholly without them. James is truer than William Blake to a vision of the world as wholly the product of the human imagination. Of course no one can be assured that James was never frightened by the silence of infinite spaces; the point is that the bias of his fiction is a convincing testimony to his sense that in art one must deal with consciousness as if it were intelligible through and through. [9] This is far more than a way of setting him off from, say, Thomas Hardy; it means that we must permit him to prune our own sense of the world severely if we are to enter into his. A great deal of what is presumed to be middlebrow animus against Henry James is a legitimate protest on the part of people who simply do not wish to submit to this process. It must be acknowledged that to read the later works of Henry James is, not infrequently,

[7] F. R. Leavis, *The Common Pursuit*, p. 226.
[8] F. O. Matthiessen seems to suggest this in saying that James's works are "novels of intelligence rather than of full consciousness." (See *Henry James: The Major Phase*, p. 23.)
[9] Cf. *The American Scene*, p. 345 and the opening of Chapter IX.

to surrender one's own sense of life rather than to enrich it. [10]

In Henry James there is no hard or brute fact before which the mind pauses and retreats; there is no tragedy, if tragedy has to do with the ultimates of the human condition; there is nothing in men which women cannot fully understand, nothing in women which men cannot fully understand; there is no realized death or birth. Always and everywhere, what exists is what consciousness has interpenetrated, and what it has not, does not exist even as a difficulty. There are difficulties in plenty, but they lie in us, not in the conditions to which we are subject; if there be a metaphysics, it must be a dynamics of the soul. Existence is made up of the great community of those who are conscious or aware. William Troy, referring to James's story *The Altar of the Dead,* seeks to describe that community: "This sense of the continuum between past and present, between all who share the memory of a common experience, is now known to be at the heart of every religion in the world. For James it is a very real religion, although wholly without any theological cast. Or, if we prefer, he emerges as one of our great humanists, the greatest perhaps, because his humanism was grounded in such a rich tragic experience. And in that case, his altar— what would it be but the sometimes splendid and exultant, sometimes mangled and ignoble, body of humanity stretched out in imagination in time and space?" [11] Although I think "tragic experience" an unsuitable term, this seems to me an excellent figure with which to emphasize the role of consciousness in James. His work is less, or

[10] The chief of Gide's criticisms of James is that he writes about a world completely cognized (*The Question of Henry James: A Collection of Critical Essays,* ed. by F. W. Dupee, pp. 251–253).
[11] "The Altar of Henry James," *The Question of Henry James,* ed. by F. W. Dupee, p. 272.

other, than tragic precisely because the role of conscious-ness is what it is. His world is one in which dramatic situations are always prior to fated conditions, in which nothing is truly immutable, and in which, from the stand-point of the philosopher, all relations are internal; nothing, that is, is known save through its relations to other things.

What may be called the *primacy of consciousness* seems altogether too systematic a notion to apply to James, and foreign to our image of him. But its artistic consequences are both familiar and attractive; it is as a matter of fact one of the secrets of his appeal to us. At the price of a certain editing of our sense of the world we gain some-thing that we greatly desire. "We are in fact hungrier than we acknowledge, hungry to the point of indiscrimi-nate excess, for the substance of the moral life. What would it be like so to act that each thought, each gesture, floated on the tide of passionate conviction; that the very shapes and colors of our day were judged and assigned a place in the measure that they contributed to our unique yet communicable sense of the world? The texture of the prose of Henry James answers this question. It is the result of just such a passionate absorption and conviction." [12] James's scene is a scene which the imagination controls completely, no matter how complex it becomes. It is mis-leading to speak of James as both subtle and complex with-out making this qualification. He is both subtle and com-plex in the mode of Dante; these qualities in him relate to a total vision, the principles of which have a profound simplicity. There are important exceptions to this rule, but these do not inform us about the nature of that moral outlook which is peculiarly Jamesian.

To get at the roots of his vision we must turn back to the period in which the notion of the primacy of con-sciousness was arrived at in America—say from 1820 to

[12] Introduction, *Henry James: Selected Short Stories*, ed. by Quentin Anderson, pp. xvii–xviii.

1850. I should like to avoid the use of the term "transcendentalism" as the most general label for the attitude in question. Most of the existing analyses of transcendentalism seem to me to be somewhat affected by the genetic fallacy—its imputed origins outweigh, and are not commensurate with, its significance for those who are said to have professed it. For my limited purpose here I shall employ a term which expresses more clearly the nature of the most important goal of the transcendentalists and certain of their intellectual kindred, including the elder Henry James. Let us provisionally call what they fostered the "bootstrap myth." What Lowell suggested in dubbing Emerson a "Plotinus-Montaigne" (*A Fable for Critics*) was that he stood for a contradiction, an empirical or perhaps a "democratic" idealism. I should describe this species of idealism as attributing to individuals a capacity for insight into the nature of things so profound that men may be thought of in their plurality as incarnating an ideal order which will one day visibly prevail. Single and sundered as we are, we shall somehow lift ourselves by our spiritual bootstraps into a total order in which the qualities of *each of us* will somehow be preserved and be acknowledged by all the rest. [13]

The first point about this belief, of which the term transcendentalism suggests only a part, is that it is self-contradictory. How can an individual perceive an order that requires the collaboration of all other individuals to make it apprehensible? The contradiction is minimized, but not done away with by the interposition of an indefinite temporal span between the moment at which the experience of individuals as individuals is the sole index of reality

[13] For indications of how Emerson conceived of the power of diverse individuals to bring about a unity among men—an idealism in which the prototype of order is the mutual recognition of *moral* claims— see *The Complete Works of Ralph Waldo Emerson*, ed. by Edward Waldo Emerson, III, 70, 113–114, 215–216, 267; X, 352, 353.

and the moment at which, as Emerson puts it, we shall "meet again on a higher platform." [14] Initially, there is no such time interval in Emerson; *Nature* (1836), for example, does not temporalize the transition from individual awareness to immersion in what he later called the "Oversoul." This temporal emphasis did, however, appear rather early in Emerson's work, and grew increasingly important. If one puts the emphasis on the development of moral order in the individual—a growth which is expected to culminate in a true community—it is the bootstrap myth which is in question; [15] if one puts the emphasis on the capacity of individual moments of experience to attest to the existence or the possibility of such an order, it is the metaphysically transcendent powers of individuals which are in question.

Among the transcendentalists the two emphases were not systematically separated, largely because they were not concerned with the metaphysical implications of the authenticating moment of experience. If we are to understand Emerson (or Thoreau, or Whitman, or even the final metaphysical speculations of William James), we must consider the paradox of the individual who is somehow to be universalized and yet in essence remain himself. We must, that is, take it for granted long enough to see what needs it fulfilled. Why was order said to be either present or nascent in individuals and denied to existing cultural reality?

This question cannot be answered by bringing forward the array of notions from Coleridge, the Orient, German idealism, Cousin, and so on, which were employed to support the assertion. These importations filled a need, and were therefore adopted with various degrees of en-

---

[14] Emerson, "Friendship," *Complete Works*, II, 214. ("Ah! seest thou not O brother that thus we part only to meet again on a higher platform, and only be more each other's because we are more our own?")
[15] Emerson, "Experience," *Complete Works*, III, 70.

thusiasm and understanding. Had they been cherished as prime intellectual instruments rather than as "aids," [16] they would have undergone development at the hands of their users; and in general they did not.

The insistence that the fact of diversity promised unity seems to have had a native source. I wish to suggest that was a response to a social structure which could not in certain respects be taken for granted. These Americans were trying to reassert certain elements in their own past—to put old wine in new bottles.

Intellectual history need not be rewritten to establish those aspects of it that seem to have had a compelling effect on the elder Henry James and his two great sons. My hypothesis—the one which they at least seem to validate—in its most general form is this: The most percipient members of the generation from which the transcendentalists emerged tried to maintain, by individual and endlessly recapitulated assertion, the moral and religious sanctions which, for their fathers and grandfathers, had been institutionalized. They tried to stuff into the self what the society had ceased adequately to represent. What for Lowell and Longfellow seemed an adequate set of institutions, appeared empty to these men. Their situation was in some ways analogous to that which Weber described as characterizing the Reformation. Weber's rising Protestant class is held to have internalized certain sanctions which had formerly been explicitly the business of the priest in the confessional. What seems to have taken place in America is that, with consciences already thus burdened, the men of the 1830's and 1840's sought to bring into being a vision of a satisfactory earthly kingdom as well. I am not speaking of those who turned to Utopian experiment, or Fourier or the Catholic Church; or, more precisely, I am not concerned with them *after* they had fallen back on these ex-

[16] Coleridge's *Aids to Reflection* is the work most often cited as influential among American transcendentalists.

pedients. After they had done so they may be characterized as persons unable to bear the burden which Emerson, Thoreau, Whitman, and others sustained. Brownson and Ripley each found a public image of unity in diversity and clung to it.

But Emerson tried, in a more literal way than we acknowledge, to be his own church and state. He tried to do for himself what church and state had done for his long line of preacher ancestors. This is an attempt even more radical than it at first appears. We are prone to think of the interplay between individual and institutional life as a transaction between fixed quantities: the fewer institutional demands, the more individual freedom, and so on. But the elements are not fixed in this fashion. On occasion the functions performed by institutions have been taken over by individuals, and our own days are full of instances of the reversal of the process. Moreover, the assumption by the individual of certain cultural tasks may limit his freedom by imposing so much work on him that he becomes the monk of a very strict order indeed, living the life of a Carthusian individualism. This is the obverse of Emerson's self-reliance.

The capacity of individuals to incorporate a new kind of society and bring it into being, or the power of diversity to create unity, is one of the assertions of the bootstrap myth. But the supremacy of the individual over the coercive aspects of the environment—over pain, evil, and death itself—had to be asserted also, largely because the modes in which these things had been experienced in the church, the town, and even in the family, were held to be empty and destructive of individual growth. These lost or discarded ways of regarding pain, evil, death, and sex had filled out the picture of man's place in the world. How were they to be replaced or supplanted? It is pretty plain that Emerson had difficulties with these questions. But he did have a rather general answer.

This answer was derived from Sampson Reed or directly from Swedenborg. [17] The compelling conditions of human life were representations, symbolic exfoliations, of our existing limitations. Nature was a set of correspondences exemplifying our nature, not its own. These difficulties would therefore disappear when men changed. To explicate the ways of "the Ideal journeying always with us," we may look to nature, but only for an image of what wells out of the human spirit, for what originates within us. No man can afford to be a "hater of the wind," in Yeats's phrase, for the wind blows from him, and he alone can temper it. In Emerson's account of nature we find of course the same implicit dialectic between the eternal now and the promise of our future glorious union. The paradox of the bootstrap myth recurs and is projected in nature.

The most important consequence of the views of nature, society, and the individual which the primacy of consciousness and the bootstrap myth entail is, for my present purpose, their effect upon the sense of self. Under the pressure engendered by packing nature, history, providence, creativity, and political and moral sanctions into it, the self (as the writings of the transcendentalists represent it) becomes a species of universal register or "transparent eyeball" (the phrase is Emerson's), and the chance for a dramatic, an actively social life seems to diminish. One feels that among the transcendentalists the ordinary sustaining relations of the self, to wife, to children, to friends, are hardly represented; while with regard to its posited universality the self appears hypertrophied, as it does in Whitman.

It is at this point in American intellectual history that the elder Henry James steps upon the scene, vehemently denying that the self can perform all these tasks for us and praying for "deliverance from that puerile Pantheistic gabble which is fast strangling the higher faculties of the mind under the grasp of an all-devouring Imagina-

[17] Emerson, *Complete Works*, I, 113.

tion. . . ." [18] His Presbyterian youth and his schooling at the Princeton theological seminary had pricked him to rebellion against the figure of God as arbitrary and angry, while at the same time preparing him to criticize Emerson and his fellows. He described with passion and precision (and in Emerson's case, with tender solicitude) the disastrous moral consequences of transcendentalism, and the necessity of grounding the bootstrap myth on a different account of the self and its powers.

He was wholly sympathetic to the idea that all values must be found in and certified by the individual consciousness, and an established church or any sort of externalized conscience was as antipathetic to him as to Emerson. His sense of the divinity was that it was wholly involved in man—on this point he is both clearer and more emphatic than Emerson—but he did not regard this as a reason for honoring individuals. In the chapter called "Emerson," which William James printed in his father's *Literary Remains*, the latter observes: "One cannot be by nature universal and particular, or public and private, both, short of being infinite or creative, which man surely is not. [19] Yet each of us does possess an invaluable individuality which will be realized in the perfect society: "No one doubts that in every person existing there is a special aptitude to some divine end if we could only get at it, a special potency for some beautiful function which no other person embodies so highly." [20] And when the elder James permits himself to anticipate this era, he plainly parallels the Emersonian assertion that the particular power of each of us will be universalized; "The distinction which sense alleges between us and nature becomes completely wiped out in

[18] *Substance and Shadow: or Morality and Religion in Their Relation to Life: An Essay on the Physics of Creation*, p. 253n. (Cited hereafter as *Substance*.)
[19] *The Literary Remains of the Late Henry James*, ed. with an Introduction by William James, p. 245. (Cited hereafter as *Remains*.)
[20] *Lectures and Miscellanies*, p. 81. (Cited hereafter as *Lectures*.)

the higher fusion operated by consciousness; so that we feel ourselves expand as it were for the moment into universal dimensions and lap up all nature in the bosom of our individuality." [21]

When the apocalyptic society is realized, all nature will be imprisoned in particular individual forms; what is now public (church and state, for instance) will appear simply as a reflection of what is private, the hidden divinity of man. Meanwhile, we must not forget, as Emerson does, that this state of things cannot be brought about by the efforts of single and consequently *self*-assertive men: "No man can be truly himself as long as any inequality exists between himself and his fellow." [22] The student of philosophy may be reminded of Scotus Erigena, who was condemned for asserting that we would (in our individual worth) persist as so many points of light in God, thus by implication enriching His substance. The elder James almost always, and Emerson frequently, suggested that the final order of the world would be one in which the unique function each of us has would be combined with those of all other men. In the view of the elder James the result would not simply enhance God, it would *be* God.

But Emerson could not wait, so to speak, and often suggests that we are even now able to rise through the grades of being to a union with the One. The elder James found this irritating in the extreme; he could not understand how Emerson could employ two ideas which seemed to him profoundly antithetical. Nevertheless, he himself was forced into some inconsistency on this point, because whenever he tried to illustrate what the future divinity of the race would be like—how it would feel to "expand into

---

[21] *Substance*, p. 300.
[22] *Lectures*, p. 128. In *Remains* (p. 299) the elder James says of Emerson's opinion of the "State": "It was only in his enfeebled later years that he ever lent himself to the idea of society as its destined divine form."

universal dimensions and lap up all nature in the bosom of our individuality"—he tended to sound like Emerson. Yet the likenesses between them throw the differences into sharp relief. Emerson tended to ignore or to call unreal those very aspects of the existing state of affairs which the elder James thought a necessary preparation for the realization of the divine community. Emerson exhibited what James called a "profound incredulity" [23] with regard to church and state, as if they were already "dead" and man already divine. But if we do not see the preparatory significance of these institutions, we cannot understand how we are to be saved. "It is not true abstractly, or apart from fact, that God is life and gives life to man; but *really* true, or true to fact, true, *that is, to the experience of the creature;* and so far as it is untrue to that experience, it is manifestly not true at all. Man's rational development demands, then, a theatre of experience, by means of which he may become built up and established in the truth. For the truth being that God alone is life and the Giver of life to man, it is evident that man must strictly ignore it, until it become experimentally demonstrated." [24]

What the elder James says is "evident," will take a good deal of explaining, but the force of the phrase "experimentally demonstrated" may be indicated here: What is demonstrated to man must be demonstrated *in* society; the demonstration must lie in the individual's perception of his actual relation to his fellows. Nature and the existing society make up our "theatre of experience," and we must judge of its inequities on the basis of the difference between existing social relationships—based on self-righteousness—and existing attitudes toward nature—based on acquisitiveness—and the very dissimilar state of affairs which our hearts prompt us to wish for. The difference cannot simply

[23] "Emerson," *Remains*, p. 299.
[24] *Christianity: The Logic of Creation*, p. 24. (Cited hereafter as *Logic*.)

2

be ignored, the existing society dismissed—we are implicated in it—its inequities are simply our faults in magnified
form. Individuals cannot intuit the divine save as they can
envision the coming of the universal brotherhood, "the divine-natural-humanity," since it is only in this union with
our fellows that the divine can be realized.

At this point a summary of the differences and likenesses
between the elder James and Emerson will be useful. First
of all, both men insist on the primacy of consciousness and
are believers in the bootstrap myth. Men collaborate to
build moral reality, and from it all else flows. (The naïveté
they exhibit on the issues of philosophic idealism enables
them to be all the more thoroughgoing on this point.) [25]
As proponents of the bootstrap myth, both hold that we
must look to a future democracy of the spirit in which the
values of a spontaneous and pluralistic world will somehow be ordered into a grand chorus: The traits of each
individual (who is truly an individual) will be universalized
without interfering with the simultaneous apotheosis of
every other individual. [26] In the elder James this order is
the explicit end of providence, and we may trust in the
God within us for its realization; in Emerson it is the hope

[25] *Notes of a Son and Brother*, page 238, on which the son quotes
from one of his father's letters. I quote a sentence to indicate how
moral and metaphysical terms converge in meaning: "Precisely what
I like, to get extricated from metaphysics, its encouragement from
a few persons like yourself, such encouragement as would lie in your
intelligent apprehension and acknowledgement of the great *result* of
metaphysics, which is a godly and spotless life on earth."
[26] *Society: The Redeemed Form of Man, and the Earnest of God's
Omnipotence in Human Nature: Affirmed in Letters to a Friend,*
p. 183: "Dear friend, if men could but once livingly swing free of
these *personal* implications in their thoughts and aspirations towards
God: that is to say, if they could, even for a moment, spiritually feel
themselves as no longer visible or cognizable to God in their atomic
individualities, but only as so many social units, *each* embracing and
enveloping *all* in affection and thought: the work would be forever
done, as it seems to me." (Cited hereafter as *Society*.)

which makes individualism vigorous and legitimates our present refusal to assent to an imperfect social order.

It is this withdrawal, this refusal to acknowledge one's moral implication in the existing society, which the elder James condemns; in Emerson he finds it innocent, but highly dangerous. His exasperation with Emerson arose out of a sense that Emerson might, by a slight correction of perspective, be led to express his own conviction that as persons, men are nothing, that work, activity, is everything, so that the best man is exemplified in the artist, a man wholly sunk in his work, who makes no personal claims. When Emerson said "Trust thyself!" James winced, because Emerson might mean (and often did)—harken to the insights which come from the divine power within you; or he might mean (and often did)—the individual is sufficient unto himself; a sense of sin is unmanly weakness. The latter position, innocent though it might be for Emerson, was calculated to encourage self-righteousness in others.

The elder James believed that we have two selves, a false and a true self, and that the latter, our "spiritual individuality" (most generally our style), cannot now be fully enjoyed. Emerson had a giddy way of proclaiming that it could—that he had had the experience yesterday; or again, one might find him asserting that an atomized Lockean society had made such experience unobtainable for most men. The elder James was less giddy. If we are to be "true to the experience of the creature," we must steadfastly acknowledge that the society in which our spiritual individuality is to be manifested has *not* come. Finally, the elder James had to make an intellectual disposition of Emerson that would fit his own views; he concluded regretfully that Emerson was literally an innocent who had not even started to grow up morally; he was unaware of having any self at all. He was therefore unable to confront his present unsatisfactory self and begin the process of getting rid of it which culminates in the divine society.

This sketch of the views of the elder James will be filled out later when I examine the particular ties which linked him to his son, the novelist. Here I wish to posit my principal contention about the latter's American roots: To call *him* an American is to call him a son of the bootstrap myth; in other highly important respects he was, or became, British, but in this one his Americanism, though qualified and occasionally obscured altogether, was early acquired, persistent, and grew in strength with the years. It was hardly conscious filial piety which led him to adopt his father's version of the bootstrap myth, but rather a combination of temperamental inclination and his cultural situation. He did not go to Europe unequipped to meet the poignancy of its appeal and the weight of its massed cultural sanctions. No man could have survived such an assault and developed into a great artist without some version of tradition to sustain him; his avenues into his own past would have been blocked by denial and suppression, his palette muddied by unresolved conflict.[27] James remained *in general* an American; in particular, quite the reverse. An Americanism so generic precluded being *an* American, a particular voice in the great ragged chorus. Instead, it became an identification. The Henry James who wrote *The*

[27] See the chapter called "In the Great Grey Babylon" in F. W. Dupee, *Henry James*, for a somewhat different emphasis on the question of James's disposition of his personal resources as a man and a writer. One may say of the differences between my treatment and Dupee's that we have different goals. He wishes to determine the conditions under which *What Maisie Knew* and *The Awkward Age* became biographically possible, whereas I have undertaken the inquiry: What shaped the last three novels? The present study is concerned with the American attitudes which sustained James even after he had ceased to regard himself as an American in Europe. These, as will appear, seldom found explicit expression. They are described as aspects of James's psyche in Saul Rosenzweig's article "The Ghost of Henry James" (*Partisan Review*, XI, 1944, pp. 436–455). The writer finds Rosenzweig remarkably accurate, but incomplete and inclined to underplay James's own awareness of his character. These matters are more fully dealt with in Chapter XI, below.

American Scene had gone, so to speak, on a visit to himself, and the discovery of an America in some ways unanticipated brought on a final stage in the development of the artist. His sense of America had up to that time been precisely that it furnished spiritual admonition, which he figured in a fashion that is familiar to his readers. For example, he speaks of himself, in *Picture and Text,* as "haunted by a type," that of the young American girl. A fresh visit to America, given over to the observation of *American* particulars, led him to reverse his field. The generalizing eye he casts on Newport in *The Ivory Tower* reminds us much more sharply than James's works for the theater of the great tradition of comedy—this is, if I do not push such broad terms too far, his most "European" work.

As a thinker, Henry James is an exquisitely ordered version of the most general manifestations of the culture of his origin. The questions he raised in his work about the uses and the worth of possessions, the standards of individual accomplishment, the cultural ties which bind man to man, the function of art in realizing human potentialities, are all answered as his father had answered them. His sense of history is just as unhistorical as was his father's or Emerson's, and for the same reason. The past was a record of man's situation in the universe and an indication of his prospects; the actual plurality of pasts, the actual discontinuities, the sharp reminders of human limitation history contains, meant little to a man endlessly weaving a web of aesthetic and moral order. James's mode of recording the inescapable anomalies of human life, death, evil, and sex, is compatible with his father's and incompatible with a tragic view, or indeed any view which acknowledges the main stream of the Western tradition. In short, the middle term between the crudeness of James's ideas (for in any account that includes the achievement of European writers they must be called both crude and bare) and the fineness of his accomplishment is supplied by the context of American experience in which those ideas had originally flourished, an experience which justified their bareness and necessitated their crudity.

To put the matter historically: The Henry James who settled in Europe in the seventies brought with him a fully articulated attitude toward European culture, worked out in the household in which he had lived and among the people he had known—a theater of experience had been constituted for him. He never questioned the primacy of consciousness, his father's monistic account of the growth of moral order, the Promethean mission of art. These things fell in so well with the nature and needs of his talent; braced him so strongly against the rush of European sensations; were in fact a passport, the best America had devised, to the kingdoms of this world. Emboldened by them, he pitted the spontaneous moral sense of the young American girl against the massed sanctions of European society and dared to give her the victory. He came inevitably to his greatest theme, redemption, in a rendering "true to the experience of the creature." Europe was the only possible scene for such a redemption as the Henry Jameses imagined. It could only exist in subjugating the most complex and cultivated consciousness imaginable to American "good faith," without losing the least of the fruits of culture in the process (XVII, xvii-xvii). [28]

[28] This is the form in which citations from the New York Edition of *The Novels and Tales of Henry James,* New York: Charles Scribner's Sons, 1907–1909, 24 vols., will be made hereafter. Volumes XXV, *The Ivory Tower,* and XXVI, *The Sense of the Past,* were added in 1917, and the whole was reprinted in 1922. Wherever the text does not incorporate a reference to the title in question and the matter is relevant, a title or short title will be included in the note.

References to works not included in the New York Edition are to *The Novels and Stories of Henry James,* London: Macmillan, 1921–1923, 35 vols., or to the separate volumes in which they appear. Citations from the Macmillan edition will follow the same form as those from the New York Edition, with the addition of the word "Macmillan."

His father had also sought to show that the contrast between America and Europe was the chief contemporary illustration of a recurrent theological and philosophical anomaly: Mankind's moral consciousness is developing under providence according to a foreseeable pattern, hence we may judge no man and entertain no respect of persons; but only those who act from quite spontaneous and, in effect, antisocial motives are to be praised. We are familiar with this difficulty as a contradiction in the Marxist view of history, which is said to have an inevitable course yet permits of individual insights which affect its issue. The elder James found his version of this anomaly in St. Paul and embraced it: [29] Europe was steeped in the providentially necessary delusion that the works of the Law alone profited a man; America, again providentially, was the scene on which men had begun to realize that the Law was but scaffolding surrounding the glorious tabernacle of individualism universalized. It is this contradiction which provides the rationale of the "international situation" in the works of the novelist. Technically it was a godsend to his drama, affording not simply an opportunity for a realistic commentary on manners, but a chance to clothe in circumstance conflicts of an elemental sort: it became the basis of James's profound melodrama which employs aspects of human consciousness as characters. [30]

The "international situation" was of course liable to misapprehension on the part of his readers. They were prone to take his use of it too literally, as if he had meant to furnish a moral guide book, and he finally came to call it the "international fallacy," implying, I take it, that he had unduly narrowed its meaning in writing certain stories

[29] *The Nature of Evil: Considered in a Letter to the Rev. Edward Beecher, D.D., Author of "The Conflict of Ages,"* p. 148. (Cited hereafter as *Nature of Evil.*) See also *Moralism and Christianity: or Man's Experience and Destiny,* p. 139.
[30] See Jacques Barzun's essay "Henry James, Melodramatist," *The Question of Henry James,* ed. by F. W. Dupee, pp. 254–266.

(X, xvii).[31] The opposition of American spontaneity to
institutionalized European manners is a way of figuring a
conflict which all men must undergo, a conflict through
which we may reach what the novelist calls (in another
connection) a "sublime consensus." The American who
thought James was suggesting how Americans in general
were related to Europeans was badly mistaken The question for James was how to symbolize our relation to ourselves—how spontaneity in the given situation was related
to righteousness or greed. European manners and artistic
achievements came to stand for the realm of the particular;
American spontaneity and good faith for that of the universal. The antithesis turned out to be indispensable to the
artist. It gave body, gave dramatic and circumstantial significance, to the conflict within mankind. A *nouvelle* on the
scale of *The Beast in the Jungle* might represent this conflict stripped almost to its psychic elements, spontaneous
love and spiritual greed; might place its action everywhere
and nowhere. But the last three novels, in which the bootstrap myth found its Dante, required the density of symbolism which only the familiar can provide.

The contrast between European and American manners
is in this sense a device, just as the discrimination of James's
characters into men, women, and children is often a device,
for enforcing a point about our relation to ourselves. In
this sense we must qualify our assertion that James is
wholly devoted to his art—to the exclusion of a general
moral intention—by recalling that James's father never
tires of asserting that universal truth must get its living by
finding its embodiment in social and aesthetic form. It
cannot be revealed in any other way. This is what a rendering "true to the experience of the creature" means. It
is part of my purpose to show that James's morality did
not flow out of the demands of his art; that those who

[31] See also *The Letters of Henry James*, sel. and ed. by Percy Lubbock, I, 143. (Cited hereafter as *Letters*.)

think it did, make him less substantial and more anomalous than he is; and that the assertion itself stems from a failure to investigate his American heritage.

One ought rather to say that James was happy (to some tastes a little *too* happy) in the specific kind of freedom the bootstrap myth gave him. A conception of the world in which consciousness made all the differences exempted him from the tyranny of conditions, external compulsions, and from the unblinking pressure of the unaware. In the freedom he enjoyed he could chronicle every imaginable struggle of the spontaneous spirit with institutionalized manners without the acrid partisanship which beset those artists who cried up art for art's sake, or socialism, or the right to be decadent, or symbolism. His world, crude though its basis might be, was safe, because its dialectic involved everything he perceived in human life—it was total vision. All the aspects of humanity were necessary; we should have no Milly Theale without a Kate Croy, no America without Europe. He did not have to overlook any part of what he saw in order to celebrate what he most prized. To be able to believe, in his age, that the possibilities of triumph and defeat, of good and evil, of fellowship and hatred, all lay within the human spirit was his great strength, his secular religion; and in those years it was, as an individual achievement, almost without parallel.

To return to his great symbolic antithesis, and to put the question once more in the terms it affords, James could not condemn Europe because it had so thoroughly defined itself, in art, in letters, and in politics. Europe was one of the contraries without which no progression was possible. What he called the "extraordinary American good faith" could not mean anything until it had assimilated the wealth of culture, until its "desire for taste" [32] had been fulfilled, and it had incurred the guilt of acquisitive-

[32] *The American Scene*, p. 429.

ness. Nor could Europe escape its self-righteousness and its greed without that good faith. He felt confident that "the American, the assumed, the postulated, would, in the particular case of its really acting, count double." [33]

In *The American Scene* he is forever marveling in his teasing way over the quantity of things Americans take for granted. This is not a fresh observation; it is part of the bootstrap myth. The quantity taken for granted is precisely the quantity which Emerson had assumed we were all to possess, and which, in *The Golden Bowl*, James represents the world as finally providing. It is, in the end, "the extraordinary American good faith" whose bowl is filled to the brim; the cracked bowl of self-righteousness and greed is smashed. The posterity of the earlier generations of American tourists who were like "dispossessed princes and wandering heirs" (XIII, xix) was finally crowned and endowed with the vast objective complement of Europe's beauty, taste, and power.

That America's bowl should be filled, that all Europe should be tumbled (one hopes with some guidance from poor Charlotte Verver) into the temple of the muses at American City, is of course a kind of joking symbol too, for no such cartage was really necessary. [34] What was finally necessary was a reconciliation of man with himself, an ideal sufficiently familiar, but in Henry James, the novelist, not to be realized save on the terms his father had laid down.

[33] *Notes of a Son and Brother*, pp. 367–368.
[34] "The aesthetic need," as James calls it in *The American Scene*, p. 440, must somehow be fulfilled.

II *The Sources of Appearance*

THE LETTERS IN WHICH JAMES WROTE OUT HIS AMERICAN bias are often so large that they escape the diverted eye. The European of James's century would not have been disposed, as James and his compatriots were, to ask when discussing an acquaintance, "What has he made of himself?" The European would more likely have asked, "What's become of him?" What, given his birth, fortune, and talents, has the world done to him? Americans, as James fondly tells us, were forever holding people up to the mark—largely the mark of business success, but in the situations in which James found artistic profit, the mark of moral achievement as well. [1] Despite the fun James makes of the self-made man, [2] he is quite as ready as the most blustering millionaire to assume that a man is wholly responsible for his character. The characters who are the product of conditions are always at the periphery of his drama.

This does not mean, however, that his characters are lined up as in the schoolrooms of our childhood and asked

[1] In *The Ivory Tower* James rings an amusing change on this attitude (XXVI, 81).
[2] For example: the millionaire who orders the statue of "Intellectual Refinement" in *Roderick Hudson;* the "self-made" girl, Pandora Day (XVIII).

to show the shining teeth of those whose motives are pure. This is the fashion of New England and New England's fiction, the heritage of the Puritan preoccupation with the question of election. [3] It is the self-righteous who hunt motives. What James makes his characters accountable for is the use they make of their experience. Here, in brief, are the conditions of much of James's fiction: One must be "American" enough to be called to account for the use one makes of experience; one must have had enough of the "European"—have had enough of the realm of represented experience—if one is to make any use of it. There is a famous passage in James's biography of Hawthorne in which American poverty in this respect is detailed; [4] his description attains a more striking compression in *The American Scene*, in which he notes that there is not enough history in the country "to go round," and upon encountering a group of Indians in Washington, writes, "One rubbed one's eyes, but there, at its highest polish, shining in the beautiful day, was the brazen face of history, and there, all about one, immaculate, the printless pavements of the State." Where history leaves no impress on the state one may well speak of the people as fostered by a sparse social order, a "great blank unnatural mother." If we add "the truth that production takes time, and that the production of interest, in particular takes *most* time," [5] and note James's negative answer to the question provoked by

---

[3] James often used one form or another of the contention between Yankees and Yorkers to inform his moral geography. (*Notes of a Son and Brother*, pp. 86–87, 117, 188; see also his father's *Nature of Evil*, pp. 151–152, 173.) James generally found New England's self-righteousness more useful in fiction than the values obtainable from a more sympathetic treatment. Susan Shepherd Stringham's conversion to Milly Theale is archetypal (*The Wings of the Dove*). The pleasant genre piece, *A New England Winter*, is an exception.

[4] For the passage on Hawthorne's situation, see James's *Hawthorne*, pp. 30–31.

[5] This and the three brief passages preceding it are from *The American Scene*, pp. 346, 350, 415, and 148.

the Congressional Library—Can money create form?—his demonstration seems complete. America does not provide experience.

I mean, of course, represented experience, an array of manners, of settled social expectations, monuments, paintings, institutions, historically charged scenes. The list is familiar enough. What people on James's European scene do *with* the impressions these things make on them is the point. Simply to take possession of them, to "do" them as a tourist "does" a castle, is *not* the point. James's Europe appears to Americans in the guise of people who have been nurtured by it; who exhibit its effects. The American is like a child at the fair, though what he sees is not the Coliseum but people who have all their lives been conscious of the Coliseum. Or, to shift the figure, the American steps ashore and confronts his heritage; to confront it is only secondarily to look at it; primarily, James expects him to deal with people who are acting out its meaning. Let us suppose that he meets Maria Gostrey of *The Ambassadors* (XXI, 18, 35),[6] or Mrs. Assingham of *The Golden Bowl*, or Mme Merle of *The Portrait of a Lady;* he will find that each of them knows all there is to know about Europe; they have been so assimilated to it that they also feel that nothing really changes, nothing is transformed. To get at James's elemental contrast we simply put it that the spiritually American know that the world of *their* particular situation is unique. Characters who are in this sense "American" may be Europeans; contrariwise, the Mme Merles, the Maria Gostreys, may be American in origin, although they have ceased to be so in spirit. Since I am using a broad brush here, I will put it that in general the contrast between moral spontaneity and institutionalized manners involves Americans and Europeans respectively.

[6] See also *Mrs. Medwin* (XVIII), in which another of James's American guides to Europe, Mamie Cutter, appears.

What I have said so far may suggest that the uses Europeans make of experience are less subtle than those of which Americans are capable. Less loving, less generous, less creative, yes, but not less perceptive or less intelligent. Moral spontaneity does seem closely allied to the artist's endowment in James, but those who lack both, though their expectations be circumscribed, their vision limited by what they have known, are quite as capable of complex behavior in pursuing their aims as are artists or Americans.

It may also appear that I have *identified* European manners with experience, that what the American encounters is simply the rituals of another society. To dispel this impression I must amplify my description of what, for a Jamesian character, experience consists of. The first element in this description must take the form of a warning. Nothing is to be taken for granted; no such conception as "human nature" or "realpolitik" functions as current coin either for the character or James's reader. Nor does James permit himself reference to historical events or color which is merely "local." Whatever the work aims at doing, must be done within it. If we encounter a character who relies on such things as his class position, or takes a moral stand because "everybody" knows that it is the appropriate one, we may be sure that this character is not, in the Jamesian world, having any experience at all—he is morally dead. Moreover, the sense of the European world which one of James's works conveys may not properly be assumed in reading another; nothing, I repeat, can be taken for granted. Every story or novel—at least in James's intention—starts afresh, and even those in which James uses a sort of emblematic shorthand which does carry over from work to work do not depend on these emblems alone for the realization of their intention.

Second, everything which is presented in the story has a meaning for the story; we enter a world in which every glance, every overhead sentiment, every bit of embroidery or park bench is clamoring for attention as a meaning. Somebody in the story is responsible for it: he or she characteristically observed it, characteristically listened for it, characteristically made it or sat on it. Experience is *of* a series of meanings, not simply of impressions which one has to think about and turn into meanings—it comes to begin with as "significant form." Fond as James is of speaking of the pictorial as having a value equal to that of the dramatic, he set himself a rigorous standard governing its use—a standard which clearly subordinates it to the dramatic. The pictorial must be rendered as something that a particular character saw in a particular situation. It must not be used as something detachable which might be called "atmosphere." Here are two sentences from a story published in 1870, which James would not have permitted himself ten years later: "It was the middle of August, and summer sat brooding fiercely over the streets of Milan. The great brick-wrought dome of the church of St. Mary of the Graces rose black with the heat against the brazen sky." [7] The James of *The Portrait of a Lady* (1881) marshals his weather as he needs it and is not concerned with Milan as an object to be described.

What has not taken on form as a meaning for somebody, what has not been dealt with by someone's intellect, is not material for James's art because it cannot manifest life. The power of art is simply an exaggeration of the power of life to create form. Or, to reverse the emphasis, the power of art is that it strips life of excrescence and waste; the pure energies of life cannot manifest themselves except *as* art. Many instances of this tendency to assert art as the prime exemplar of life suggest themselves.

Children take more than one role in James's work, but they function oftenest as aesthetic objects representative of the moral quality of their parents. Arbitrary and even latently cruel as this use of children may seem to us, it was

[7] *Travelling Companions*, p. 1.

quite consistent on James's part. Children *are* works of art in a real sense, and James simply pushes the point a little further: Ideally reflective of the love and wisdom of their parents, children will, if these fail, become perverted or die. If we assign false or distorted meanings to life, these will be pictorially apparent in our children. Little Dolcino Ambient of *The Author of Beltraffio* dies of his mother's righteousness and his father's greed (XVIII, 21); Pansy Osmond is a perverted sacrifice to her father's self-love. Most of the *jeunes filles* we encounter and even the lost little American, Aurora Church (of *The Pension Beaurepas* and *The Point of View*), are sacrifices of the same sort.

It may seem that in seeking to define experience as James's characters have it, I have simply found elaborate ways of stating the famous Jamesian doctrine of the "point of view": nothing should enter into fiction except through the sensibility of one character or another. What this does not suggest is that there are two broad ways of *taking* experience, the way of the morally spontaneous and the way of those circumscribed by institutions, by greed, by a variety of life-denying impulses. Nor does the doctrine of the "point of view" make it clear that the consciousness of the lone Jamesian observer has a power not granted us—although James's own family came close to having it. Since this observer does not face any brute or unassimilated facts, or any merely public objects or events, what does he have in common with his fellows in the story? What he has in common with them is a universe, not of discourse merely, since forms and shapes too have meaning, but a universe of meanings which he and they have an almost magical capacity to detect; this applies even to those whom we might think morally or intellectually incapable of doing so. It is as if his fiction realized the conditions of his father's apocalyptic society in which each person embraces the spiritual intent of all other persons in some region uncluttered by space and time.

One more observation of this general sort: Since the Jamesian character is primarily responsible for his use of his experience, we may call him "American" in the measure that he recognizes that no instituted observances, no advices from Mrs. Grundy, no simply inherited loyalty to principle, can justify his behavior. His values must be re-created from moment to moment through his fidelity to the meanings he finds in his world. His world depends on this continual re-creation, as Berkeley's world depended on God's thinking it.

Of the boarders he encountered while staying in Palm Beach (the account is in *The American Scene*) Henry James found those who wore the look of "business success" the most easily discriminable: "Since there were no other sources of appearance," the rest had to be content with no definable appearance at all. To find such "sources" [8] in people's occupations, their professional idioms, and their regional marks is just what we expect the novelist to do. Balzac's enormous canvases are filled with just such details, and James wrote with high appreciation of Balzac's power to find in people's callings, their social tasks and social status, the roots of their attitudes and their actions. But the novelist who seeks to establish every detail in his work through the use that a character makes of the things that have happened to him in the course of the work itself is employing a method completely opposed to Balzac's; his sources lie in moral and psychological principles nowhere available to the social observer. That James could work in Balzac's vein we learn from a long series of his fictions. But he also worked in another way, dictated by another view of the "sources." I shall catalogue those works in which the first of these two modes is ascendant, and undertake a comparison between two novels representative of the two modes.

First, however, let us recall the properties of the second

[8] *The American Scene*, p. 438.

mode. What I call the "primacy of consciousness" entails
—on the part of those who *are* conscious—that accountability for our use of our experience which I have been
describing. If man makes his own reality partly through his
own efforts, partly through his capacity to recapitulate the
experiences of others as they are represented in art and
manners, the community to which he really belongs is the
community of those who are conscious and therefore responsible. All the rest of the world, both natural and social,
becomes a set of rootless appearances, by-products of the
achievements of those who are or have been conscious.[9]
The burdens borne by those who are in this onerous sense
conscious are heavy; the morally spontaneous or the artists
must be forever spinning their world into a web of meanings—a web as responsive as the spider's, so that a touch in
one place is felt in every other.

Henry James did on occasion permit himself to refer to
this view of the "sources of appearance." Most of these
passages in his letters and notebooks deal affectionately
with his own consciousness, which gives him a world so
much richer than the one he is ostensibly inhabiting. In a
letter to Grace Norton, he describes consciousness as an
"illimitable power." [10] Late in life he contributed to a
symposium on the possibilities of immortality and was led
to define its intimations, though hardly to plump for the
fact. These intimations are to be found in consciousness,
especially the artist's.

The point is . . . that in proportion as we (of the class I
speak of) enjoy the greater number of our most characteristic
inward reactions, in proportion as we do curiously and
lovingly, yearningly and irrepressibly, interrogate and
liberate, try and test and explore, our general productive
and, as we like conveniently to say, creative awareness of

[9] Or, as he put it to his amanuensis, Theodora Bosanquet, "simple
organisms." (Theodora Bosanquet, *Henry James at Work*, p. 24.)
[10] *Letters*, I, 101.

things—though the individual, I grant, may pull off his job
on occasion and for a while and yet never have done so
at all—in that proportion does our function strike us as
establishing sublime relations. It is this effect of working it
that is exquisite, it is the character of the response it makes,
and the merest fraction or dimmest shade of which is ever
reported again in what we "have to show"; it is in a word
the artistic consciousness and privilege in itself that thus
shines as from immersion in the fountain of being. Into that
fountain, to depths immeasurable, our spirit dips—to the
effect of feeling itself, *quâ* imagination and aspiration, all
scented with universal sources.[11]

This, if we like, is James's piety, and his "proof" consists
in the disproportion between what consciousness gives and
what he can "show." It would be amusing to trace here the
likeness between this disproportion and the "overflowing"
cups, springs, and fountains in father and son, but the point
now at issue is this: which of James's works do *not* reflect
such a view of the sources of appearance? They will
clearly be those works in which a radical commitment to
variety and spontaneity does not involve the writer in any
reference, express, implied, or emblematically figured, to
"universal sources." They will not be Emersonian or
"American" because they will not invoke unity as the
promise of multiplicity; they will not offer the artist or the
young American girl as the forerunner of an apocalyptic
union in consciousness—each embracing all.

The first group in such a list is of course made up of
prentice work, such stories as reflect the Hawthorne influence, for instance, yet do so with respect to superficial
matters only. *The Romance of Certain Old Clothes* (1868)
sounds like an addition to Hawthorne's "Legends of the
Province House"; *Professor Fargo* (1874) is reminiscent
of *The Blithedale Romance*; and it is not simply the

11 "Is There a Life After Death?" *In After Days: Thoughts on the
Future Life,* by W. D. Howells, Henry James, et al., pp. 227–228.

fictional atmosphere but the moral conclusions of this group which suggest second-rate Hawthorne. Others of later date (*The Ghostly Rental*, 1876, for example) might be added to this first group. A second group of still other early stories reflect an attempt to come to terms with the Hawthorne vision. They cannot be discriminated chronologically, by date of publication (it seems likely that James reworked some of his very earliest efforts and published them after he had in a measure outgrown them); what is apparent in this second group is that they employ Hawthorne's themes only to vary their significance. *Adina* and *The Last of the Valerii*, both published in 1874, have Hawthorne affinities which run deep. Yet the latter story effectually subordinates its "faun" (*both* stories have a figure reminiscent of Hawthorne's character in *The Marble Faun*) to his American wife, who has a moral authority which Hilda never gains.

Benvolio (1875) seems an attempt to throw a bridge between Hawthorne's chief concerns and the problems besetting the young James—who was chiefly occupied, it appears, with the question of the "right" and "wrong" uses of European experience by a young American writer. The dashing young Benvolio (an abstract sketch for the figure later realized in Felix Young of *The Europeans*, 1878) is both gay and deeply serious: "One was often idle when one seemed to be ardently occupied; one was always idle when one's occupation had not a high aim. One was idle therefore when one was working simply for one's self. Curiosity for curiosity's sake, art for art's sake, these were essentially broken-winded steeds. Ennui was at the end of everything that did not multiply our relations with life. To multiply his relations, therefore, Benvolio reflected, should be the wise man's aim." (Macmillan, XXIV,300) That we may "multiply our relations" we must be involved with the world, and even with the "worldly." Benvolio tells the Countess: "You represent the world and everything that the world can give, and you represent them at their best—in their most generous, most graceful, most inspiring form. If a man were a revolutionist you would reconcile him to society." (Macmillan, XXIV,309) [12] But when the Countess plots against Scholastica, who represents his commitment to his muse, Benvolio gives up the Countess. "Multiply our relations" we must, but we cannot do so under the banner of society itself. Society exhibits life, but it does not create it; it is the consequence of variety and spontaneity, but it is not the *source* of these things. That source is to be found in the poet's imagination. In Hawthorne the fear of the awful impersonality of intelligence is complemented by the only deep and abiding trust in the power of society as a great *existing* brotherhood to be found among our nineteenth century authors. In this story James turns on Hawthorne, saying in effect, "There is no need to fear the impersonality of intelligence—your awful scientists and reformers are just specters; intelligence is manifest only in *persons*, in style, whereas the 'great warm human heart' [13] with which you figure brotherhood cannot really be trusted at all." With the impulse to say something of this order to his first master, he, I suspect, took *Rappaccini's Daughter* and turned it topsy-turvy: Scholastica and the father who had trained her are wholly benign; they have separated themselves from the world on the world's behalf. Or, to put it flatly, the poet is the man who sees the world under the aegis of the imagination—incomplete as the imagination may be if it does not seek out the world. *Benvolio*, then, does not figure in the list I am now compiling, and it marks the end of James's Hawthorne discipleship, though not the end of the Hawthorne "influence."

Hawthorne, who greatly preferred to trust the world,

[12] This sentence, from a story published in 1875, presages the theme of *The Princess Casamassima*.
[13] Hawthorne's phrase in *The Scarlet Letter* for the court of last resort on moral issues.

as he knew it, to arrive in its slow, bumbling, and incomplete fashion at a sense of moral reality, was largely unintelligible to James. The moral vision of Henry James was at once more completely unified and more diverse; he found in social fact, not the hard floor of inescapable circumstance, but an array of symbols useful to depict spiritual flux, and was ultimately an Emersonian. The contrast is an enlightening one; it affords the clearest evidence that James was incapable of seeing an alternative to the bootstrap myth, even though it was given him in his most brilliant and admired predecessor. For Hawthorne the world was largely intractable to our purposes, offering conditions both foreign and fatal to us; while in James nothing is discernible save the triumphs and defeats of the imagination.[14]

Although I use the term in a less honorific sense than that in which James employs it himself, "anecdote" (X, xxiv) is a useful word to describe those stories with which I am not concerned here. Such stories are stories because the world has agreed on the interest of the chosen situation; its appeal is a public fact on which James relies. Another way of suggesting the general nature of this group of short fictions (although it is technically applicable only to those published after the seventies) is to call them "notebook" stories, since they characteristically employ some rather neat notion for a story and work it out in a fashion which does not startle one who has read the preliminary entry in James's notebooks. Many of the stories I have put to one side are very good indeed, but we are concerned with James insofar as he exhibits his "American" attitudes, and in this group these are muffled or absent.[15] The story which

[14] An able discussion of the relation between Hawthorne and James appears in *The Complex Fate*, by Marius Bewley.
[15] The stories I have in mind are *The Romance of Certain Old Clothes, Professor Fargo, The Ghostly Rental, A Landscape Painter, A Day of Days, DeGrey: A Romance, A Problem, Osborne's Re-*

clearly belongs in this category is one in which James has invoked a ghost, a daughter jealous of her father, a gorgon like Georgina Roy, a pretty inversion of the commonplace (as in *The Chaperon*, in which a daughter regains social standing for her mother). Such stories engage his talent, but fail to tap his hidden imaginative resources. He does his best work in the short story when employing the simplest of *données*. My stricture does not apply of course to situations which look like commonplaces in the notebooks and flower into something extraordinary—the first notebook entry for *The Golden Bowl*, for example—but rather to those situations the interest of which is predetermined for the reader and is not transformed in the course of the work.

The novels I do not propose to consider are of greater interest as works of art than a good many of the stories ignored here. It is a curious fact that those who cannot stomach James's American piety in extended form find themselves able to admire such *nouvelles* as *The Birthplace* and *The Beast in the Jungle*. Their preferences among the novels, however, mark out with precision the group I shall not treat. The list is an impressive one: *The Europeans, Washington Square, The Bostonians, The Reverberator, What Maisie Knew*, and *The Awkward Age*.

In general, a discrimination between the stories and novels I have listed and those which will be treated is a discrimination between those in which James takes the full burden of vision on himself and those in which he does not.

venge, *Master Eustace, Rose-Agathe* (also called "Théodolinde"), *The Diary of a Man of Fifty, The Siege of London, Lady Barberina, A New England Winter, The Path of Duty, A Light Man, Georgina's Reasons, Mrs. Temperley, Louisa Pallant, The Modern Warning, A London Life, The Patagonia, The Solution, Brooksmith, The Marriages, The Chaperon, Sir Edmond Orme, Lord Beaupré, Collaboration, The Wheel of Time, Glasses, The Great Condition, The Given Case, The Third Person, Paste, The Tree of Knowledge, Broken Wings, The Two Faces, The Beldonald Holbein, The Story In It, Julia Bride, Fordham Castle.*

Those in which he does not are "novelistic" in the sense that they depend primarily on attitudes assumed to be ascendant in the reader, or attitudes which the reader may be led to assume as the historically grounded attitudes of the time and place of the story or novel. The work in which we are forced to acknowledge that values are re-created in individual consciousness at every moment is a work with which I must deal; the work in which we may fall back on some sort of moral convention independent of it may in this place be neglected.

Both of the two possible "sources of appearance" give rise to fiction of high merit; both are responsible for second-rate things as well. A juxtaposition of an example from each class will make the grounds of my division clearer.

The Bostonians and *The Portrait of a Lady* fall within the span 1881–1886. They are different in a number of obvious respects, of which the American setting of *The Bostonians* is perhaps the most important. With the exception of the unfinished *Ivory Tower*, only three other novels have an American setting, and one of these, *Watch and Ward*, is rather a document for the student of James's life than an object for criticism. Another obvious distinction lies in the presence in *The Bostonians* of Basil Ransom, the only free-standing male figure in James's whole output. Basil has not heard of the necessity of redeeming anyone or subordinating himself to a woman, and he is nevertheless offered for our sympathetic consideration. It is perhaps less obvious that his antecedents are nearly as important as his actions in our judgment of him. Just as we are asked to believe in Olive Chancellor's Bostonian genesis, so we are asked to accept his Southern upbringing and his result-ant cultural "set" as in large measure accounting for him—accounting for him, not to the exclusion of interest in him as a person, yet in a measure which is reminiscent of Howells, or rather, Balzac, since Howells never contrived such a thicket of social circumstance as we get in *The*

Bostonians. Accustomed as the reader of James may be to characters whose substance is that of the tradition they represent (Major and Mrs. Monarch of *The Real Thing* are examples), he is hardly accustomed to finding such a character put forward as the representative of life, growth, and possibility.

The Bostonians is a surprising exception among James's novels, a novel which seems quite *open* to our inspection because it makes the assumption that certain traditions speak for life or for death; it neglects the characteristic Jamesian assumption that it is only within the presented experience of the characters that such values can be elaborated and chosen. Basil Ransom seems to come into the book from outside; there is a world outside—there are perhaps a number—and he has been chosen in part because he represents the one best qualified to cast light on the others which appear in the book. Again, Ransom has been determined to see what in a certain instance we want him to see—the waste of life which Verena's enslavement entails—but we are conscious that this is the sort of thing he *would* see, since he is from the South, the South of a familiar and widely shared fictional convention.[16] Olive Chancellor too has found at the service of her temperamental inclination a whole spectrum of conventions which may, although at the price of some distortion, be made the aids of a life-denying purpose; she is not fully responsible either, since her particular evil is so largely the fruit of a particular social soil.

In *The Bostonians*, therefore, we see James making a bold and assured use of novelistic techniques foreign to the chief assumptions I have attributed to him: (1) the primacy of consciousness, here supplanted by "given" social data;

[16] It is notable that James puts in Ransom's mouth a cultural observation on the "feminization" of the South which later crops up in *The American Scene*, pp. 401–402. See *The Bostonians*, Macmillan, IX, pp. 137–138.

(2) our accountability for our experience; (3) the grand division between the closed or greedy and the open or spontaneous ways of *taking* experience; (4) art as the primary expression of life; (5) that independence of moral conventions which leads him to create or to *re*-create them within each work; (6) the radical commitment to variety and spontaneity, which involves implicit reference to "universal sources"—the bootstrap myth.

The Portrait of a Lady is a novel in sharp contrast to *The Bostonians*. Its moral data are not "given," and it relies on no convention with which the reader is familiar. This does not mean that its conclusion—or those of the works which are like it in this respect—is something new, but it does mean that we cannot anticipate this conclusion. The grounds for this conclusion are wholly supplied by the book—it draws on no other world. The reader will recognize in this assertion about the book's moral basis a form of the critical commonplace about James's virtues as a writer. In James everything must be represented, and what is not represented does not count artistically. What I add is simply that it does not—with the exceptions we have been noting—count morally either. And just as James is said to make heavy demands on our sensibility, he may be said to be urgent with our moral sense, to demand of us that we be active readers.

To find our bearings in *The Portrait of a Lady* we must reflect at each stage of her career, not on what has become of Isabel Archer, but on what she has made of herself. We may say that the difference between what is required of us in dealing with Isabel Archer and what is required of us in dealing with Basil Ransom, Olive Chancellor, and Verena Tarrant is complete. Isabel's history is prefigured in the image of her speculation before the locked door of the "office" in Albany, but we cannot initially know this, and it is only after reading (and perhaps rereading) that we perceive that she has gotten in Osmond what she was foolish enough to imagine as desirable, an opportunity to be "exquisite." [17] This is what lay beyond the door, but nothing less than an earnest collaboration with the novelist will suffice to make it plain. In this work the sources of appearance are hidden—in *The Bostonians* they are, by another convention, made to seem apparent. It is not directly our affair to discover why, in particular works, "the struggle with the reader" [18] lapses, but I should like to indicate some of the conditions for a solution of this problem.

First of all, since the works which exhibit the assumptions I have catalogued begin to appear early in James's career, and works of the other sort persist to the end, no single line of development provides an answer. Second, I note that *The Europeans* and *Washington Square*, among the novels which may be classified with *The Bostonians*, have American settings, and that *The Reverberator*, although laid in Paris, employs, as do the other three, a society which is taken for granted—in this case the French aristocracy. Just as in *The Bostonians*, we have to do with certain constituted values, which the course of the book does not affect, which remain unchanged. Having gone so far, one perceives a suggestive anomaly. Is not the basis of the "international" stories and novels exactly this: that the mores of one society are contrasted with those of another? The answer of course is No; in fact, it is only in the open, or public, works that such contrasts are fundamental. And

[17] F. W. Dupee (*Henry James*, p. 122) calls Isabel a "*self*-seeker," an excellent term, though less invidious in his reading than in mine.
[18] Introduction, *Henry James: Selected Short Stories*, ed. by Quentin Anderson, pp. viii–ix. Cf. Edna Kenton's discussion of the "active" reader (Introduction, *Eight Uncollected Tales of Henry James*, p. 20). On the question of the demands James makes on his reader, an essay of Kenneth Burke's "Psychology and Form," is useful. I detach a sentence: "Or, seen from another angle, form is the creation of an appetite in the mind of the auditor, and the adequate satisfying of that appetite." (See *Literary Opinion in America*, ed. by Morton Dauwen Zabel, pp. 667–676.)

it appears that the best of these are actually confined to American settings. The international theme represents inner conflict; *The Bostonians, The Europeans,* and *The Reverberator* juxtapose conflicting cultural assumptions. James seldom deals with European society as such—he can so seldom afford to sacrifice it as an array of symbols. Moreover, his happiest attempts to handle a society are to be found in *The Bostonians* and *The Europeans,* novels laid in America. James's attempts to use European society as a fictional entity—not to "go behind" it—are generally less happy. This approach yields one great story (*The Pupil*), a light novel (*The Reverberator*), books of travel, and a number of inferior short stories. The travel books cannot stand comparison with *The American Scene,* a fact which seems to confirm the conclusion that the only society James could render on its own terms was that of his origin.

I think it plain that the relation between Europe and America as Henry James treated it, is at the bottom a relation between aspects of Henry James himself. When we discuss the international theme, we are in effect investigating the tension between James's American and European or "other" self. We must at the same time be conscious that his account of Europe was not simply private or arbitrary. I have taken pains to show that his sense of America was profound; his sense of Europe, although sharply limited by the role his imagination had assigned it, was, in virtue of the poetic precision of the part it played, apprehended with a firmness that reminds us of the way in which *Gulliver's Travels* grasps the England of Queen Anne. The open or public works show no such firmness. They offer us a margin for reflection and amusement; they seem almost abundant in piquant detail. (This is of course an illusion; the other works have just as much detail, but James will not let us play with it; he keeps it all to serve his overriding intention.) The oppositions which *The Bostonians* or *The Europeans* set up, that between New England and the

South, or between New Englanders and Europeans, owe so little to James's own imagination and so much to the popular imagination that we may describe them as books in which much of the imaginative *work* has been done by the culture itself. This is hardly to say that without James we could have had the delightful *Europeans,* but simply that the book amounts to a talented disposition of elements ready to the hand of Howells as well as James—ready to the hand of any American novelist of talent.

The contrast between *The Bostonians* and *The Portrait of a Lady* is so sharp that it is puzzling. Does my inversion of the meaning often attributed to the international theme help us here? It is said that the juxtaposition of America and Europe gave James an objective field, a fabric of tough social circumstances which his imagination went to work upon. I have taken the position that this process is indeed found in James, but that it is largely found in the American novels and their kindred, and that the international situation is from the beginning an invocation of the depths within us, or an account of inward conflict in which nationality has an emblematic function. If this be granted, the international theme is seen to have an ancestry in very early and somewhat uncertain essays in the "deeper psychology," such as *The Story of a Year, A Most Extraordinary Case* and *Watch and Ward. Travelling Companions* and *A Passionate Pilgrim* then appear as representative early attempts to give the "deeper psychology" an adequate poetic body by employing the array of symbols Europe afforded. The saturation of *Travelling Companions* with the moral doctrine of the elder Henry James serves as confirmation. James took his conception of the nature of man abroad with him; he was not provoked to formulate it by European experience. In fact, he never gave up the attitude toward Europe which his father had elaborated in his own published work.

I have quite failed to discover how James, having come

to write in the vein which runs through *Travelling Companions* (1870) and *The Portrait of a Lady* (1881), could on occasion shift his ground as radically as he does in *The Bostonians*. This novel seems to use as its point of departure a shared mass of social perceptions and judgments; *The Portrait of a Lady* does nothing of the sort. James does put our assumptions to work in this book—our assumptions, let us say, about the English aristocracy—but instead of relying on them, he regularly controverts them.

I leave this question to James's biographers, and proceed with the task of making its importance apparent. James's moral innovations—his employment, that is, of his father's version of the bootstrap myth—are present in those works which owe least to the techniques and conventions of other novelists; particularly the convention of the defined social scene of which the reader is presumed to have had experience, direct or vicarious. James is most original when he is exhibiting filial piety, though one can hardly say that the piety is the cause of the originality. He is a man set apart from both his naturalist and romantic contemporaries, since the naturalists sought to define the social scene with precision, and the romantics recognize it in the act of creating a fictional world in which its compelling character is denied.

James does neither of these things; he undercuts both, as had Hawthorne and Melville before him. He creates his own version of tradition to serve as frame for his art. He became, in the light of his father's work, one of the nineteenth century naturalists of the self, among whom Blake, Nietzsche, Goethe, and Stendhal may be numbered. The view of human nature with which his father had provided him was rather crude and constricted. But it was radical; it embraced a conception of psychic dynamism which undercut the traditions available in the novels of his day. And it carried him, at a bound, from provincialism to a very wide, though sharply edited, vision of man and his destiny.

James's version of tradition is what this book is about, although I seem to promise more than I mean to give in saying so. That the framework James employed was a wambly and transparent construction—like those which served Hawthorne and Melville—seems evident when we consider how disastrously it could at times affect his work. This question must be reserved for a later chapter, but I wish at this point to make clear my sense of the importance of the function which these versions of tradition fulfilled in Hawthorne, Melville, and James.

These three had to find elements in the common life of living Americans, and in the American past, which might serve as symbols of extensive reference. They chose with astonishing perspicacity, and though the very attempt to find such things on one's own hook may appear desperate when we consider the cultural situation of George Eliot, or that of Balzac, the record persuades me that their choices were not arbitrary. They made plain what was in the lives of other Americans obscure; and *what* they made plain turned out to be important to all Americans who were in the least exercised about their heritage and its preservation.

To name some of the things they chose is to open a chapter of American cultural history which cannot, in this place, be carried very far. Consider the part played by the journey as an epitome of life in the works of Twain, Howells, Henry Adams, and Henry James; by the young girl as the arbiter of values formerly watched over by organized religion in Howells and Henry James; or by the quest for an absolute in Whitman, Henry Adams, Twain, and William James. A theme still more general carries us back to Emerson and forward to the last American breath: What does it mean to be a person in a society which has largely transformed or discarded the old sanctions of class and Christian belief? This is pervasive among these writers, although it is more sharply defined as a theme in some (Emily Dickinson, for example) than in others.

What the Jamesian version of tradition meant in its specific applications will be apparent below. It is, however, important to note here that those critics whose preferences among the novels lie with *The Bostonians, The Europeans, Washington Square, What Maisie Knew,* and *The Awkward Age* are in my eyes ducking the problem of tradition as it affects James, since they are occupied with those of his works which are, in the sense suggested above, open, depending as they do on a spectrum of moral judgments and presumptions about the social scene which the reader possesses before he begins to read.

III "Father's Ideas"

IN 1885, THE YEAR OF THE PUBLICATION OF *A Little Tour in France* and the serialization of *The Bostonians*, Henry James received copies of *The Literary Remains of the Late Henry James*[1] from his brother William. The father they both admired and cherished had died in 1882. In his letter of thanks and appreciation Henry Junior is forthright about what had been called, in the family circle, "father's ideas."[2] Referring to the extracts William had selected from their father's work, he writes: "It comes over

[1] Brilliantly edited, this volume affords a foretaste of *The Varieties of Religious Experience* (1902), since William here views religion as primarily a personal experience. This emphasis was no doubt inevitable in the sons of such a father, whose religious sense was nothing if not an expression of his own character. However, the psychological categories William employs are, by contrast with those to be found in the work of his father, heavily moralistic. The title he gave the volume is somewhat misleading, since his Introduction is over a hundred pages long, and may be called an essay in filial apologetics. It presents his father as a man who had worked out an exceptionally appealing variety of theism, in that "it is monistic enough to satisfy the philosopher, and yet warm and living enough to speak to the heart of the common pluralistic man." The remainder of the volume consists of a fragment of an autobiography by the elder James, a draft of an unfinished work called "Spiritual Creation," and a brilliant essay on Carlyle, originally published in the *Atlantic*.

[2] *Notes of a Son and Brother*, pp. 156, 161.

3

me as I read them (more than ever before,) how intensely original and personal his whole system was, and how indispensable it is that those who go in for religion should take some heed of it. I can't enter into it (much) myself—I can't be so theological nor grant his extraordinary premises, nor throw myself into conceptions of heavens and hells, nor be sure that the keynote of nature is humanity, etc. But I can greatly enjoy the spirit, the feeling, and the manner of the whole (full as this last is of things that displease me too,) and feel really that poor Father, struggling so alone all his life, and so destitute of every worldly or literary ambition, was yet a great writer." [3]

This is, and was meant to be, a rather complete disavowal of interest. It is also plainly uninformed, since the elder James for many years before his death had not been much concerned about "heavens and hells," [4] though he formally granted a plurality of both. These regions may indeed have bulked large in the infant Henry's fancy, which must have found Blakean imagery by far the most arresting part of his father's spate of talk on these topics. It is in keeping with this sense of his remoteness from his father's "system" that he speaks of the elder James's originality, his sometimes deplorable, though often admirable, "manner," and his greatness as a *writer*.

The question William raised for Henry in putting together the *Literary Remains* is hardly the one William had posed himself. We may imagine William to have asked: "What capacity for seizing the flux of experience in discussable terms did my father have?" But the novelist (who was not concerned with his father's technical competence in philosophy) makes a response to the *Literary Remains* which is really a response to the question, "May my father be called a writer, a person who makes solid, grace-

---

[3] *Letters*, I, 111–112.
[4] See the reference to the physical appearance and titles of the elder James's Swedenborgian library, *Notes of a Son and Brother*, p. 158.

ful, appealing, his rendering of experience?" Henry has found a tactful way of replying, but he has not even conceived of William's question. And he is *not* "sure that the keynote of nature is humanity": precisely the view that I have attributed to him. He doesn't "go in for" religion, and that seems to be that.

Yet, when one turns to *A Small Boy and Others* (1913) and *Notes of a Son and Brother* (1914), one finds that the matter is a good deal more complicated. The period which James calls *The Middle Years*,[5] is long over, and James's sense of his father's work and the part his father had played in his childhood and youth testifies to a grasp of his father's most general intentions which, in the middle years, he had not explicitly acknowledged. The two volumes of reminiscences make it plain to those who know the elder James's work that it was finally Henry, not William, who best understood his father's spirit.

The view of the elder James that one might expect from the child of the "visiting mind" and from the youth who wanted to be a writer is clearly expressed in a number of places. The following passage concerns the fact that the family did not in any way publicly celebrate the faith which so pervaded the family atmosphere: "Well do I remember . . . how I was troubled all along by just this particular crookedness of our being so extremely religious without having, as it were, anything in the least classified or striking to show for it; so that the measure of otherworldliness pervading our premises was rather a waste, though at the same time oddly enough a congestion—projecting outwardly as it did no single one of those usual symptoms of propriety any of which, gathered at a venture from the general prospect, might by my sense have served: I shouldn't have been particular, I thought, as to the

[5] The title of James's unfinished third volume of reminiscences, issued in 1917. All three volumes have been reprinted as the *Autobiography of Henry James*, ed. by F. W. Dupee.

selection." [6] The child, as well as the man, hungered for things *represented*—things which asserted themselves with a "European" salience.[7]

The oddity of my own case, as I make it out so far as it involved a confused criticism, was that my small uneasy mind, bulging and tightening in the wrong, or at least in unnatural and unexpected, places, like a little jacket ill cut or ill sewn, attached its gaping view, as I have already more than enough noted, to things and persons, objects and aspects, frivolities all, I dare say I was willing to grant, compared with whatever manifestations of the serious, these being by need, apparently, the abstract; and that in fine I should have been thankful for a state of faith, a conviction of the Divine, an interpretation of the universe—anything one might have made bold to call it—which would have supplied more features or appearances. Feeling myself "after" persons so much more than after anything else—to recur to that side of my earliest and most constant consciousness which might have been judged most deplorable [8]—I take it that I found the sphere of our more nobly suppositious habitation too imperceptibly peopled; whereas the religious life of every other family that could boast of any such (and what family didn't boast?) affected my fancy as with a social and material crowdedness.[9]

All this has the note of the deprivation we might have expected James as child and youth to feel. He felt that the "sources" were superabundant, the "appearances" meager. But at the time of the writing of these reminiscences, the question of the "sources" wears a different face. In a passage immediately preceding the first of those quoted above he says that "such invidious homes," homes, that is, where religious observances took on apparent form, "under

[6] *Notes of a Son and Brother*, p. 167.
[7] The marvelous romance of "Europe" is one of the prime themes of *A Small Boy and Others*.
[8] That is, by his father, who denounced a "respect of persons."
[9] *Notes of a Son and Brother*, p. 169.

my subsequent observation of life, affect me as so much bleak penury or domestic desert where these things of the spirit, these genialities of faith were concerned." And in an earlier passage in his *Notes* he puts the emphasis where it was finally to rest for him.

It was a luxury, I to-day see, to have all the benefit of his intellectual and spiritual, his religious, his philosophic and his social passion, without ever feeling the pressure of it to our direct irritation or discomfort. It would perhaps more truly figure the relation in which he left us to these things [10] to have likened our opportunities rather to so many scattered glasses of the liquor of faith, poured-out cups stood about for our either sipping or draining down or leaving alone, in the measure of our thirst, our curiosity or our strength of head and heart. If there was much leaving alone in us—and I freely confess that so far as the taking any of it all "straight" went, my lips rarely adventured—this was doubtless because we drank so largely at the source itself, the personally overflowing and irrigating.[11]

Just what James had in this way absorbed I shall try to show; my present concern, however, is with the meaning of his disavowal of interest in 1885.

His letter to William, with its emphasis upon his father's comparative success as a writer, provides a biographic clue which takes us back to the *Notes of a Son and Brother*. Conscious as critics and biographers have been of the rather overwhelming character of the paternal inheritance of William and Henry James, they have not in the case of the younger Henry emphasized the particular embarrassment of his father's influence as he himself emphasized it. James notes his own "detachment of sensibility from everything, everything, that is, in the way of great relations, as

[10] On the previous page (156) James had compared "father's ideas" to so many gold coins left about "to be 'taken' or not according to our sense and delicacy. . . ."
[11] *Notes of a Son and Brother*, p. 157.

to which our father's emphasis was richest." The next passage incorporates both his youthful sense of an activity on his father's part competitive with his own, and his matured sense of his father's capacity for "active observation and contact."

There was the dim dissociation, there my comparative poverty, or call it even frivolity, of instinct: I gaped imaginatively, as it were to such a different set of relations. I couldn't have framed stories that would have succeeded in involving the least of the relations that seemed most present to *him;* while those most present to myself, that is more complementary to whatever it was I thought of as humanly most interesting, attaching, inviting, were the ones his schemes of importances seemed virtually to do without. Didn't I discern in this from the first a kind of implied snub to the significance of mine?—so that, in the blest absence of "pressure" which I just sought here passingly to celebrate, I could brood to my heart's content on the so conceivable alternative of a field of exposure crammed with those objective appearances that my faculty seemed alone fitted to grasp. In which there was ever the small torment of the fact—though I don't quite see today why it should not have been of a purely pleasant irritation—that what our parent most overflowed with was just the brave contradiction or opposition between all his parts, a thing which made for perfect variety, which he carried ever so easily and brightly, and which would have put one no less in the wrong had one accused him of knowing only the abstract (as I was so complacently and invidiously disposed to name it) than if one had foolishly remarked on his living and concluding without it. But I have already made clear his great mixed range—which of course couldn't *not* have been the sign of a mind conceiving our very own breathing humanity in its every fibre the absolute expression of a resident Divinity. No element of character, no spontaneity of life, but instantly seized his attention and incurred his greeting and his comment; which things could never possibly have been so genially alert and expert—as I have, again, before this, superabundantly recorded—if it had not fed on active observation and contact. He could answer one with the radiant when one challenged him with the obscure, just as he could respond with the general when one pulled at the particular; and I needn't repeat that this made for us, during all our time, anything but a starved actuality.[12]

The succeeding passage exhibits the son returning upon himself once more, to say that he had as a youngster thought of his father's young manhood as involving scenes which, unlike those he himself witnessed, "might have met in some degree my appetite for the illustrational."

Four expressions, given here in the order in which they occur, above, indicate how faithful James was, both to the feelings of his youthful self and to his ripest judgment. He and his father each employed a distinct "set of relations"; he felt in this "a kind of implied snub to the significance of mine"; yet the novelist acknowledges that no one spoke so tellingly, nor with such immediacy, for every "element of character," every "spontaneity of life." James insists a little too much that no doctrinal "pressure" was felt by the James children, and he is formally accurate, as we know, not simply from his own evidence, but from the very nature of the elder James's principles, and from everything his letters say. But there *was* serious pressure. The young writer felt that his father's vision was competitive with his own. His father was forever explaining what human actions revealed; making of the whole universe a tremendous and continuing "yarn," which absorbed the whole array of particular events and feelings on which a storyteller might have based his work.

He rejected his father's manner of telling the universal story; he never seems to have doubted his father's account of human motivations. The antithesis between the pictorial and the dramatic, which flowers into so many interesting

[12] This and the two brief passages preceding it are from *Notes of a Son and Brother*, pp. 171–172.

and suggestive discriminations in the novelist's criticism of his own work and that of other writers, is *primal:* for when he had satisfied his hunger for the pictorial, or even before he had done so, he was forced to ask himself *what set of relations*, what dramatic oppositions, would serve to organize his fictional scenes. Yet when he asked himself, let us say, "What are the sources of appearance in this particular situation? what motives inform? what elements of character determine? who speaks for life or spontaneity? who denies life and how?"—his father's spirit rose up in him; his father's account of human nature offered itself insistently. The consequences of this fact were clearly mixed. As we shall see presently, the need for his father's version of tradition as a counterweight to Europe was very great; yet the danger of relying too much on the views of "the great explainer" was a real one; one might *become* a great explainer to the detriment of one's art. [13] In 1885 James responded to this threat (which lay below the threshold of consciousness) by associating his father with himself as a writer; he was clearly the better writer, so what had he to fear?

William, on the other hand, had not since his crisis in 1870 [14] feared identification with his father. The explicit assertion that he had a will and a power to choose, which resolved that crisis, was also an explicit defiance of "father's ideas"; his father's crisis of 1844 had been resolved with the declaration that one must abandon the moral will in order to know the "resident Divinity"! William had to keep on asserting the power to choose; he was throughout his life hobbled and constrained by the need to keep on opposing his father, to keep on asserting that moral order is being

[13] See Chapter I, note 27. Rosenzweig holds that it was James's fate to identify himself with his father. See also the cited chapter bv F. W. Dupee, esp. pp. 138–139.

[14] Ralph Barton Perry, *The Thought and Character of William James*, I, Chapter XIX.

won *now* by namable persons, and in this way took up an Emersonian position against his father.

More important still for the question of the difference between the brothers with respect to "father's ideas" is the fact that William did not in his Introduction to the *Literary Remains* emphasize the part played by personal bias in the making of his father's philosophy. Had he done so, he would have been obliged to comment on his father's claims as a psychologist, and these, I venture to suggest, he could not acknowledge, simply because he found them threateningly persuasive; these psychological principles anticipate Freud in a fashion which tends to break down one's belief in the efficacy and reality of the moral will. William James took a friendly and intelligent interest in his father's "theism," just the sort of interest he had in the work of such an intellectual odd fish as Benjamin Paul Blood, the Albany mystic of the "anaesthetic revelation"; he turned away from the spectacle of a psychological dynamics which suggested that *within* our moral selves there is inescapable conflict.

Henry Junior, however, seems to have swallowed his father's psychology whole, and although he never undertook any systematic exposition of his father's thought, as William did, the two volumes of his reminiscences show that he was in possession not simply of his father's spirit but of a sense of his father's characteristic judgments. There is a familiar passage which many persons have quoted without any awareness of its force as evidence of the novelist's sympathetic comprehension. It is found in *A Small Boy and Others*. James has just been saying that the household rang with but a single imperative, "Convert, convert, convert!"—convert, that is, "every contact, every impression, and every experience." These, he goes on, "were to form our soluble stuff; with only ourselves to thank should we remain unaware, by the time our perceptions were decently developed, of the substance finally projected

and most desirable. That substance might be just consummately Virtue, as a social grace and value—and as a
matter furthermore on which pretexts for ambiguity of
view and of measure were as little as possible called upon
to flourish." James quickly adds that this household was
not in the least instrumental "to the formation of prigs."

Our father's prime horror was of *them*—he only cared for
virtue that was more or less ashamed of itself; and nothing
could have been of a happier whimsicality than the mixture
in him, and in all his walk and conversation, of the strongest
instinct for the human, and the liveliest reaction from the
literal. The literal played as small a part in our education as
it perhaps ever played in any, and we wholesomely breathed
inconsistency and ate and drank contradictions. The presence
of paradox was so bright among us—though fluttering ever
with as light a wing and as short a flight as need have been—
that we fairly grew used to allow, from an early time, for
the so many and odd declarations we heard launched, to the
extent of happily "discounting" them; the moral of all of
which was that we need never fear not to be good enough if
we were only social enough: a splendid meaning indeed being
attached to the latter term.

Thus we had ever the amusement, since I can really call
it nothing less, of hearing morality, or moralism, as it was
more invidiously worded, made hay of in the very interest
of character and conduct; these things suffering much, it
seemed, by their association with the conscience—that is the
conscious conscience—the very home of the literal, the haunt
of so many pedantries.[15]

Two or three other passages must be added to this, and
use made of the whole group collectively in order to introduce the reader to certain essential points in the writings
of the elder James. A passage of some six pages in the
Notes of a Son and Brother is probably the most illuminat-

[15] Quotations in this paragraph are from *A Small Boy and Others*,
pp. 215–216. For another use by the novelist of "social" in this sense,
see *Notes of a Son and Brother*, p. 274.

ing as to the son's feeling for his father and those ideas from which he was hardly separable. I abstract two fragments:

Detached as I could during all those years perhaps queerly enough believe myself, it would still have done my young mind the very greatest violence to have to suppose that any plane of conclusion for him [his father], however rich and harmonious he might tend to make conclusion, could be in the nature of a fool's paradise. . . . If it didn't sound in a manner patronising I should say that I saw that my father saw; and that I couldn't but have given my own case away by not believing, however obscurely, in the virtue of his consequent and ultimate synthesis. Of course I never dreamed of any such name for it—I only thought of it as something very great and fine founded on those forces in him that came home to us and touched us all the while. As these were extraordinary forces of sympathy and generosity, and that yet knew how to be such without falsifying any minutest measure, the structure raised upon them might well, it would seem, and even to the uppermost sublime reaches, be as valid as it was beautiful. If he so endeared himself wasn't it, one asked as time went on, through his never having sentimentalised or merely meditated away, so to call it, the least embarrassment of the actual about him, and having with a passion peculiarly his own kept together his stream of thought, however transcendent, and the stream of life, however humanized? There was a kind of experiential authority in his basis, as he felt his basis—there being no human predicament he couldn't by a sympathy more like direct experience than any I have known enter into; and this authority, which concluded so to a widening and brightening of the philosophic—for him the spiritual—sky, made his character, as intercourse disclosed it, in a high degree fascinating.[16]

This section of the book is one of the finest things in James—in or out of fiction. In saying, "I couldn't but have

[16] *Notes of a Son and Brother*, pp. 229–230. The six-page passage begins on p. 224.

given my own case away"—the case for his possession of the artist's faculties—had he failed to find in his father's expressive humanity precisely the grounds appropriate to a valid "synthesis," James shows a noble consistency. The artist has the power to recognize the philosopher. But such noble consistencies must on occasion be disingenuous: James knew more about his father's scheme, and knew it more explicitly, than he allows the uninformed reader to see.

These next lines follow James's praise for the "masterly clearness and justice" of his brother's Introduction to the *Literary Remains,* and his own characterization of his relation to his father's thought in the years when he was exposed to it as "a total otherness of contemplation." He proceeds to state the underlying principle of "these things":

. . . the active, not to say the obvious, moral of them, in all our younger time, was that a life of the most richly consequent flowed straight out of them, that in this life, the most abundantly, and above all naturally, communicated *as* life that it was possible to imagine, we had an absolutely equal share, and that in fine I was to live to go back with wonder and admiration to the quantity of secreted thought in our daily medium, the quality of intellectual passion, the force of cogitation and aspiration, as to the explanation both of a thousand surface incoherences and a thousand felt felicities. A religion that was so systematically a philosophy, a philosophy that was so sweepingly a religion, being together, by their necessity, as I have said, an intensity of relation to the actual, the consciousness so determined was furnished forth in a way that met by itself the whole question of the attitude of "worship" for instance; as I have attempted a little to show that it met, with a beautiful good faith and the easiest sufficiency, every other when such came up: those of education, acquisition, material vindication, what is called success generally. In the beauty of the whole thing, again, I lose myself—by which I mean in the fact that we were all

the while partaking, to our most intimate benefit, of an
influence of direction and enlargement attended with scarce
a single consecrated form and which would have made many
of these, had we been exposed to intrusion from them,
absurdly irrelevant.[17]

Two things have perhaps kept us from seeing what a
deep and intimate comprehension of his father's work
James exhibited in his reminiscences. First, we are naturally
skeptical as to the intelligibility of the elder James—whose
abstruseness has been a byword ever since Howells's remark
that in writing *The Secret of Swedenborg*, James had kept
the "secret." Second, the novelist was incapable of convey-
ing information simply *as* information; he had to give a
kind of dramatic form to everything. What this means in
the present instance is that we are so absorbed in his
wonderful capacity to catch up the elements of his past
into form that we don't serially note how many things he
initially perceived. To begin with the passage quoted on
page 54, why should the fact that James was " 'after'
persons" have been considered "deplorable"? Well, simply
because for the elder James (who of course followed St.
Paul in this) a "respect of persons" was a great sin.[18] Note
also the implied stricture: the "serious" apparently had to
be the "abstract." In the next long passage we find James
explaining that he "drank so largely at the source itself" that
he had no need of the offered "cups." (The reader may
remember the tremendous number of cups, bowls, vessels,
fountains, overflowing tides, and so forth, in the novelist's
work. We shall come to these; meantime it is enough to
know that the relation between "sources" and containers
is derived from the elder James.)

In asserting that he went to his father himself for

[17] *Notes of a Son and Brother*, pp. 165–166.
[18] *The Secret of Swedenborg: Being an Elucidation of His Doctrine
of the Divine Natural Humanity*, p. 163. (Cited hereafter as *Secret.*)

knowledge of his beliefs, James is displaying a fidelity that would have delighted his father. To be "true to the experience of the creature" is to have a living experience of the "resident Divinity," not to seek Him in books. Again, the son is aware (page 56) that his father held that God is imprisoned in man. It appears (pages 56 and 57) that the "perfect variety" and the "spontaneity of life" (the novelist's own announced values) had as their sanction a mind which conceived of God as within us. Such a mind, in other words, is exactly the sort which characteristically pays tribute to variety and spontaneity. (If the reader feels that this is the prime characteristic of the *artist's* mind, he is in agreement with *both* father and son, and not the novelist alone.)

I come now to the passage (page 59) which deals with the unspoken exhortation of the parents, "Convert, convert, convert!" Make, that is, the whole of your experience serve your sense of "Virtue, as a social grace and value. . . ." Now if virtue is truly *social*, it is a new kind of thing which needs the explication supplied by the familiar phrase (page 60), "We need never fear not to be good enough if we were only social enough. . . ." The passage condemns the "literal"—the letter, in the elder James, is likely to be an *inversion* of the spirit—condemns prigs and the "*conscious* conscience," which is the "haunt" of "pedantries." What then does "social" mean to the son? It means not being persuaded of one's *personal* rectitude, not attributing virtue to other *persons* as such. His father was a "source" of the kindliest and most attaching virtues, but the son is perfectly aware that the father would have been horrified had he been regarded as more, or less, righteous than anyone else. It is, then, on a social scene, or within the family itself, that these powers his father exhibited, "these things of the spirit, these genialities of faith," were to be found.

James has stated the alternative possibility, that which begins with a "respect of persons," in *A Small Boy and*

Others: "I never dreamed of competing—a business having in it at the best, for my temper, if not for my total failure of temper, a displeasing ferocity." He continues: "If competing was bad, snatching was therefore still worse, and jealousy was a sort of spiritual snatching." [19] Self-righteousness, spiritual greed, is the greatest possible sin in father and son alike. Theodora Bosanquet perceived the importance of this in James; although she missed his belief (once again his father's) that we cannot altogether avoid spiritual greed: "When he walked out of the refuge of his study into the world and looked about him, he saw a place of torment, where creatures of prey perpetually thrust their claws into the quivering flesh of the doomed defenceless children of light." [20] The elder James, in a letter printed in *Notes of a Son and Brother*, shows the impartiality on the score of our virtues which is more characteristic of his son: Before the coming of his apocalyptic society "we shall be utterly unworthy to love each other or be loved in return. We shall do nothing but prey upon each other and turn each other's life to perfect weariness." [21]

Theodora Bosanquet, in seeking to describe James's own vision of our perfect state, has hit on a description very close indeed to that used by the elder James in this letter. The novelist's father writes: "The first requisite of our true relationship to each other (spiritually speaking) is that we be wholly independent of each other: then we may give ourselves away as much as we please, we shall do neither them [*sic*] nor ourselves any harm." [22] (We may "give ourselves away" freely when what we love in other people is simply their reflection of a unique aspect of "the abounding divinity"—that is, their style.) Miss Bosanquet writes of the novelist: "His Utopia was an anarchy where nobody

[19] *A Small Boy and Others*, p. 176.
[20] *Henry James at Work*, p. 32.
[21] *Notes of a Son and Brother*, pp. 239–240.
[22] *Notes of a Son and Brother*, p. 239.

would be responsible for any other human being but only for his own civilized character." [23]

The sentences in the last of my series of extended quotations come close to being a summary view of the elder James's *Weltanschauung*. I have already referred to James's complaint that the "serious" was unfortunately "abstract." Here, though "not concerned with the intrinsic meaning of these things" (to which William, he feels, has done far more justice than he could), he is concerned with their "moral." His statement of the moral amounts to saying that his father's abundance, fidelity to particulars, and so forth, "flowed straight out of them." In other words, his father's abstract universality *was* somehow consonant with particularity.[24] This is the first point in a list of the elements of his father's belief which the novelist clearly comprehended. The second is that his father was utterly faithful to the abstract demand that all men be treated alike, in that each member of his family had an "equal share" in what emerged from his father as "source." An important corollary to these two points is James's awareness that his father believed his own good qualities to be due to a "resident" God; he knew that his father did not believe that religious *experience* was something "other" than what was "communicated *as* life." What was experienced was the very life of the hidden cause itself, for God had no other way to *be*. Third, James recognized and repeatedly celebrated his father's power to make sense of the world the family saw, not by excising or distorting bits of it in the manner of humdrum rationalists, but by reconciling the whole. Frequently, of course, this reconciliation was effected through the desperate logic of paradox, but what more clearly testified to his father's refusal to blink the least scrap of actuality? Fourth, the younger son has

[23] *Henry James*, p. 33.
[24] See the discussion of the bootstrap myth in Chapter I, esp. pp. 11–21.

clearly taken in the burden of his father's strictures, not on *personal* claims alone, but on the whole fabric of institutional life in church and state. He knows that success is to be claimed for the thing one has done, not for the thing one is, or the place one has attained in any sort of hierarchy.

If the reader has taken in the aspects of the elder James's system that the novelist understood, he is in possession of a number of clues needed to lead him through the "system" I shall summarize. It may be concluded, on the question of the relation of Henry and William to their father's beliefs, that William's excellent Introduction proves that he understood the relations between "father's ideas" very well; but the passages I have quoted here, and those I quote from *The Tragic Muse* in the following chapter, show that Henry understood their possible applications in a degree that makes William's knowledge seem pedantic. The younger son is, to my knowledge, the only man who has ever *used* the elder James's beliefs. By the time he wrote *The Golden Bowl* his "faith in the power of the moral to offer a surface" had become nearly as unqualified as his father's.

The interpreters of the elder James have made little of that "experiential authority" which the younger Henry James felt so deeply.[25] The theologian's admirers are keenly aware of his acuteness as a judge of character (is there a better sketch of Emerson's or Carlyle's?), but they betray no consciousness that this acuteness had a systematic basis; that the charming man with the queer notions actually put

[25] An excellent bibliography of works by and about the elder Henry James is to be found in *The Philosophy of Henry James, Sr.*, by Frederic Harold Young. (See my review in *American Literature*, XXIV, 1953, pp. 556–557.) In addition to Ralph Barton Perry's admirable chapters on the elder James in *The Thought and Character of William James*, and Dr. Young's book, I should mention C. Hartley Grattan's *The Three Jameses* and Austin Warren's *The Elder Henry James*.

some of these to work when he made judgments of people.
These queer notions themselves were of course completely
caught up in the theology and the philosophy. They were
couched in symbolic terms, and in the period before Freud
and the existentialist vogue it was very difficult to attach
them to anything. It does not appear so difficult now, and
the basis on which his father analyzed human nature seems
to have been from the very start the younger Henry
James's psychological stock in trade. It follows that some
of the lovers of the novelist's work have been *elder*
Jamesians without being in the least aware of it.

I shall not, however, attempt at the outset to discriminate
psychological principles from the rest. To get at the elder
James, one must first look at him whole and thereafter try
to suggest how the parts were used. This is because his
universe is one of moral energies in motion; his principles
are co-ordinates of the flux and reflux of creation.

Creation, as his son William says in his Introduction to
the *Literary Remains*, is his leading idea. The image of
God as a detached watch-maker and the opposed image of
an arbitrary and angry God were equally repugnant to
him. His God is a god of love unalloyed, and evil is, in
his universe, a species of psychological and metaphysical
necessity. The argument as to creation runs as follows:
God cannot create perfect beings who share His nature;
to do so would merely and meaninglessly diffuse His
essence into so many godlings. Man must be given, from
the very outset, a wholly different nature. God therefore
creates an "other," a creature who will be as different
from himself as is the greedy and psychically unformed
infant from his loving and self-forgetting mother.[26] God
would surely not exhibit His power of selfless love in
creating replicas of himself—this would be simple narcis-

---

[26] This, of course, suggests the alienation stressed by some varieties
of existentialism, as does the fact that our existence precedes (or
is the ground of) our awareness of being.

sism. Instead He makes receptacles or molds which must be filled with the divine love to give them "life."

Still, these creatures God has made will not be independent of Him if He simply endows them with a consciousness of selfless love to begin with; they must first believe themselves independent of each other and of God, and thereafter come to realize, as grown-up moral agents, that God alone is worthy of love. So the first stage of creation —the making of the molds—is followed by a second stage in which man declares his moral and material independence, but is finally faced with the knowledge that without God's love he is a mere hollow receptacle, that the cup of the self cannot really be filled by righteousness or material possessions.

This second stage of creation occupies the whole of human history from the beginning to the realization of the apocalyptic *union* of God and man in society. I will rehearse this stage once again, using an alternative set of terms which the elder James derives from *Genesis*. The life to which Adam (perhaps it is better to say "the Adam," since this is a technical term) awakes is a mere confusion of appearances to him. Yet all these appearances are susceptible of arrangement into an order which would exhibit the union of God and man—all are representative of the divine nature which man embodies. Adam is seeing the cosmos within himself, but he thinks it is outside him—his senses tell him so. If he proceeded to arrange these appearances in the order of their final meaning, he would not, to repeat the point made in the paragraph above, become an independent moral agent. He would not feel himself possessed of that agency which he will finally resign to God. There would be, in still other words, no merit in the whole creative transaction either for God or His creature. But if the Adam cannot use God's power to arrange the appearances about him without interrupting the creative process, whose power *can* he use? God provides Eve,[27] who institutes the delusion which is necessary if man is to arrive at a separate consciousness. Eve incites us to appropriate and order the shows of appearance as *possessions*. God is a benevolent cheat. He gives us a false self first, to teach us what the true self is.

The Eve has a number of names, but "selfhood" is the simplest. (She is also the "receptacle" or "mold," and in Swedenborgian parlance she is the *proprium*.) When we seize on money, power, status, goodness, aesthetic experience, or anything else and hold it as a *possession*, we are responding to our selfhood's urging. Before we begin to do this we are not men at all, but innocents, spiritual Emersons, "mere dimpled nurslings of the skies,"[28] to use the elder James's phrase. We are lapped in the divine love and wisdom, but the divine power or "use" has not begun to work in us. (This is the elder James's trinity—love, wisdom, and use.)[29]

What the Eve gives us is not simply undifferentiated greed; she gives us an "identity." Through our possessions, moral, material, aesthetic, we become somebodies. (Here James approaches Veblen's thesis about the function of owning things in *The Theory of the Leisure Class*.) We get from our possessions a sense of personal fullness. From them we learn who we are, and with them we make distinctions between ourselves and other men. We judge them better or worse, richer or poorer, endowed with more or less sensibility. Every man tries to fill the cup of his selfhood with those things that will enable him to lord it over his fellows.

It would be misleading to suggest that it is simply our

---

[27] See *Society*, pp. 170–171, for an account of the succession of selfhood by conscience. Both are symbolically feminine.

[28] *Logic*, p. 120.

[29] Frederic Harold Young, *The Philosophy of Henry James, Sr.*, p. 168, has a useful series of "triads" derivable from this original trinity.

individual selfhood which gives us identity; the church as we know it is also a great vessel of lies, chief of which is the assertion that God prizes us as individuals; rejects some of us and favors others. The state, however, imperfect and oppressive though it may be, is an emblem of our future union with God and our fellows in the "divine-natural-humanity." The state must finally disintegrate, that is, surrender the function of controlling our passions into the hands of a new society, which will supplant both church and state. In the meantime the state has quite properly the ascendancy over the church, for it is at least a symbol of our future destiny, and its powers serve to keep its citizens from each other's throats. The church, having lost its symbolic function, must perish, because it is dedicated to the maintenance of the lie that God does not share His love of us with absolute equality.

But where is God now to be found? To answer this question it will be best, since we are trying to describe a process, rather than a static order, to start once more at the beginning. I have been talking about God's activity without acknowledging His part in it. Using the terms from Genesis once more, I shall amplify the description of the Adam. The elder James thought of mankind as containing all nature. Nature is simply a reflection of our spiritual contents. Adam, earth, universal man, the Grand Man or Maximus Homo, all these are interchangeable terms expressive of the fact that the divine wisdom is actually present within us.[30] We see it as outside us and call it nature. God's love is also within us. James sometimes calls this love the "female Adam," making symbolic use of the fact that Genesis refers to the creation of man, male and female, *before* Eve was made.[31] So the "female Adam," or divine

[30] *Secret*, p. 48.
[31] James does not often use this convenient designation. In general we may say that man is given a moral life by Eve in order that he may become aware of the spiritual life through conscience. (See

love, dwells within us, though the Eve screens us from awareness of her presence. The divine love takes the form of the "female Adam," or the conscience which struggles with the Eve. The triumph of conscience results of course in our union with God and our fellows—the "divine-natural-humanity."

Although the elder James is a bit hard on Kant in *Substance and Shadow*, he seems to have found him very useful. By giving the Kantian intuitions of space and time a beginning and an end, he succeeded in clarifying his own scheme considerably. Space and time are the conditions necessary to knowing phenomena. What we know while the Eve is driving us to appropriate [32] goods, status, scientific knowledge, is the phenomenal. But what we know is truly a reflection of the divine wisdom in us. The Eve simply gets us to *take* it in the wrong way. We ought to see that everything that is deployed in space and appropriated in time is actually a reflection of our own nature. We ought to take it as the divine love urges us to— as a reflection of our own nature. If we can for a moment do this—view all nature as God views it—we will on that instant be united with God. Simply by inverting our perspective, and crying out, "Behold, all this is humanity!" instead of saying, "Lo, how many things I can grab and keep all to myself!" we can put an end to these preliminary delusions, space and time. Once we have learned to take experience for what it is, testimony to the presence within us of the divine wisdom and the divine love, time will have a stop, space will become simply our spiritual perception of the being of God-Man, the "divine-natural-humanity." To introduce the last of the terms from

Secret, p. 49; *Society*, pp. 170–171; and "The Woman Thou Gavest With Me," *Atlantic Monthly*, XXV, 1870, pp. 66–72, esp. pp. 66–67.)
[32] This word usually means "to fill the *proprium* with," and is therefore pejorative. Occasionally James used it with another theological emphasis: to take one's share of the grace offered by God and known through Christ's example.

Genesis, the coming of the *second* Adam, or God-Man, reduces the chaotic consciousness of the first Adam to its final order.[33]

The elder James was reluctant to make a distinction between the history of individuals and that of the human race, and he often uses the same terms for both. For example, we may say of the race and of individuals that their history is that of a struggle between the conscience and the selfhood, the one seeking to refer all that exists to the divine nature common to us all, the other seeking to engross all existence and separate man from man. In the following passage on our moral history James uses the term *"vir"* instead of Eve for the selfhood, and "goodness and truth" for the love and wisdom within us. "All the phenomena of our moral history go to show the *homo* or created man, the man of interior affection and thought, utterly unconscious of the infinite goodness and truth which alone give him *being*, and joyfully allying himself with the *vir* or finite conscious man, the man of mere organic appetite and passion, who gives him contingent *existence* only, or renders him phenomenal to himself; shows him as the symbolic narrative phrases it, *'leaving his father and his mother, and cleaving unto his wife until they become one flesh.'*"

Since the delusion Eve fosters is a *necessary* preliminary phase for humanity, no one can be condemned for adopting it. Man must pile up goods, pile up knowledge, and accumulate works of art in order to learn that he is a nullity, that all these represent a reality he has denied. He must even obey the laws and conform to his neighbor's standards. Nothing is more ridiculous than the reformer, who forgets that we are not ready for our union with God; who tries to make a new church or a new state,

[33] The fact that the elder James deals with the flux and reflux of creation limits his psychological principles. See "Henry James and the New Jerusalem" (*Kenyon Review*, VIII, 1946), p. 524.

or advocates communism. We are not ready for these things, and we shall not, in the end, need them. There is, however, an effective mode of being evil, of arresting, if but momentarily, the march of providence. I quote a passage on the evil the church (any church, since James is not tilting at a particular faith) encourages in us.

The Church studiously fosters the sentiment of moral worth or dignity in its disciples . . . and thus delivers them over bound hand and foot to spiritual pride. . . . However selfish or worldly a man may be these are good honest natural evils, and you have only to apply a motive sufficiently stimulating in either case, and you will induce the subject to forbear them. But spiritual pride is inward evil exclusively, pertaining to the selfhood of man or livingly appropriated by him as his own, and cannot therefore become known to him save in the form of an outward natural representation; for it is not like moral evil, mere outward oppugnancy to good, but it is the actual and deadly profanation of good, or the lavish acknowledgement of it with a view of subordinating it to personal, or selfish and worldly ends. It is the only truly formidable evil known to God's providence, being that of *self*-righteousness, and hence the only evil which essentially threatens to undermine the foundations of God's throne.[34]

Just as children pursue the images cast by a projector, men grasp at nature. The delusion that their senses and intellects are the arbiters of reality does not damn them. We must all incur the guilt which comes with acquisition. Persuaded by our selfhood that the phenomenal is the only reality, we must painfully live the error down. The last step in philosophy will be the *docta ignorantia*, the conclusion that without knowing God we can know nothing truly; the last gasp of the strenuous moral will is to be

[34] *Society*, pp. 202–203; see also pp. 191, 415, 416. Reinhold Niebuhr's description of Kant's "radical evil" suggests that it is of the same order: "Radical evil, for Kant, is man's inclination to corrupt the imperatives of morality so that they become a screen for the expression of self-love." (*The Nature and Destiny of Man*, I, 120n.)

the admission that we cannot will the good; and the final meaning of acquisition of every sort is that nothing can be owned. These are "good honest natural evils"; forms, identical at bottom, of what the novelist called "spiritual snatching," attempts, in his father's terms, to fulfill the demands of the selfhood. But the evil of self-righteousness makes an "outward natural representation" of the self, and calls it God; it is the ultimate evil.

What we deludedly call "human nature" is simply the relation between love of one's self and love of one's fellows. Our "identity" *is* simply the form that the struggle between these two loves takes in us. An individual is not so much a *thing* as an *event;* a focus at which these moral energies intersect. Hence the subtitle of *Substance and Shadow—An Essay on the Physics of Creation.*[35] The consequence is that to love our fellows exclusively would be to revert to the state of the first Adam, not to attain that of the second. Innocents and moral idiots may display such a love now, but they are simply evading the conflict with the Eve which we must go through. But at the other end of the spectrum we discover something very nearly absolute, a love of self which has become a love of spiritual death. This is *self*-righteousness. The self-righteous seek to make God a possession.

The attempt to appropriate conscience must take the

[35] See *Nature of Evil,* p. 112: "There is no such *entity* or *thing* as human nature." See also *Society,* p. 433, where James speaks of nature as the "human realm . . . a certain undefined or purely potential and promissory existence which subjectively never *is* but is always *becoming* or *to be.* . . ." William James did not have to go far to find such descriptions of consciousness as fill his *Psychology.* William Troy, in his essay "The Altar of Henry James" (*The Question of Henry James,* ed. by F. W. Dupee), finds that the whole attitude of the younger Henry James toward experience may be expressed by his reverence for the network of enjoyed and suffered personal relations: "The individual, in the language of modern physics, is only an 'event,' to be defined in terms of a given field of forces."

form of grasping some "outward natural representation" of the divine in us. The selfhood is limited by Kant's intuitions of time and space; it can deal only with the phenomenal, what *appears* to it. "Bodily" churches, any ecclesiastical organization we can see, are such representations. The man who appropriates a woman, not simply to allay his lust, but because he sees in her a chance to gain glory for himself, is such a sinner. He tries to make the boundless source of good his own. (He takes the portrait for the lady; or sees the "heiress of all the ages" as simply the inheritor of millions and of wasted flesh.) To appropriate our spiritual superior damns us.

This very general view of the elder James's "spiritual cosmology" lacks the dramatic force which he tried to give it. It may be possible to suggest this more directly by describing the process from the standpoint of one of its three protagonists. We may discuss the regeneration of a particular man; we may describe the historical movement from formation to the coming of the divine society; or we may speak of what God undergoes for our sake. I reserve the first approach for the next chapter in which I deal with the elder James himself. Since the elder James regarded himself as a Christian, it is necessary to explain his Christology, and I shall therefore begin with God. It has been said above that men are created as a kind of limit or antithesis. Otherness to God, alienation from God, is what defines us. Having made us other, God enters into us in order that we may become like Him, or, to put it in Swedenborgian terms, as does the elder James, that the Lord or God-Man may come into being. God submerges himself in men in order to make them divine—*not* to make them God, but to enable them to join Him in an order in which both men and God will be swallowed up. Creation is not simply a putting-forth of God's energy; it is not complete until that energy has flowed back into the divine-natural-humanity. "Creation necessarily *in*volves the crea-

tor and obscures his perfection in the exact ratio of its
evolving the creature and illustrating his imperfection.
Unless therefore the creature *himself* reproduce the creative infinitude concealed in his nature it must be forever
obliterated from remembrance." [36]

In the sight of God, therefore, the selfhood, Eve, or
proprium is morally neutral. The self exists so that we may
become aware of our otherness to God and overcome it.
"Nature" and "history" are the record in space and time of
our delusion that we do not share the divine nature and are
not at one with God. The delusion, the positing of self-
consciousness, is the necessary ground of our perception of
our otherness to God. This is perhaps the most sporting
theory of redemption ever devised. James's God puts
himself completely at man's mercy. The descent of God
into man makes possible the ascent of man to God, who
subjects Himself to the conditions of human life so that
man may become His equal. Christ was simply the first
man to do this; the first man in whom God *showed*. By
acknowledging the divinity within, Christ revealed the
"creative infinitude" which lies in all of us. His feat was
an utter denial, under the most extreme temptation, of the
self. To be hailed as the Messiah is, according to the theologian, the most enticing bait for our self-righteousness that
we can imagine. The incarnation is then simply the type of
the activity of the divine love in man. "The truth incurs
this humiliation, undergoes this falsification on *our* behalf
exclusively, who, because we have by nature no perception
of God as a spirit, but only as a person like ourselves, are
even brutally ignorant of the divine power and ways." [37]
Christ revealed the divine life in us by renouncing the life
of selfishness as factitious, frustrating, and vile.

What thereafter takes place from the point of view of
the divinity I shall give in shortened form. When the

[36] *Secret*, p. 48.
[37] *Secret*, p. 185.

Eve's phenomenal understanding has built (for example) a scientific account of the world which is complete save that it lacks the meaning which it has when we invert our perspective and see that it describes "the spiritual or invisible contents of the human mind," [38] or when individual selfishness has in a thousand ways discovered the frustration and futility of acquisition, we finally see, with horror and loathing, the self which has contrived these inversions of significance—and the divinity within us is released from bondage.

The moment the selfhood becomes "other," the experience of God and of man are united, not in some other world, but in this one. It becomes "natural" to us to be divine; it becomes "natural" to God to be human. The alienation which had heretofore defined us we now see as the *other self*. In our spiritual geography, America comes to rule over Europe; the feminine over the masculine; the artist over the king and priest. We now order nature as a true cosmos, an image of God's wisdom shaped by God's love. Man, says the elder James, "has the task and the power divinely given him of subduing all nature to himself, and so leading it back to him from whom it originally comes." [39] Or, to use the set of terms from Genesis once more: What has taken place is a "marriage" [40] of the infinite and the finite; the Adam has broken off his "liaison" with the Eve and has been wholly vivified by the female Adam, thus becoming the second Adam; while the Eve has been deprived of phenomena and forced to accept the fruits of the divine wisdom. Or, to use terms from physics which emphasize the fact that the elder James is describing a process or event: The "field" of creation reaches an equilibrium in the unified consciousness of God and man.

[38] *Substance*, p. 121; for a less lofty account of nature, see *Society*, pp. 237–238. Also see *Substance*, p. 317; and *Logic*, pp. 183, 195.
[39] *Secret*, p. 116.
[40] *Society*, p. 143.

If this be what happens to God, what happens to individuals in this divine society? What is left of us when we have perceived the self as "other," [41] as alien? We become utterly spontaneous, seeming precisely what we are, and being precisely what we wish to be. But again, what is left of us? The elder James calls what remains to us "spiritual individuality." It is no more and no less than our style. When we are apotheosized, the content of our selves is nothing less than the whole of God's nature; it is universal, but the form or style is our own. Each of us recapitulates the whole, as if we were a community of artists, each giving his individual stamp to a single subject matter. The union of universality with true particularity which Emerson projected is thus worked out by the elder James. He alone, in his generation, made a complete version of the bootstrap myth.

I turn to an abbreviated sketch of the history which culminates in the divine society. Out of Swedenborg's long tale of successive "churches" on earth, the elder James chose only three to represent the sum of our history. The first two have been manifest; the third is wholly spiritual and now arising, though invisible, amongst us. The first or Jewish church is the church of the law which makes God completely external: "In short, the Jew was notoriously a frivolous subject—as near to worthless as a people could well be that still wore the human form—and cultivating only such base ideas of the Divine righteousness as stood in a mere 'outward cleansing of the cup and platter, while inwardly they were full of extortion and excess.' " [42] When America disavowed England's church and state, Americans became *as a people* the first effective manifestation of the possibility of living by an inward law. But this means that America is the promise of the real "third

[41] The process of self-confrontation is illustrated, in the elder James's own case, in the following chapter.
[42] *Society*, pp. 84–85.

force," [43] the divine society. What is the second of these churches?

It is the Christian church, the Christian church not as an organization but simply as the chance that Christ offered individuals to anticipate in themselves the state of redeemed man. This anticipation can be only partial, but without it God would have been imprisoned within us forever: "Accordingly unless the Divine Providence had all along the course of history singled out such persons as were capable of spiritual regeneration without detriment to their conscious freedom, evil would have reigned uncontrolled throughout history, and creation consequently have been stifled in a vain effort to get birth or put on form." We discover on surveying history itself "that the exact meaning of the Providential administration of human affairs has been to give man social and aesthetic form or consciousness, by means of a sickening experience of the endless disease disorder and death wrapped up in his physical and moral consciousness. . . ." [44] What Christ has done for individuals we perceive to be an "at-one-ment"— evidence that God is "naturally" joined to us; this is redemption,[45] not regeneration or salvation. (The theologian's use of these terms is not wholly consistent in appearance, because he sometimes compresses, and at others expands, his account.) But, on the basis of our seeing that a *vir* or Eve need not take the form of selfishness, that Christ was a *vir*, a particular form, really adequate to contain the *homo* [46] or universal nature, we may attain as individuals something very like regeneration.

We must not attempt to do this prematurely through

---

[43] *Substance*, pp. 153–154.
[44] This and the preceding passage are from *Substance*, p. 152.
[45] "Redemption" technically begins when the "sleeping Adam," or "fossil infinitude," has been endowed with a consciousness in Eve. Christ makes us aware of the *natural* conjunction—as opposed to the non-natural one which Eve institutes—that we have with God.
[46] *Secret*, p. 103.

moral strenuousness. We have to make a form or style fit
to contain the universal sources, to hold the waters of life.
I quote the epigraph on the title page of *Society: The
Redeemed Form of Man:* "Man during his earthly life
induces a form in the purest substances of his interiors, so
that he may be said to form his own soul, or give it quality;
and according to the form or quality of soul he thus gives
himself will be his subsequent receptivity to the Lord's
inflowing life: which is a life of love to the whole human
race." [47] This directly suggests the novelist's most general
observation about the famous "ideas." It runs: "His *tone*,
that is, always so effectually looks out, and the living parts

[47] This epigraph is drawn from Swedenborg. Its emphasis on the
individual's preparation for a future life is actually somewhat at
odds with the elder James's "spiritual socialism," to use Frederic
Harold Young's term. The elder James was rather impatient of the
religious stress on "post-mortem consciousness," presumably because
he did not think of death as in that degree important. We shall, while
in the body, and afterwards, continue to enjoy that grade of awareness for which we have qualified ourselves: "Thus when we die . . .
we wake in a world perfectly conformed to our ideal." (*Substance*,
p. 522.) He elsewhere quotes Swedenborg: "The good appertaining
to man makes his heaven, so that every man's heaven is exactly what
his good is." (*Secret*, p. 220.) The younger Henry James appears
inclined to sympathize with this view; he does not have any interest
in a prolongation which is not "a renewal of the interest, the appreciation, the large and consecrated consciousness, in a word, of
which we have had so splendid a sample in this world." And—delicately putting to one side the claims of those who do not want any
renewal, or have nothing to renew—he writes: "How *can* there be
a personal and a differentiated life 'after,' it will then of course be
asked, for those for whom there has been so little of one before?—
unless indeed it be pronounced conceivable that the possibility may
vary from man to man, from human case to human case, and that the
quantity or the quality of our practice of consciousness may have
something to say to it." ("Is There a Life After Death," pp. 199–200,
201.) When these quotations are juxtaposed with Miss Bosanquet's
testimony as to James's Utopia (*Henry James at Work*, p. 33), we
have an interesting light on James's story, *The Great Good Place*.
The theory of the "place" and the protagonist's qualifications for a
stay there seem to be an aspect of the "religion of consciousness"
which father and son held in common.

of him so singularly hung together, that one may fairly say his philosophy *was* his tone." [48] His father's great achievement was not the construction of an intricate system, but the development of a form, a style, a "tone," by which he was able to express it in his personal discourse.

"Father's ideas" had a simple basis, which made possible their ramifications and involutions. What the novelist was from infancy so sure of that he never dreamed of questioning it, was that his father had been quite right about experience. There were two ways of *taking* it, the selfish way and the loving way, and those who took it in the former, accepted conventional forms, while those who took it in the latter, made their own forms, and arrived at a style which was a worthy container of all that was precious and noble. When he found *both* these modes of appropriating experience at work in his own mind and soul, he began to write and—genius aiding him—became Henry James.

[48] *Notes of a Son and Brother*, p. 230.

IV *The Great Explainer*

THE TWO HENRY JAMESES ADDRESSED THEMSELVES TO experience with an almost military rigor. The father was obliged to *represent* the presence of the spiritual exclusively in the natural [1] (in his own days and ways), while the son had undertaken to give *form* to whatever aspect of the world he touched. Both efforts involved denying one's *personal* importance and asserting the worth of things done or executed.[2] However, the father's task involved him in difficulties and apparent contradictions. Was he not after all claiming a closer aquaintance with the spiritual than other men had? His books describe our regeneration as the process which frees us from self-righteousness and spiritual pride. No one can assert that he has completed this process until he has joined the perfect society. Still, a very important stage can be clearly marked. In his own case, the elder James calls it "My Moral Death and Burial." [3] In *Society: The Redeemed Form of Man* he tells of an experience which he later learned to call a "vastation," [4] after Swedenborg. It may be figured as a loosening of the moral

[1] *Secret*, pp. 119–120.
[2] *Secret*, p. 180.
[3] *Society*, p. 71 (page heading).
[4] See also the fragmentary "Autobiographic Sketch" in the *Remains*, pp. 123–191. In *Logic* (p. 233), menstruation is held to symbolize "vastation."

4

bowels, since James borrowed from Swedenborg the notion that celestial influences feed us, and devilish influences are discharged like excrement. The crucial passage in this account has often been quoted, but its significance with respect to the elder James's beliefs does not seem to have been clearly understood. James first explains that in the year 1844 he had been much occupied with what he felt to be an important discovery in theology; he was thus in the full flush of pride in *personal* achievement.

One day, however, toward the close of May, having eaten a comfortable dinner, I remained sitting at the table after the family had dispersed, idly gazing at the embers in the grate, thinking of nothing, and feeling only the exhilaration incident to a good digestion, when suddenly—in a lightning flash as it were—"fear came upon me, and trembling, which made all my bones to shake." To all appearance it was a perfectly insane and abject terror, without ostensible cause, and only to be accounted for, to my perplexed imagination, by some damned shape squatting invisible to me within the precincts of the room, and raying out from his fetid personality influences fatal to life. The thing had not lasted ten seconds before I felt myself a wreck, that is, reduced from a state of firm, vigorous, joyful manhood to one of almost helpless infancy. The only self-control I was capable of exerting was to keep my seat. I felt the greatest desire to run incontinently to the foot of the stairs and shout for help to my wife,—to run to the roadside even, and appeal to the public to protect me; but by an immense effort I controlled these frenzied impulses and determined not to budge from my chair till I had recovered my self-possession. This purpose I held to for a good long hour, as I reckoned time, beat upon meanwhile by an ever-growing tempest of doubt, anxiety and despair, with absolutely no relief from any truth I had ever encountered save a most pale and distant glimmer of the Divine existence, —when I resolved to abandon the vain struggle, and communicate without more ado what seemed my sudden burden of inmost, implacable unrest to my wife.[5]

[5] *Society*, pp. 44–45.

This experience of panic was followed by bouts of acute anxiety which persisted for more than two years. That it *was* panic in the clinical sense we cannot doubt, and one marvels at the capacity exhibited by the elder James and his two famous sons to achieve a workable emotional economy under the stresses they report.[6]

When his anxiety had become somewhat less acute, James was told by a lady of his acquaintance, Mrs. Chichester, that he had undergone something very like a Swedenborgian "vastation."[7] James got hold of Swedenborg's works and found in them a clear and sufficient explanation of the meaning of his disorder: "For while these remarkable books familiarized me with the angelic conception of the Divine being and providence, they gave me at the same time the amplest *rationale* I could have desired of my own particular suffering, as inherent in the profound unconscious death I bore about in my *proprium* or selfhood."[8] James had, as he puts it, "been in the habit of ascribing to the Creator, so far as my own life and actions were concerned, an outside discernment of the most jealous scrutiny, and had accordingly put the greatest possible alertness into His service and worship, until my will, as you have seen—thoroughly fagged out as it were with the formal, heartless, endless task of conciliating a stony-hearted Deity—actually collapsed." He had in vain tried to pour his feelings into a form prescribed by a church—to carry forward the symbolic rendering of the

[6] Perry's account of William's crisis is cited in Chapter III, note 14, above. For my treatment of Henry's description of *his* crisis, see Chapter VI and Saul Rosenzweig's article, cited in Chapter I, note 27.
[7] *Notes of a Son and Brother*, pp. 173–174. James looks back wistfully on Mrs. Chichester's intervention and the drama which he might have found in its success—had he been more than an infant and able to take it all in. Of Mrs. Chichester he says that she had been one of the family's shared reminiscences ("the sweet legend of his [father] and my mother's charmed impression of whom had lingered with us . . .").
[8] *Society*, p. 54.

matter which the novelist seems to have understood best.
He had now to find a mode of living which did not dramatize moral self-assertion, but, rather, dramatized moral self-
abnegation. Not only had he lost "the moral or voluntary
power" but also he felt "an actual acute loathing of the
moral pretension itself as so much downright charlatanry."
He continues:

No idiot was ever more incompetent, practically, to the
conduct of life than I, at that trying period, felt myself to
be. It cost me, in fact, as much effort to go out for a walk,
or to sleep in a strange bed, as it would an ordinary man to
plan a campaign or write an epic poem. I have told you how,
in looking out of my window at the time at a flock of silly
sheep which happened to be grazing in the Green Park
opposite, I used to envy them their blissful stupid ignorance of
any law higher than their nature, their deep unconsciousness
of self, their innocence of all private personality and purpose,
their intense moral incapacity, in short, and indifference. I
would freely, nay, gladly have bartered the world at the
moment for one breath of the spiritual innocence which the
benign creatures outwardly pictured, or stood for to my
imagination; and all the virtue, or moral righteousness,
consequently, that ever illustrated our specific human
personality, seemed simply foul and leprous in comparison
with the deep Divine possibilities and promise of our common
nature, as these stood symbolized to my spiritual sight in
all the gentler human types of the merely animate world.[9]

James now felt that there was more "heavenly sweetness
in the soul of a patient overdriven cab-horse, or misused
cadger's donkey," than in the whole calendar of saints. It
was after all our "common nature" that counted, not our
individual moral pretensions: "You may easily imagine,
then, with what relish my heart opened to the doctrine I
found in these most remarkable books, *of the sheer and
abject phenomenality of selfhood in man. . . .*" James's
self-loathing, so vividly figured by the "damned shape"
[9] *Society*, pp. 71–72.

which he encountered in the dining room, is a consequence of our delusion of personal identity: "But though man starts with this feeling of his own absoluteness, or of his being life in himself, he is by no means left without a divine witness in his own bosom to the profound untruth of the feeling. For he feels, at the same time that he feels his existence, that there *is nothing in himself to warrant or justify such existence*. Let him start then never so gayly in the career of existence, he nevertheless starts with a threatening bombshell in his very vitals, which is ready to explode and lay him waste every moment that he remains unreconciled to the essential truth of things; or, what is the same thing, unenlightened as to the essential emptiness, imbecility, and charlatanry he carries about with him under the name of selfhood." It is selfhood with which all men contend rather than any external evil: "We may say then that God's creative purposes towards the human race necessarily involve a long preliminary wrestle or tussle on the part of the individual or self-conscious man *with himself:* a long, toilsome, most bitter, and vexatious conflict on his part with his own puny, crooked, insincere and ineffectual ways: before he can attain to that steadfast peace in God, which shall eventually leave him profoundly disinterested, indifferent, and actively inert in his own behalf." [10]

We must look into the question of just what the novelist's father thought *he* ought to do in the world, having had the good fortune to become "actively inert in his own behalf"; but first let us see how he makes the transition from individual career to society, in his own terms. The first point is that the casting out of the selfhood is coeval with the acceptance of a *social* as against a *moral* standard: "Let us understand then that the destiny of a man is to be made social out of moral; to attain to a conscience of perfect

[10] Quotations in this paragraph are from *Society*, pp. 72, 170–171, and 172.

social unity and order, through a previous conscience of complete moral discord and disorder. In a word our universally admitted spiritual or individual regeneration, has always been but a Providential stepping-stone and type of our universally ignored natural or common recreation." [11]

A favorite figure from mechanics, which explains how man moves closer to his divine nature in the very measure that he learns more, accumulates more, and is increasingly convinced of his individual nullity and loathsomeness, helps also to make plain the parallelism between the history of persons and that of the race.

The moral experience of the race necessarily involves this double or divided movement which we name Church and State; the former a descending or centrifugal movement by means of which the creature becomes self-convinced of his essential antagonism, as naturally constituted, to the Divine perfection: the latter an ascending or centripetal movement, by means of which the creature acknowledges himself as such recognized antagonist of the Divine perfection, to be rightfully under law to his fellow-man. In other words our moral consciousness as negatively reflecting our social destiny, is made up of two opposing elements, *self* and *the brother*. But inasmuch as the virus of their oppugnancy inheres only in the former or active element, *i.e.* in the selfishness of the human heart, so the Church as representing this element is bound to serve the State, or assume a secondary place with respect to it. . . . The play of these two forces fills the page of human history, until they succeed at last in generating a third or grandly unitary force which we call society, in which they both willingly coalesce and disappear, and which consequently thenceforth assumes the undivided responsibility of human destiny.[12]

His works and his letters represent the elder James as happily engaged in watching the unfolding of providence;

[11] *Substance*, p. 154.
[12] *Substance*, 153–154; see also *Nature of Evil* (p. 74) for the opposition between "self" and "the brother."

in detecting the signs of that reconciliation which will issue in the divine-natural-humanity, and inverting the literal meaning, both of revelation and existing institutions and conventions, to get at their spiritual meaning. He weaves everything he sees and hears into the web of providential activity. He is no less a "restless analyst" [13] than his son Henry, since he feels obliged to gloss and connect every impression and experience. He is endlessly receptive and interpretive. Politics, personalities, the theater, and the arts in general are all grist to his mill. His delightful letters testify that between such abstractions as the one in the next passage and his daily life there was the liveliest reciprocity: "The law of the image is subjectively to invert the lineaments of its original, or reflect them in so negative a form as that the original shall be wholly lost sight of in itself and the image alone appear; all that is light in the one being dark in the other, and vice versa." [14] The man who knew the world under the aegis of conscience or "God-in-us" was continually staggering his friends with such assertions as these. He found it perfectly axiomatic and intelligible that nature was an inversion of the Divine Wisdom and history an inversion of the Divine Love; and no doubt he took out a daguerreotype to illustrate the fact.

On contemporary social questions his capacity for indignation was nicely balanced by his trust in a providence as busily at work before his eyes as that which Cotton Mather had envisioned. Much of his indignation falls on reformers. American popular government does everything to "irritate and inflame" our "fallacious sentiment of selfhood";[15] *but* this is so much the better, for it brings on the crisis, which the comparative rigidity of church and state in Europe serves to postpone.

[13] As the novelist frequently calls himself in *The American Scene*.
[14] *Secret*, p. 48.
[15] *Remains*, p. 199. American society does this partly by giving us many opportunities for acquisition.

His general position on social amelioration is made clear in this passage on man's nature in the *Nature of Evil*: "Make him the subject of brotherly love alone, or self-love alone and his manhood becomes merged immediately in the purely natural innocence of the dove, or the purely natural subtlety of the serpent. Accordingly, the attempt to simplify the human constitution by making man subject in the social sphere to the influence of good alone would be to the last degree destructive of his rational character, and end by relegating him to the ranks of mere animality." [16]

Some of his applications of this principle sound like Lincoln Steffens grown up: "No man of truly angelic possibilities is ever greatly up to the demands of the actual life. If such a man manages to avoid stealing or doing other palpable mischief, it is as much as we may reasonably ask of him. But put him in a post of eminence or of large responsibility, and he will be sure to go on blundering at such a rate, and putting things to such confusion by his most unseasonable simplicity and good nature, by his most unreasonable confidence in exactly the least deserving and most designing persons, that you are forced erelong to send to Wall Street for some remorseless financier to straighten his accounts and save the world from bankruptcy." [17] The man of "angelic possibilities," since he has moved a little further than the rest toward the reconciliation of the dove and the serpent, is out of step, and an inevitable butt for his fellows. There is no reproach which we can properly address to God about this; he has taken his chance on us, shut himself up within us and given us freedom. To take away that freedom by constraining the whole race to good behavior would make the freedom meaningless, and the eventual society a tyranny instead of the spiritual democracy James foresaw.

[16] *Nature of Evil*, p. 226.
[17] *Substance*, pp. 251–252.

James's transmogrified version of Fourierist association-ism does not, as far as I can tell, jibe with Swedenborg's emphasis on the earthly state as a preparatory one. James was not technically a Swedenborgian (for a reason which will appear in a moment), but after he had read Sweden-borg he used very few ideas which were not to be found in the vast reservoir of Swedenborgian reports from the angels. The question of the relation between the work of the two men is really a question as to what James selected and emphasized, with the exception of the emphasis on the bootstrap myth. James was scornful of the New Church because he believed it to have betrayed the principles of Swedenborg by coming into existence in the first place. The church announced by Swedenborg was, as James conceived of it, the third and final dispensation (the first two being the Jewish and the Christian, the former stand-ing for all those which, in Swedenborg, are said to have preceded it). It was to arise with the coming of the Lord or God-Man, in the form of a new society. Since no new society was manifest to James, he thought it highly idiotic of the followers of Swedenborg to attempt the founding of such a church. Its most important characteristic was surely to be its root in universal brotherhood, and universal brotherhood did not exist.[18]

James seems to have browsed widely and eagerly in the sere pastures of Swedenborg, although he carefully guards himself against attributing to him any *personal* spiritual heroism. It was the fact that the "seer" had had the *self*-abnegation required to go and *listen* to the angels which made him, in James's well-known phrase, "insipid with veracity." The divine economy is of course a far more complex affair in Swedenborg than in James, who sought

[18] On the general question of the likeness of Swedenborg and James, see Alice Spiers Sechrist, "James's Debt to Swedenborg" (*The New Christianity*, XVIII, 1952, pp. 6-15). For the shift in James's empha-sis which I find and Miss Sechrist does not see, see page 93, below.

FORSYTH LIBRARY
FORT HAYS KANSAS STATE COLLEGE

to reduce his account of it to a few basic antinomies (or a few well-chosen paradoxes). These he told over and over as if they had an incantatory power. In each case it is over their coming reconciliation in the divine-natural-humanity that he rejoices. The angels, each of whom is complemented by a devil, will give way to the divine natural man, who has the power to use the "waste human force" which the devil represents. Angels give up something of their humanity to be conjoined with God; the divine natural man will not need to do so. Of this the resurrected Christ of flesh and bone is our example.[19]

We may say that the ideas were derived from Swedenborg; but the role of the man who employed the ideas is strikingly different. To make this plain, I turn to James himself. I have quoted him as saying that Swedenborg had informed him about the "angelic conception of the Divine being and providence." James was very grateful indeed for the discovery of the provisional and phenomenal nature of selfhood, and for the doctrine of the divine natural man, but he regarded the "angelic conception" of God and providence as a severely limited one. Swedenborg had been narrowed by an exclusive converse with angels. It was after all men, rather than angels, who were to compass the millennial changes James anticipated. He had learned this from Swedenborg himself. An angel has no *spontaneity;* his being is derived immediately from God, on whom he depends as the divine natural man (who will *consciously* give his allegiance) will not. Angels have no news to impart; nothing fresh happens to an angel. Well-grounded as they are in the doings of providence, they cannot anticipate the divine-natural-humanity itself.[20] James, however, could.

This apparently innocent difference with his "seer" tells

[19] *Secret*, pp. 45–46 (a list of God's attributes which are to become ours).
[20] *Remains*, pp. 310–314.

us something of the greatest biographical importance about
the elder James himself. I have tried to show in my first
chapter that there is a case for the assertion that the
proponents of the bootstrap myth were culturally determined; there is also evidence as to how the elder James was
emotionally determined—as to the psychic need which
Swedenborg's notions answered in him. One may put the
question that his behavior poses in a number of ways. Why
was he so fond of standing reality on its head? What
fantasy lay at the root of his genuine self-abnegation? A
brief inquiry into this matter may bring the reader closer
to the meaning of his imaginative adventure. I employ a
more recent version of one of those polarities within
personality which the elder James was so fond of describing. When his encounter with the "damned shape" in the
dining room had left him in a state of neurotic despair,
what did the elder James proceed to do with the emotional
resources at his command? I suggest that James came to
terms with his anxiety by adopting a role even more
fantastically presumptuous than Swedenborg's. Swedenborg had merely consulted God's understrappers, the
angels; James would take Swedenborg's scheme and apply
it to the nascent divinity—mankind. This involved an emotional polarity of the sort familiar in those who assume a
messianic role: a terrible arrogance completely disguised by
a maternal care for the whole world. The disguise served
to conceal from him his own masculinity, which he deeply
feared, and it entailed an incessant compulsive activity.
"The great explainer" [21] must be forever telling himself
that he made no claims which would estrange him from the
figure of *his* father. The "Autobiographic Fragment" in
the *Literary Remains* lends some weight to this supposition.

One cannot, however, derive this evidence from an

[21] The epithet applied to Gabriel Nash by Miriam Rooth in *The
Tragic Muse* (VIII, 54).

explicit account of the elder James's relations with his parents. Full as he is of vehement denunciations of types and classes, James is quite free of particular animadversions. He appears to have hated nobody, and borne no ill will—characteristics which we should of course expect him to show in the role I impute to him. His father, the millionaire merchant of Albany, had surrounded him with comfort and left him provided for to the end of his days. The son never even troubled to visit Syracuse and inspect his inherited holdings there; the source of his income was something with which he had no personal concern. What we do learn of his father in James's own account fills out this intimation that he felt more dependence on his father than he acknowledges. He informs us that when he lost his leg at the age of thirteen, his father was so deeply affected that his mother had to recall him to himself.

This picture is oddly at variance with the public image of "Billy James of Albany," the merchant who rivaled the Van Rensselaers in wealth and prestige, and was noted for his Presbyterian strictness.[22] It is also at odds with the remainder of the "Autobiographic Fragment." James complains of a *lack* of emotional warmth in the family circle, which, combined with external religious observances, made the James home an illustration of the "common vice of contented isolation." [23] If the tenderness the father showed in the months following the accident (an accident of a character particularly likely to disturb a boy of thirteen) had been more or less suddenly withdrawn, and the mother (who had a large brood to tend) had been persistently matter-of-fact, a brilliant and sensitive youngster might have developed just such a compulsion as the elder James exhibits. His attempts to get other people to acknowledge that God is infinite love *and* that they are totally estranged

[22] See Harold A. Larrabee, "Henry James, Sr., '30, at Union" (*Union Alumni Monthly*, XV, 1926, pp. 236–247).
[23] *Remains*, p. 152.

from Him, might, on the basis of this supposition, be translated: "My father looks stern and demanding to the world,
but I—even though he has temporarily abandoned me, and
I need him terribly—*I* know him to be truly loving and
kind, and I will so proclaim him to the world." The tension
between the "appearance" of God's estrangement (an appearance too bitter to accept) and the "reality" of His loving kindness is, at any rate, precisely the emotional burden
of the writings of Billy James's son. The primal importance
of the father as against the mother in James's imagination
is confirmed by certain figures of speech recurrent in
James's writing, and by a physical symptom, his stammer.

The place of women in the theologian's universe is so
exalted that it is not surprising to find that it has a most
unpleasant obverse: Women are split in two, and those who
want something other than worship are properly addressed
as Jesus addressed Mary, "Woman, what have I to do with
thee?" [24] (Mary must, by his logic, have been the epitome
of Jewish righteousness, in order that the Christ might, by
the fullest abasement, testify to his utter humiliation.)
Women *ought* to comport themselves as priestesses of the
divine love which they represent. American women are
reduced to a symbolic role as prophetesses of our "unseen
spiritual manhood," while European women are said to
be subject to masculine lust. The elder James himself
sought to represent his "unseen spiritual manhood" by be-
having like an "American" woman, seeking no power in
society, but simply acting out the precepts of universal
love and wisdom.

In all this there is an interesting congruence with Rosenzweig's thesis about Henry Junior's "passional death," [25] a
renunciation of all positive sexual aims, resembling the elder
James's explicit renunciation of his assertive selfhood. The

[24] *Moralism and Christianity*, p. 134.
[25] "The Ghost of Henry James" (*Partisan Review*, XI, 1944, pp.
436–455).

father's characterization of the man who has resigned his moral will is that he becomes "actively inert in his own behalf." The mood which prevails in him is one of eager receptivity—and assured dependence. Such an attitude assumes a world completely ordered, and a benign power engaged in its administration.[26] One of James's sentences about Swedenborg betrays his hidden awareness of the role he himself had assumed (it also accounts for his fondness for the figurative use of breasts and udders): "I have tried to bring out the motherly character of his teaching, the incomparably tender and succulent aspects which it bears to the guileless unmercenary heart of man . . . Swedenborg's primary demand on his readers is a heart attuned to goodness; and he leaves what subsequent truth he reports to his intellect fearlessly and without argument to the heart's sole arbitrament." Swedenborg is not creative but motherly; he just tells us what the angels said. The "actively inert" are, then, the delightedly dependent, yet their delight is their own: ". . . the babe leaps up on his mother's arm," in response to his own feeling, though he does so in a world of fostering power. In his study James played both these roles—that of mother and of babe—but out of it he seems to have been able to muster a gay acceptance of the differences between the behavior the world exacted of him and the convictions he so laboriously elaborated. The conflicts his public role involved may have been responsible for his stammer, but like many people whose emotional lives center about their mouths, he was at the same time a lively and even brilliant talker.[27]

[26] Edwards and Emerson both adopt this attitude at times. See Emerson, *Complete Works* (I, 182): "The Student, as we all insist, is great only by being passive to the superincumbent spirit." Perry Miller, in his *Jonathan Edwards,* refers to Edwards's "empirical passivity" as a "program of action" (see esp. pp. 47, 57, 65).

[27] Henry Senior's stammer is mentioned in a letter from Carlyle to Emerson. See C. Hartley Grattan, *The Three Jameses,* pp. 45–46. Henry Junior's stammer is discussed in Edith Wharton's *A Backward Glance,* pp. 178, 185, 195.

To accept the fact that his religious impulses were not unique, and his particular formulation not altogether novel, proved impossible. His work was too much for himself and not enough for the world. He tried, almost singlehandedly, to construct a scheme which would represent the stresses of his feelings about God, the self, and the world, and the dynamism of the elements he sought to employ was such that he did himself more empirical justice than reason was prepared to countenance. Freud had not yet made it plain that conflict is an inescapable fact in individuals as well as societies, and this particular precursor seldom hit upon the vocabulary or the images appropriate to the character of what he wanted to say about people. He can attain to profundity about human emotions, but he does so with such a clanking of conceptual machinery that few people have had the patience to discover the fact. The thing he wanted us to feel—that human beings *are* the locus of tensions and oppositions, of fields of moral force—he could never quite articulate. The necessity was too much his own, and the act of explaining too often subsides into ritual and privacy.

This description applies to the elder James's books, although they contain many passages of lively and telling discussion of problems of the day, of personalities, even occasionally of philosophic issues. From this point of view *Substance and Shadow*, because of its comparatively relaxed tone, is the best of the lot, and, perhaps for the same reason, the work which oftenest recalls William James's ability to make philosophic discourse take on the directness of the spoken word.

If the books have, on the whole, the teasing, evasive quality of neurotic compulsion, James's letters often do not. Indeed, I have been harsher than his son Henry in the measure that I know the books instead of the man. The capacity he shows for imaginative sympathy—which Henry Junior found so impressive—is complementary to an emphasis which is found in the books, the emphasis on "taste or spontaneous attraction." [28] This phrase and the phrase "social and esthetic," [29] which occurs even more frequently, offer a clue to the most apprehensible and appealing side of the elder James's books. Despite all the hundreds of pages of manipulated abstractions he produced, he was an invoker of life, he wanted to open the roads to human greatness.

Up to the time the younger Henry James attained his majority, his father's chief mode of expressing this in his books was to cry up the Artist as against the Priest and King. He once called the artist "the only regenerate image of God in nature, the only living revelation of the Lord on earth." In passage after passage, in volume after volume, he uses the artist as the type of the divine-natural-humanity which is to come. This is a fact of great importance for the biographies of William and Henry James. It has much to do with William's sense that reality is somehow created out of the novelties that greatness brings down to us, and it helps to explain Henry Junior's easy and almost unconscious belief that "art makes life." [30]

The thesis on which the elder James based his extraordinary claim for the artist is that he exhibits, insofar as one now can, "spiritual individuality." The linked terms "social and esthetic," are juxtaposed with the terms "nature and society." At present we are under the dominion of material greed (we try to possess "nature") and moral greed (we try to get men to acknowledge our status), and we ask God to proclaim us spiritually fatter than our fellows. The artist, on the other hand, is the image of "social" man, because he makes no such claims; he simply

[28] *Substance*, p. 301. The use of the term "attraction" is probably the clearest mark of the fact that James had for a time been much interested in Fourier, whose American followers made "attractive industry" a byword. For another use of "spontaneous," see *Substance*, p. 12 ("spontaneous or aesthetic activity").

[29] *Secret*, p. 203.

[30] *Letters*, II, 490. For the "regenerate image," see *Substance*, p. 13.

employs appearances to reflect God's nature and makes no claims for *personal* recognition. If he is truly an artist, he is selfless. He asks no recognition for what he is, but only for what he does. His activity reveals him as a "regenerate image" of God because he orders that revelation of God's nature which is his consciousness under the auspices of the conscience or social self rather than the Eve or selfish self. Or, we may say that the true artist is not a personage in the bad sense—he is a creative force, recognizable, as the creator himself is recognizable, *only in the quality of the things he makes.* "In other words, the law of all spiritual existence is that doing determines being, or that character is based upon action, not action upon character. Whatsoever one actually does when one is free from the coercion of necessity [nature] or the constraint of prudence [society] is the measure of what one really is." [31]

He who accepts his form at the hands of nature and society is shaped by moral and material greed—he is a true son of "the church"; he who makes his own form is at least an "image" of God. [32] Moreover, the man who seeks distinction on the ground of his character alone only increases his likeness to everyone else who wants personal recognition. He is in the situation of our contemporaries who buy Cadillacs to show that they have gotten ahead; but the Cadillac is everybody's symbol and does not actually distinguish anyone. The artist who surrenders his selfhood lives by "taste or spontaneous attraction"; he acquires his own tone or style. In his later works the elder James is prone to emphasize the inability of the artist to compete with God in creation because what the former makes must be shaped out of the materials at hand, while God first forms the creature and then gives him life. (The difficulty here is the same one that confronted James in relation to

---

[31] *Secret,* p. 180.
[32] See the elder James's epigraph to *Society,* quoted in Chapter III, above.

Swedenborg: Since no live man ought to be praised, but only the "God-in-us" which animates us spiritually, praise for the Artist might be taken as moral toadying to actual artists.)

The Artist is the nearest thing we have to a truly "spontaneous" man: "Art is nothing else than the obedience of one's spontaneous tastes and attractions, uncontrolled either by nature or society, by necessity or duty." In a passage on the deprivations of angels the elder James remarks that they have a "sheer incapacity freely to image God, that is, to do good spontaneously. . . ."[33] And we know that "to do good spontaneously" is to be an artist.

It is distressing to reflect how many earnest students have tried to construct an Emersonian aesthetic (apparently on the assumption that everyone who writes must have one), the fact being that no transcendentalist can afford to have an aesthetic; he has to make use of objects in nature and works of art to reflect the moral claims of individuals, or of "the superincumbent spirit."[34] To work out a scheme as to how art functions in experience as distinct from the way in which other aspects of life affect us, one must first assert that the experience of art is terminal, or is in some other way truly discrete. But in Emerson and the elder James (and other Americans of their intellectual persuasion) art was indispensable to the exhibition of the distinctively moral. As the elder James himself would have it, we are to subdue all nature to ourselves, so that it becomes a spectacle of the divine in us.[35]

Despite the elder James's highly complimentary illustrative use of the artist, and its association with spontaneity, which is one of the novelist's prime values, the younger man was not altogether happy with his father's conception of the artist. We shall find him using his father's

[33] *Logic*, p. 235n.
[34] See note 26, above.
[35] *Logic*, p. 235n.

technical terms, for example, in describing novelists as "lovers of the image of life," a phrase in which the relation between the terms *image* and *life* is precisely parallel with his father's usage.[36] The novelist of the order of Balzac is distinct from the poet, of whom James writes: "It is not the *image* of life that he thus expresses, so much as life itself, in its sources—so much as his own intimate, essential states and feelings." [37] We are familiar with the term "sources"; we here find that "life" is a term for what flows from these, and that "image" is a term for objects and persons as *reflections* of the "sources," or (to use the term I have earlier employed) these reflections are "appearances." [38] That this congruence in the use of terms was not accident, we see from the figure of Gabriel Nash in *The Tragic Muse* (1890). James made his awareness of his father's theory of the artist apparent by undertaking both to celebrate him and to criticize his view of the artist in the same book.

Gabiel Nash is both an affectionate portrait of the elder James's "tone" or style, and an implied criticism of his personal mode of advocating his system. The character has variously (and mistakenly) been associated with the doctrine of art for art's sake, and, as a person, with the novelist himself.[39] The cumulation of detail makes it quite plain that the elder James figures in this novel about the

[36] The *Question of Our Speech*, p. 71. The use of the word "life" in this expression is apparently identical with the usage of the elder James, for whom "the life" was the in-dwelling spirit, and for whom its "image" was its reflection in the Adam, or world of man and nature.

[37] *Picture and Text*, p. 54. Here James speaks of the necessity that the artist "have a great love" in order "to see."

[38] It will further be shown, in Chapter V, that in the novelist, as well as in the father, "appearances" are sometimes *inversions* of the "sources."

[39] See Introduction, *Henry James, Stories of Writers and Artists*, ed. by F. O. Matthiessen, p. 2; and Introductory Essay, *The Complete Plays of Henry James*, ed. by Leon Edel, p. 40.

place of the artist in society. This is surprising when one considers how chary James was of the use of autobiographical material. But he could feel both justified and relatively safe; it was the meaning of his father's attitudes that he sought to dramatize, not (or only to a limited degree) his particular idiosyncrasies. (It is of course less surprising to find the elder James in the most explicitly didactic of his son's works.) This is a book animated by ideas; we may even conjecture a teasing reference to his father in the preface, in which James asserts that the virtue of the book lies in the consistency of its "tone." The word and the emphasis recur in the *Notes of a Son and Brother,* in which he remarks that one might say of the elder James that "his philosophy *was* his tone." It was his father's *tone* which held together the multiplicity of *his* ideas.

The man who acts from "spontaneous taste and attraction" and calls himself, on this ground, an "artist," is, as the younger Henry James makes plain, in an ambiguous position. Gabriel Nash is made to declare. "I work in life!" And we shall find him asserting that he acts *from* the "life"; is unconstrained, that is, by nature or society, by material greed or moral greed. But the very act of proclaiming this means that he is putting himself forward as an example. He may be a beneficent power in the lives of others (as he is in this book), but while he is trying simply to *represent* the sources, he seems to make a personal claim. The novelist, the painter, the sculptor, whose work is separable from his own person may avoid the implicit assertion that he is *the* appearance representative of the sources.

Before I deal with Nash and his "little system" I must say something about the general character of this novel. *The Tragic Muse* is in conception curiously mechanical; in execution, curiously loose. Its figures have not those ligatures binding each to each which led Eliot to call

James's chief subject a "social entity." James is perhaps trying to justify this quality in the book in the preface. Here, he says that he sought "scenic consistency, the consistency of the multiplication of *aspects*" (VII, xv) in giving us Miriam Rooth, and tells us that to his presentation of her a *"usurping* consciousness" was not germane. This, as his preface does not explicitly note, though reading makes it apparent, is a case in which method is enforced by a view of character. To invade Miriam's consciousness would be to treat a part of her which is *not* histrionic, and therefore to rob us of the representation of the great artist herself. For the mechanical juxtaposition of points of view James offers no excuse; he seems rather to think that he has succeeded in pulling the whole together through its "tone"—which in this instance may mean just its "philosophy." But I cannot feel James's confidence in his structure.

The relation of Nick, who has abandoned a parliamentary career for portrait painting, to Peter, who has "quenched a personal passion for the good of the public service," is all too artificial (VIII, 219).[40] The *idea* of the artist's relation to a world unfriendly to the artist's silent working is too important to the novel, and the dramatic consequences of Nick's situation not important enough. James sweetly explains that they could not be very interesting because the artist is not in himself a hero. This is rather a reason for not attempting the novel than a defense. There is a good deal of fun in the book, fun of the sort which James attempted less successfully to get into his comedies, disengaged little squibs of humor, such as the juxtaposition of Nick's callings—he has been "representing Harsh" (a constituency) and now as a portrait painter he is undertaking to represent life instead!

To go on with my strictures—the measure of James's

[40] For James's defense of the figure of Nick Dormer, see VII, viii–ix.

intended use of Miriam Rooth, as the preface suggests it, is by no means satisfied in the book itself (VII, xiv-xvi). He meant us to feel about Miriam as we cannot; he meant us to feel that she was representative of the situation, not simply of the actress, but of creators at large. The actress who gives her self to art cannot keep it, cannot live any other life than that of art, and is nonetheless condemned to the appearance of heartless narcissism.[41] This, James seems to have felt, is but an affecting instance of the general fate of the artist, further sharpened by the fact that the actress cannot interpose the barrier of a medium like the painter or writer; she *is* the material in which she works.

The very fact that analysis in such terms is appropriate to this novel indicates its limitations. The subject matter is here reduced to James's own rationale of the arts in society; there is nothing behind, no sense of possibilities in reserve, as in *The Portrait of a Lady*. It has been assumed that James must have decided to enrich his picture of the relation of the arts to society by introducing (in addition to his devoted artists, his philistines, and his false patron, Peter Sherringham) someone who might represent the aestheticism of the period. And this is what Nash is taken for by the uninformed characters in the book; their mistake is apparently meant to adumbrate the fact that the elder James was persistently associated with Swedenborgianism, which he detested as a sect. Any straight look at Nash belies the notion that he thinks art independent of life. He has quite another creed to offer, and it is simply a polished rendering of the views of the elder James. The anomalies he embodies are wholly intelligible on this basis, but this

---

[41] Cf. R. P. Blackmur, "In the Country of the Blue" (*Kenyon Review*, V, 1943, pp. 602–607): "Aschenbach the artist could have no life except that terrible privation of life which is art." See also *A Small Boy and Others* (p. 104), where James speaks of the "histrionic image" as it is when "reduced to its mere self. . . ."

is not of much help to the reader, who is being treated to a rather teasing dose of family piety.[42]

I infer from James's *Notebooks* that certain details about Gabriel Nash are drawn from the novelist's intercourse with Herbert Pratt in Venice in the year 1881. James expresses the intention of putting Pratt into a novel: "I shall even make the portrait close and he won't mind." Some of the traits Pratt exhibited are used in the novel. It is impossible to say when the image of Pratt and the terms of his father's system merged into the figure of Nash.[43] The biographical interest of James's invoking his father (whose passion for the theater was deep) at the time he is about to embark seriously on playwriting is considerable. Here we may note simply that the artists in this book move between society, on the one hand, and "the great explainer," on the other, and that what Nash is represented as doing for these artists is what I have represented the elder James as doing for the young man who went to Europe to become a writer. He supplies that account of the world which justifies the artist as the creator of the only forms that count; those of society—its laws for example—are of real use only to people who have no spontaneity, no love for variety, no individual style.

There is a hint in James's *Letters* that his father was very much in his mind in the early stages of composition of *The Tragic Muse*. He writes William in October, 1888, from a Geneva hotel: "I am sitting in our old family *salon* in this place, and have sat here much of the time for the last fortnight in social converse with family ghosts— Father and Mother and Aunt Kate and our juvenile selves." [44]

[42] On the other hand, these terms are not unlike those which the novelist himself uses in the essay on Flaubert, quoted in Chapter I, above.
[43] *The Notebooks of Henry James*, ed. by F. O. Matthiessen and Kenneth B. Murdock, p. 31. (Hereafter cited as *Notebooks*.)
[44] *Letters*, I, 140.

But it was not so much Father as Father's ideas and "experiential authority" [45] that he strove to represent through brilliant paraphrase. The novel opens with a scene amusingly domestic, though it takes place at the Paris exhibition. The family presented is rather more a family in a Howellsian state than any other in James, but it has no least reference to James's own family. To the Dormers—mother, two daughters, and the son and presumed heir to his father's political gifts—the son's college mate Gabriel Nash appears. I say "appears" because Nash has throughout an apparitional quality, as if he were a genie who came at call. He is most real and homely when, following Miriam Rooth's transformation from a dowdy, over-eager aspirant into an actress, he becomes her familiar, a sort of household attendant. But in these first scenes with Nick Dormer he speaks with a high impersonality of the claims of art over every other calling.

Before I present what he calls his "little system," here, in order to amplify the comparison, is one of the extended statements the elder James made about the place of the artist in the world:

If the divine man, the man of genius, the man of inward force, the man of ideas, in short, the Artist, would succumb to society; if he would say nothing and do nothing which society disallowed, nothing subversive of its customs and traditions; if he would utter no prophecies and confess no want of a superior righteousness to that which flowed from the obedience of existing institutions; then society would gladly honor him, and give him the pomp and glory of all the kingdoms of the world.

But the artist is unable to gratify society in this thing. He lives from God alone, from the inspiration of truth and beauty in his own soul, and he cannot acknowledge any law or institution which limits these. Hence in an immature or dissentient society his lot is to suffer outwardly, to be

[45] *Notes of a Son and Brother*, p. 229.

crucified in the flesh even while he is being glorified in the spirit, even in order to his being thus glorified.[46]

The first point in Gabriel Nash's "little system" (as he explains it to Nick) is "the idea of being just the same to everyone." He says: "People have so bemuddled themselves that the last thing they can conceive is that one should be simple." [47] Dormer and his family have found Nash in the highest degree paradoxical. Dormer says, "Lord, do you call yourself simple?" The reason Nash is hard to understand is that he appears to do nothing and have no personal interests. His reply to Dormer points to this freedom of his, which is a freedom from the bonds of "nature and society," as the elder James puts it, and is here rendered by "savage" and "interest." "Absolutely; in the sense of having no interest of my own to push, no nostrum to advertise, no power to conciliate, no axe to grind. I'm not a savage—ah far from it! but I really think I'm perfectly independent." Other people, Nash continues, try to get one to enter the "boats" of their interests, dogmas, or prejudices. These are the "unregenerate." He is not of their number, having "jumped over long ago." Dormer, who cannot conceive of a free man, has a suspicion that Nash belongs to a cult of aesthetes. He asks whether the regenerate do not have a narrowing creed of their own. If so, Nash is "no better" than other people. Nash's reply contains the charge, so often preferred by the elder James, that most men invert reality. "I don't pretend to be better, for we're all miserable sinners; I only pretend to be bad in a pleasanter, brighter way—by what I can see. It's the simplest thing in the world; just take for granted our right to be happy and brave. What's essentially kinder and more helpful than that, what's more beneficial?

[46] *Moralism and Christianity*, p. 49.
[47] The quotations from Nash are from VII, Chapter IX, 165–184. Nash extends his exposition of his credo in VIII, Chapter XXIII, pp. 23–28.

But the tradition of dreariness, of stodginess, of dull dense literal prose has so sealed people's eyes that they've only ended by thinking the most natural of all things the most perverse."

So far Nash has said that we ought to treat all men alike —that is, have no "respect of persons"—and that we ought renounce our animal desires and the claims of social status, or ideological pretension; that to do so is to invert conventional morality and discard materialism; and that we are all equally bad, presumably, in the sight of God. He goes on to develop the positive aspect of the elder James's faith. What is of final importance is spiritual individuality, here called "form" and "style."

Life consists of the personal experiments of each of us and the point of an experiment is that it shall succeed. What we contribute is our treatment of the material, our rendering of the text, our style. A sense of the qualities of a style is so rare that many persons should doubtless be forgiven for not being able to read, or at all events to enjoy, us; but is that a reason for giving it up—for not being, in this other sphere, if one possibly can, an Addison, a Ruskin, a Renan? Ah we must write our best; it's the great thing we can do in the world, on the right side. One has one's form, *que diable*, and a mighty good thing that one has. I'm not afraid of putting all life into mine, and without unduly squeezing it. I'm not afraid of putting in honor and courage and charity—without spoiling them: on the contrary I shall only do them good.

There is, in fact, no other way to be virtuous—for any other method involves putting one's self forward as a peculiarly valuable (and therefore self-righteous) *person.*[48]

[48] Nick has already been accused by Nash of having a "side" (VII, 35); that is, a public, status-claiming self to maintain. The way in which Nash schools Nick is, both in manner and detail, suggestive of the way in which the elder James schooled everyone, his sons included. For example, Nash maintained that "there were more ideas, more of those that man lived by, in a single room of the National Gallery than in all the statutes of Parliament" (VIII, 266). This is

Nash's three moralists were stylists. Ruskin, of course, makes much of the relationship between morality and style.[49] Nash sees an identity where Ruskin saw a relationship. Any other mode of being virtuous would involve not "being just the same to everyone," would involve asserting one's self in the way he has ruled out. The novelist has managed to put the essence of his father's moral outlook in a very few words. Life cannot be referred to, invoked, or lived save in the guise of a particular form. What James has here described implies the bootstrap myth. Formal statement in the elder James often links the elements here involved in a precisely parallel way; links what is universal —say Nash's list of virtues—to the "spontaneity" of life through expression in "form." "This is the invariable mean-

rhetorically reminiscent of the elder James, who finds "the horse-car our true shechinah at this day" (*Society*, pp. 90–91). The passage continues: "Nick had replied to this more than once that the determination of what man did live by was required; to which Nash had retorted (and it was very rarely that he quoted Scripture) that it was at any rate not by bread and beans alone." James is surely making game here; Nash is forever exhorting in the book, and we may take it, (a) that he exhorts to ends incompatible with those of Scripture; or (b) that he does not quote it as often as his *exempla* seem to require. The first alternative would surely be chosen by those who have concluded that Nash is a mere aesthete—which is the delusive appearance he wears to what he calls Nick's "poor British wit." But Nick gives up this thesis—so it is a conclusion of the book's authoritative sensibility that one *would* expect Nash to quote Scripture oftener, considering the burden of what he says. Now the real point here is that *the elder James* did not quote Scripture as often as one might have expected him to, given his preoccupations.

[49] James was not endorsing Ruskin (note the phrase "in this other sphere"), but trying to enforce the point that universal values find expression in the artist's form. The 1890 text (Boston and New York: Houghton Mifflin and Company, 1890, 2 vols., I, 188) has Macaulay in place of Addison. On Ruskin, see *Portraits of Places*, pp. 105–107 (rather stringent remarks). There is an indicative inconsistency in Nash's saying, "we must *write* our best"—since he himself defines his vocation as *talking* in behalf of the human race (VIII, 27). It is as if James had had Nash—his father—address *him*, the novelist, instead of the painter, Nick Dormer.

ing of consciousness: *the copulation of an interior object with an exterior subject; the marriage of a universal substance with a specific form.* . . . The animal does not originate his own action, that is, is destitute of spontaneity. He acts wholly from the control of his nature. And man, in so far as he is animal, does the same thing. But in so far as he is man, he acts from taste or individual attraction, that is to say, originates his own action, or exhibits spontaneity." [50] The god seated within (the "interior object") gets expression in this way; is released through man's capacity to express him in "form."

These early scenes with Nash are capped by the one in the second volume in which Nash confirms and blesses Nick's talent. A quotation will complete this account of Nash's "system." Nick has shown his paintings to very few people; in this scene he gets out the whole lot for Nash, and waits while Nash walks about the room, observing and considering. "He had stayed in town to be alone with his imagination, and suddenly, paradoxically, the sense of that result had arrived with poor Nash." (This suggests the "apparitional" quality I have ascribed to Nash; it is as if he were Nick's and Miriam's good genius.) After his inspection he asks Nick: "Don't you recognize in *any* degree the grand idea of duty?" Nick attacks in return.

"My dear fellow, duty is doing, and I've inferred that you think rather poorly of doing—that it spoils one's style."
"Doing wrong, assuredly."
"But what do you call right? What's your canon of certainty there?" Nick asked.
"The conscience that's in us—that charming conversible infinite thing, the intensest thing we know. But you must treat the oracle civilly if you wish to make it speak. You mustn't stride into the temple in muddy jack-boots with your hat on your head, as the Puritan troopers tramped into

[50] *Logic,* p. 83.

the dear old abbeys. One must do one's best to find out the right, and your criminality appears to be that you've not taken the commonest trouble."

"I hadn't you to ask," smiled Nick. "But duty strikes me as doing something in particular. If you're too afraid it may be the wrong thing you may let everything go." (VIII, 25–26)

We recognize in this passage the problem the elder James posed for his sons, which Henry Junior described in his reminiscences.[51] He was most eager to get them to use their very own talent, and to encourage them to find it; he was also likely to feel that any particular vocation was narrowing. But here the novelist has him pronounce judgment. James has also brought in a figurative description of the relation of conscience to the selfhood. The "temple" is not to be entered with one's "hat" on, as the Puritans entered "the abbeys"; judgments made by the self-righteous are desecrations of "conscience." Nash goes on as follows:

"Being is doing, and if doing is duty being is duty. Do you follow?"

"At a very great distance."

"To be what one *may* be, really and efficaciously," Nash went on, "to feel it and understand it, to accept it, adopt it, embrace it—that's conduct, that's life."

"And suppose one's a brute or an ass, where's the efficacy?"

"In one's very want of intelligence. In such cases one's out of it—the question doesn't exist; one simply becomes a part of the duty of others. The brute, the ass," Nick's visitor developed, "neither feels nor understands nor accepts nor adopts. Those fine processes in themselves classify us. They educate, they exalt, they preserve; so that to profit by them we must be as perceptive as we can. We must recognize our particular form, the instrument that each of us—each of us who carries anything—carries in his being. Mastering this instrument, learning to play it in perfection—that's what I call duty, what I call conduct, what I call success."

[51] *Notes of a Son and Brother*, pp. 48–52.

Nick listened with friendly attention and the air of general assent was in his face as he said: "Every one has it then, this individual pipe?" [52]

" 'Every one,' my dear fellow, is too much to say, for the world's full of the crudest *remplissage*. The book of life's padded, ah but padded—a deplorable want of editing! I speak of every one who's any one. Of course there are pipes and pipes—little quavering flutes for the concerted movements and big *cornets-à-piston* for the great solos."

"I see, I see. And what might your instrument be?"

Nash hesitated not a moment; his answer was radiantly there. "To speak to people just as I'm speaking to you. To prevent for instance a great wrong being done."

"A great wrong—?"

"Yes—to the human race. I talk—I talk; I say the things other people don't, the things they can't, the things they won't," Gabriel went on with his inimitable candour.

"If it's a question of mastery and perfection you certainly have them," his companion replied.

"And you haven't, alas; that's the pity of it, that's the scandal. That's the wrong I want to set right before it becomes too public a shame. If I called you just now grossly immoral it's on account of the spectacle you present—a spectacle to be hidden from the eye of ingenuous youth: that of a man neglecting his own fiddle to blunder away on that of one of his fellows. We can't afford such mistakes, we can't tolerate such license."

"You think then I *have* a fiddle?"—and our young man, in spite of himself, attached to the question a quaver of suspense finer, doubtless, than any that had ever passed his lips.

"A regular Stradivarius! All these things you've shown me are remarkably interesting. You've a talent of a wonderfully pure strain." (VIII, 26–27) [53]

[52] See an early work of the elder James's in which he holds that a true socialism will, by freeing us from nature and society, make man "a mere pipe for the finger of the Deity to play what stops it pleases" (*Moralism and Christianity*, p. 80).

[53] The effect of the revision for the New York Edition was slightly to intensify the apparent anomaly of Nash's use of the vocabulary of

Once again, James has phrased his father's cardinal principle: "Conduct" consists in finding the "particular form" which will relate us to "the conscience that's in us —that charming conversible *infinite* [italics mine] thing, the intensest thing we know." One of the most interesting things in this passage is the way in which Nick is made to question Nash's consistency. What is his instrument? Nash's answer, though it is in fact the answer of the elder James, is not, according to the novel, quite sufficient. He seeks to prevent a "wrong," not to persons, about whom he doesn't care, but to "the human race." (Henry Senior would of course say "humanity.")

To bring out the correspondences between the father and son, I have been emphasizing a species of equation, one form of which runs: Universality plus particular form equals conduct, which in turn equals art, *impersonal* art. I should like to add (as the novel does) that such particular forms are those which reveal the universal. Peter Sherringham's highest flight in the book is his perception that Miriam's marvellous beauty is in this way connected with what I have been calling the sources: "He could but call it a felicity and an importance incalculable, and but know that it connected itself with universal values." This is a question of the book, of course, as well as an observation; it helps us to see why Miriam is a wonderful creature to paint; why she cannot be loved as a *person*, but only as a kind of mobile vision; why she wants Nick to paint her, but does not want him to make love to her, and so on. At

morality to enforce the worth of the artistic career. For example, the 1890 edition (II, 430) has "elevated idea of duty"; the revision substitutes "grand" for "elevated" (VIII, 25). Nash's insistence that the practice of art *is* the way to be moral is reminiscent of the passage in *A Small Boy and Others* (pp. 216–217), which begins: "Thus we had ever the amusement, since I can really call it nothing less, of hearing morality, or moralism, as it was more invidiously worded, made hay of it in the very interest of character and conduct. . . ."

this point I should like to anticipate far enough to associate this beauty of hers with the "infinite" thing that is "conscience," and the following passage from the preface to *The Golden Bowl*: ". . . it is clear to the most limited intelligence that the title we give him [James has called novelists 'poets'] is the only title of general application and convenience for those who passionately cultivate the image of life and the art, on the whole so beneficial, of projecting it. The seer and speaker under the descent of the god is the 'poet,' whatever his form, and he ceases to be one only when his form, whatever else it may nominally or superficially or vulgarly be, is unworthy of the god; in which event, we promptly submit, he isn't worth talking of at all. He becomes worth it, and the god so adopts him and so confirms his charming office and name, in the degree in which his impulse and passion are general and comprehensive." The relation of the artist's or "poet's" form to the "general and comprehensive" is the same in the novelist, his father, and the character of Gabriel Nash. It is apparent, moreover, that the novelist's avoidance of general *ideas* is a principled avoidance. It is not in the interest of art alone that he eschews generalization; it is also in the interest of life, which generalization cannot represent.

Certain additional details which relate Nash to the elder James should not be missed. The irruption of Nash on the scene at the outset takes place at the moment when Nick and Miriam are struggling out of the chrysalis of selfhood and becoming artists. When they have become firmly settled in their callings, he vanishes. He has no function except to serve their talents, and though he has written a book, this is not what distinguishes him. When Miriam Rooth asks Nick, anent one of Nash's absences, whether Nash is jealous of Nick, the latter replies: "Not in the least, for from the moment one does anything one ceases to compete with him. It leaves him the field more clear."

(VIII, 395) [54] Nash's club is the "Anonymous"; he repels with something close to indignation (an exception to the unvarying sweetness of his temper) the notion that he belongs to a cult af aesthetes. James makes some play with his name. It is clearly meant to point to the angel who announces the consummation of humanity's career with a trumpet. Nick muses at one point: "Gabriel might have been the angel of that name, but no angel could assist him much henceforth." (VIII, 190) He has Nash remark about Miriam Rooth, "Ambition, in her, was always on the rush, and she was not a person to conceive that others might in bad moments listen for the trumpet in vain." (VIII, 265) (The elder James, who does not often celebrate angels, mentions this one three times.[55] But the novelist may not have known this. He may, on the other hand, have recalled his father's fondness for the illustrative use of this angel in conversation.

Nick's portrait of Nash will be a "feather from the angel's wing" (VIII, 408). The name popularly suggests a prophet, and Gabriel functions as one. He foretells Miriam's marriage to Dashwood and Nick's final summons from Julia.[56] Nash is called by Miriam "the great explainer" (VIII, 54), but Nick is conscious that his explanations often fail to explain: "Nick had no wish to get rid of his private philosopher; he liked his philosophy, and though of course premeditated paradox was the light to read him by

[54] See *Notes of a Son and Brother* (pp. 50–51, 112–113) on the elder James's feeling that any *particular* vocation his sons considered pursuing was "narrowing."

[55] *Nature of Evil*, p. 37; *Logic*, p. 50; *The Church of Christ not an Ecclesiasticism: A Letter of Remonstrance . . .*, p. 20. The Elder James here employs the "angel Gabriel's plenary illumination" for illustrative purposes.

[56] In *Lectures* (p. 134) the elder James speaks of the artist's "prophetic worth," but this is a general rather than a specific capacity. The title of this lecture is more to the point; it is called "Universality in Art," and of course repeats the emphasis on the power of artistic particularity to embody generality or "life."

5

he yet had frequently and incidentally an inspired unexpectedness." (VIII, 400) Prophets must be listened to, though one does not always understand. When Biddy (his sister) asks Nick whether he has quarrelled with Nash, Nick asks in turn, "Does the nightingale quarrel with the moon?" (VIII, 419) Still, at certain crises Nash does not serve Nick, precisely because his allegiance is so sure and so general—it does not take account of the particular difficulties. This must have been one of the chief annoyances of having Henry James, "the great explainer," for a parent. Moreover, his talk had the prime disadvantage of unsupported talk: "That was one's penalty with persons whose main gift was for talk, however inspiring; talk engendered a sense of sameness much sooner than action. The things a man did were necessarily more different from each other than the things he said, even if he went in for surprising you." (VIII, 191) [57]

Chapter XLIX is a gamesome and affectionate portrait of the elder James in Nash's person. It turns on Nick's decision to ask Nash to sit for his portrait. Nash becomes "silent, restless, gloomy, dim, as if on test the homage of a directer attention than he had ever had gave him less pleasure than he had ever supposed. . . . He was so accustomed to living upon irony and the interpretation of things that it was new to be himself interpreted and—as a gentleman who sits for his portrait is always liable to be—interpreted all ironically. From being outside of the universe he was suddenly brought into it, and from the position of a free commentator and critic, an easy amateurish editor of the whole affair, reduced to that of humble ingredient and contributor." (VIII, 410) [58] Not to be

[57] James went so far as to have Nash accuse Nick of thinking him a bore (VIII, 407).

[58] It has been noted in Chapter III that the son felt an "implied snub" to his view of the world in his father's so inclusive and so different view. The "easy amateurish editor," who was his father, here sits for his portrait in a double sense: He is being portrayed in a *novel*,

pinned down, not to be identified: this was the desire not only formally demanded by the elder James's idea of the role of the invoker of human spontaneity—it was also something apparent in his daily life.[59] Peter Sherringham's comment on Nash fits in here: "If we paid ten shillings to listen to Mr. Nash we would think him very fine. But we want to know what it's supposed to be." (VII, 208) James is very amusing in *A Small Boy and Others* on the embarrassment which their father's lack of a namable calling created for his sons.

It is during these sittings that Nick asks what will happen to Nash when he is old. Nash replies that he is "immortal" (VIII, 411),[60] but he very soon disappears altogether, and it is Nick's impression that the unfinished portrait itself is fading, as might a portrait in a Hawthorne tale if the subject were reluctant to leave a record of himself. There seems to be a tender allusion to the placid and unshaken

that is, in that form which his son had embraced; he is at the same time being commemorated as the man who talked in behalf of the human race, with as much fidelity to his spirit—or, as I should say—more fidelity to his spirit, than he had been elsewhere, in particular by the able and devoted, but not quite sufficiently sympathetic, William James in the *Literary Remains*.

[59] *Notes of a Son and Brother*, p. 274. James here says that his father was engaged in behalf of the activities of his sons insofar as they were truly "*personal*" or "social," making it apparent that he understood his father's conception of the artist's "spiritual individuality" as primarily devoted to social ends.

[60] Nash says: "For me there'll be no collapse, no transition, no clumsy readjustment of attitude; for I shall only *be*, more and more, with all the accumulations of experience, the longer I live." This leads, on Nick's insisting further, to Nash's declaration: ". . . I dare say I'm indestructible, immortal." The elder James, as I have noted, dislikes the notion that death is a finality (*Nature of Evil*, pp. 132, 206). In *Substance* (Appendix, Note F, p. 522) he writes: "Thus, when we die, we wake without any shock or lapse of consciousness in a world perfectly conformed to our ideal." Death as destructive is emblematic of the spiritual fate of those who appropriate some "outward natural representation" of the divinity—it is the fate of the "spiritually" evil, who may all the while be walking about, just as some men in Dante's *Comedy* go to hell, and yet appear to live on earth.

manner of the elder James's death in this, but it is more important to note the formal point: It is Nick's concern with Nash's *self*, or with his fleshly envelope as representative of a self, that leads Nash, true to his "little system," to vanish. As Nick puts it to Biddy, "Nash has melted back into the elements—he's part of the great air of the world."

One more of James's barely dramatized comments on the life of the artist (which accords neatly with the grand distinction between the selflessness of the artist's mode of life and the moral or material greed of other lives) is found in Peter Sherringham's relation to Miriam. Reflecting on the threat to his diplomatic career constituted by his infatuation with an actress, he concludes that it will probably involve a sacrifice: "At any rate it had never occurred to Sherringham that he himself might be the sacrifice. You had to pay to get on, but at least you borrowed from others to do it. When you couldn't borrow you didn't get on, for what was the situation in life in which you met the whole requisition yourself?" (VII, 314) It is precisely Miriam, the great tragic actress, who "meets the whole requisition" herself—and does it *with* herself, which disappears in the process. As Nash is made to say, "You *never* find the artist—you only find his work, and that's all you need to find." (VIII, 200) Nash sees that Miriam becomes, in the presence of Nick the painter, herself a "picture" (VIII, 54). The point is that an actress—if she be truly great—cannot as an "appearance" be apprehended by anyone save an artist, whose capacity to detect the "sources" equals her capacity to tap them. Her audience appropriates her appearance to its selfish uses; Nick's attention is said to give her peace because it is not an act of appropriation, but part of an act of celebration.[61]

[61] The present writer erred in asserting in his article "Henry James and the New Jerusalem" (*Kenyon Review*, VIII, 1946, p. 529) that Nick Dormer was functioning as a greedy appropriator when he painted Miriam Rooth. (For the "portrait theme," see Chapter V,

Although at least one of James's critics holds that the novelist was concerned with "artists in life" above all else,[62] and many have implied as much, the fact is that James found the artist *in* life a rather threatening figure. The artist who tries to work in life is arranging life itself—the lives, that is, of others, so that they may compose a pattern for *him*. The contradiction between dedication to life and the lack of any medium in which to express one's allegiance save that of behavior toward others is precisely parallel to the contradiction which loomed so large in the life of the elder Henry James. He too did nothing save talk and write about how people ought to be related to their own lives. The "form" which we adopt "under the descent of the god" makes us more than mere men; it makes us people who live under the dominion of that "infinite thing," conscience. The elder James was fond of pointing out that angels did not in this way give form to the divine; they were immediately dependent on God's inflowing goodness and truth, and had no basis *in themselves* for not becoming devils. It will now be apparent why the character who figures the elder Henry James depends for his ability to manifest himself, on people who can give form to the divine in us. That is why Gabriel is called "poor Nash"! It also is the reason that it is appropriate to call him "Mephistopheles." Nick addresses the question, "And what might your instrument be?" to the vulnerable aspect of the elder Henry James. The father talked of the final importance of form, but he did not commit himself *to* form

---

below.) Peter Sherringham's attempt to divert her beauty and her talent to his own use, although aware that these things were "connected with universal values" (VII, 141), makes him a classic Jamesian appropriator.

[62] Stephen Spender, "The School of Experience in the Early Novels" (*Hound and Horn*, VII, 1934), p. 422. A characteristic mistake in James criticism is to assume that he is projecting an ideal world, offering us another *kind* of life. He thought of himself as dealing with our kind in *his* mode, a very different matter.

in the same degree as his son. This is the man's answer to the "implied snub" [63] that he had felt as a boy. But it is kindly given, and serves rather to correct an emphasis than to invalidate the father's point of view. Whatever his father's form might "nominally or superficially or vulgarly" have been, it *had* been worthy of the god—to borrow the terms used in the preface to *The Golden Bowl*.

To suggest how precise was James's sense of the danger of his father's role, it is necessary to refer to *The Sacred Fount*, in which the figure of a Gabriel Nash gone astray is central. Here again we have "a great explainer," the narrator, who tries to "work in life." He does so as a kind of futile Mephistopheles who seeks to get at the "sources" in others, and is defeated in the attempt. The artist in life becomes a demon when he imagines that the particular events of particular lives can be traced to their springs. This is not the business of the artist, who may appropriate whatever appearances he chooses, provided that the fount of imagined life—the generic basis of the lives he projects —is in himself, and not even ostensibly borrowed from others. To borrow the lives of others means making an "outward natural representation" of the divine in us—a sin

[63] Earlier (VII, 177), Nick had asked Nash: "And what *is* your business?" To which Nash replies, "The spectacle of the world," a characteristic answer for the delightedly dependent Henry James, Senior. The *form* of Henry Senior's activity is no doubt best described in *The Tragic Muse* by Nash's assertion, "My only good generalizations are my actions" (VII, 31). Or, as the elder James himself puts it: "A perfect life, a life that is whose every act and word are true to the sovereign soul within, will ever be the truest revelation of God as it is the highest expression of Art" (*Moralism and Christianity*, p. 133). See also *Notes of a Son and Brother* (p. 289), for an even loftier tone about merely physical art. Nick's conclusion is not of course that *he* ought to talk on behalf of the human race; Nash has told him that he has his instrument, and it is his business to use it. In so doing he will be doing what Nash is doing—playing his unique part in the human concert. See VIII, 266, where Nick reflects: "Art was *doing*—it came back to that—which politics in most cases weren't."

not only in the father, but in the son, as we shall see in the next chapter. The enigmatic conclusion of *The Sacred Fount* is purely elder Jamesian. The narrator signalizes his defeat in the last sentence of the book: "What I too fatally lacked was her tone." It is style which contains life; no accumulation of the details of actual life can represent it. To use two of James's favorite emblems as they are used in *The Sacred Fount*, the narrator's scheme "doesn't hold water"; his "palace of thought" is "smashed." [64]

James was brilliantly successful in rendering the effect of such an act of appropriation in *The Sense of the Past*. Ralph Pendrel brings about a sudden and complete "rupture of relation" with the characters from the eighteenth century among whom he finds himself, by making it *apparent* that he thinks he understands them completely. But this is to say that the whole meaning of their lives is summed in their outward appearance; it is to deny them life. And so, under the magical conditions of the story, the people of the past come momentarily to resemble "some mechanic but consummate imitation of ancient life, staring through the vast plate of a museum" (XXVI, 212–213). A moment later they awaken, but Ralph is conscious thereafter of the danger of treating them as if he knew them completely— as if they were simply the puppets of his imagination.

Now that the reader knows how simple—even though paradoxical—the father's system was, it will be less difficult for him to see that the son made a conscious use of what he had learned so early in life. We cannot be sure that he had *read* any more of his father's work than is to be found in William's Introduction to the *Literary Remains* and the "Autobiographic Fragment" they contain. But he did not need to read at all to tell us what his father's prime principles were; the two volumes of reminiscences make this clear. Was not the scene of his father's wrestle with his selfhood, and the beneficent intervention of Mrs. Chi-

[64] *The Sacred Fount*, pp. 293, 311.

chester (who had prescribed Swedenborg) a family legend? Had he not heard endless excoriations of the "*conscious* conscience" and of the "consecrated forms" which governed the manners and the worship of other less fortunate households? Had he not heard his father's version of what he makes Gabriel Nash say, that one "need not be afraid of putting all life" in one's form? These things were the substance of breakfast table conversation.

When we find him writing in 1889 about the danger of entering the "temple" of "conscience" like a "Puritan trooper," we not only know what he means; we know also how fully, intensively, and exclusively he means what his father meant about the relation of art to morals.[65]

James knew what few people have known about his father; he knew his "secret," his essentially simple roots. The conscience, the selfhood, the importance of "tone" or style, the great brotherhood of the conscious—these things seemed neither complicated nor esoteric to him. He had a mind which *these* ideas did not violate—to wrench Eliot's

---

[65] Before concluding with Nash, I ought to say a word about Leon Edel's assumption that he not only speaks for, but resembles, Henry James (see note 39, above). The physical appearance of Nash as Biddy Dormer sees him is this: "What Biddy remarked was that this young man was fair, and fat and of the middle stature; he had a round face and a short beard and on his crown a mere reminiscence of hair. . . ." (VII, 22.) The frontispiece of *A Small Boy and Others* indicates that Henry Senior wore, in 1854, a short beard and was baldish on top. He describes himself as follows on p. 182 of *Logic*, which was published in 1857: "And I for my part have never questioned that the Divine Mind was as cognizant of my visible limitations (short stature, obese figure, fair complexion, flaxen wig, and so forth) as I myself am." (For another passage of self-portraiture, see *Lectures and Miscellanies*, 1852, p. 317.) There is nothing incompatible between these descriptions. Both men are fair, fat, short, and almost bald. The physical appearance of Herbert Pratt, to whom the novelist ascribes one of the speeches Nash makes in the novel, and of whom he writes in 1881, "I shall certainly put him into a novel," is not known to the writer (see VII, 177, and *Notebooks*, p. 31). It appears that these physical details might apply either to the father or the son, or, conceivably, to Herbert Pratt.

phrase a bit. These ideas fitted his sensibility like an old shoe. Eliot simply didn't know *what* ideas were functioning to exclude all others.

The fact that the novelist saw that his father's incessant manipulation of these ideas in a measure belied the ideas themselves is apparent in the character of Gabriel Nash. The very powers we celebrate in the son enabled him to understand his father's impulses. The character of Gabriel Nash indicates that he found his father's understanding of how art functions incomplete, not that he found it wrong, and we may say that after he wrote *The Tragic Muse* he came increasingly under the dominion of his father. Biographically, this may mean that the failure of the playwriting effort was the failure of an effort to escape the American heritage; and that the full surrender to his father in the last three completed novels is a defeat, from the point of view of both biography and criticism. The novelist himself had become a great explainer.

V *The Portrait Theme*

WOMEN DOMINATE THE FICTIONAL SCENE IN HENRY JAMES. They exhibit a greater moral grandeur than men, have a greater capacity for moral obliquity, and, in general, a fuller emotional range.[1] Of course, the frequent and emphatic appearance of these lively virgins in James's work is not unconnected with their occurrence in Howells and others.[2] James's use of the American girl, however, is like his use of the bootstrap myth, in that he relied on a rather widely diffused strain in the thinking and feeling of Americans which his father's work and his father's talk had given clear symbolic articulation. He could look from Howells's *Lady of the Aroostook* (1879) to his father's description of the symbolic significance of the sexes and marriage with a sense that the elder James had systematized a cluster of feelings which other Americans had also experienced, although they had not made them coherent, or given them, as his father characteristically did, the status of philosophic axioms.

[1] See F. O. Matthiessen, *Henry James: The Major Phase*, p. 41.
[2] See Cornelia Pulsifer Kelley, *The Early Development of Henry James*, esp. Chapters XVII and XVIII. For two early instances of the American girl, see *Professor Fargo* and *Guest's Confession* in the volume *Travelling Companions*.

His father was particularly explicit on the question of the relation of American womanhood to America's providential situation, and on the difference between America and Europe in this respect. The impulse which Howells showed to make the young girl an arbiter of values was not, on the elder Henry James's showing, inconsistent with making her the representative of freedom and spontaneity. We may imagine that from the seventies to the epoch of the Gibson girl, American writers found in the figure of the girl questioning her suitor as to his aims, pursuits, and interests, the priestess of the American heritage, untainted by commercialism, committed to the future, representative of widening possibilities. In the elder James's theory this clear-eyed, questioning figure was not simply the judge of masculine aims but the visible image of the promise life held out to all men. Here is an excerpt from *Substance and Shadow* in which he refers to his impression of European society:

One reconciles himself after a while to the sight of priest and monk abroad: for we men are such born nuisances yet everywhere, especially under our European or moral form of development, which exhibits the heart or feminine element abjectly servile to the head or masculine element, that a mere ritual righteousness would seem to be our proper badge, the only approximation we can yet make to God's image. But woman when exempted from our bedevilment, when loosed from our gross Adamic servitude, and left to herself, to her own spontaneous tendencies, is gentle and modest and good: *i.e.* lives already and does not merely aspire to live; obeys a direct Divine inspiration, conceives of the Holy Ghost, and brings forth immaculate fruit. She has no aptitude for ritual religion save as a way of escape from our brutality, from the dreariness we impose on her existence. For she herself when freely pronounced is truly the consummation of the literal church, the end of all the culture the race has undergone on earth; perfect womanhood in nature meaning nothing more and nothing less than the visible form of our

unseen spiritual manhood. Woman is the normal outcome—
at once perfect flower and perfect fruit—of human progress
in interior invisible realms of being; so that we may at any
time exactly measure the comparative advance of the public
mind; the comparative spirituality of the public conscience,
by the esteem it accords and the courtesy it decrees to
women.[3]

John Stuart Mill's praise of his wife inspires this next
passage: "It is as if he had really seen while she lived the
infinite substance shadowed in her tender and delicate
womanly form; and one yearns afresh for the time when
—humanity being lifted to a higher level of life by the
prevalence of superior social conditions—every woman
will unaffectedly recognize herself as the priestess of a
truly Divine worship, and every man shrink aghast consequently from offering upon the altar of her person the
incense, now so common, of famished appetite and mer-
cenary lust." The elder James's use of "moral" to characterize the European scene refers to those who "appropriate"
righteousness—claim a kind of property in virtue, and
attempt in this way to distinguish themselves from others.

That the prime distinction between Europe and America
in the novelist's work is precisely his father's distinction may
or may not appear important when one considers this likeness in isolation.[4] But when the views of father and son on
the position of women in Europe and America are linked,
and the position accorded women is seen to be derived, not
from their sexual differentiation, but from their possession,
in common with the artist, of *spontaneity*, one begins to
make out a symbolic pattern. The woman "loosed from our
Adamic servitude, and left to herself is gentle and modest

[3] This and the passage below are from *Substance*, pp. 210–211, 322.
See also *Lectures*, pp. 74–75.
[4] For the novelist's sense of the relative position of men and women
in America, see *The American Scene* (1907), pp. 62–64, 157–159,
243, 332, 414.

and good . . . lives already and does not merely aspire to live; obeys a direct Divine inspiration, conceives of the Holy Ghost, and brings forth immaculate fruit." She is filled with the *life*, and in the *forms* of her behavior we may see *represented* "our unseen spiritual manhood."

The young American girl may therefore be an arbiter of values and a representation of the promise of life at one and the same time. She may ·function, as the work of art does, to contain and express through the forms of her behavior the universal life—Love and Wisdom: ". . . for Art viewed as the distinctively feminine evolution of human activity, in which freedom supplants force, or what is spiritual, individual, private, governs what is natural, common, public—makes Nature as furnishing the material in every work, purely ancillary and subservient to the Artist as furnishing its form, under penalty of defeating the work or rendering it imperfect." [5]

Impregnated by universal love, the artist likewise "brings forth immaculate fruit"—particular forms, though not forms of behavior, but works detached from his own person. The artist and the spontaneous American girl are thus spiritual allies, and in the work of Henry James, the novelist, they are the voices of affirmation and celebration. It is not surprising to discover that Gabriel Nash is in this way "feminine." Miriam Rooth explains that he is a "lady" in tact and sympathy (VIII, 38),[6] and we see this when he urges Nick Dormer to cease "representing" Harsh in Parliament and to represent life instead, urges him to take experience in the "free brave personal way" (VII, 180); we see that Nash is pleading for the "feminine" against the "masculine." Parliament is one of the provisional forms

[5] *Substance*, p. 465.
[6] See the elder James's admiring account of Emerson in *Remains* (pp. 296–297): ". . . Emerson himself was an unsexed woman, a veritable fruit of almighty power in the sphere of our *nature*." Also (p. 300): "He was like a vestal virgin, indeed, always in ministry upon the altar. . . ."

which we are constrained to accept by our subjection to nature and society, necessity and prudence, savagery and interest. The behavior of women who are not subjected to "gross Adamic servitude" is "free brave personal," just as the behavior of the painter who leaves Parliament and undertakes to create form on his own hook is free and spontaneous.

Let us juxtapose a letter to Thomas Sargent Perry, written in 1867, with a passage from the commemorative chapter about Minny Temple in *Notes of a Son and Brother*. As the reader considers these passages, I must ask him to recall the character of the novelist's praise of his father: praise for his father's capacity to make the particulars of experience reflect the universal with a peculiar "experiential authority." Here is an excerpt from the letter to Perry:

When I say that I should like to do as Sainte-Beuve has done, I don't mean that I should like to imitate him, or reproduce him, or reproduce him in English: but only that I should like to acquire something of his intelligence and his patience and vigor. One feels—I feel at least, that he is a man of the past, of a dead generation; and that we young Americans are (without cant) men of the future. I feel that my only chance for success as a critic is to let all the breezes of the west blow through me at their will. We are Americans born—*il faut en prendre son parti*. I look upon it as a great blessing; and I think that to be an American is an excellent preparation for culture. We have exquisite qualities as a race, and it seems to me that we are ahead of the European races in the fact that more than either of them we can deal freely with forms of civilization not our own, can pick and choose and assimilate and in short (aesthetically &c) claim our property wherever we find it. To have no national stamp has hitherto been a regret and a drawback, but I think it not unlikely that American writers may yet indicate that a vast intellectual fusion and synthesis of the various National tendencies of the world is the condition of more important achievements than any we have seen. We must of course have something of our own—something distinctive and homogeneous—and I take it that we shall find it in our moral consciousness, our unprecedented spiritual lightness and vigor. In this sense at least we shall have a national *cachet*.—I expect nothing great during your lifetime or mine perhaps; but my instincts quite agree with yours in looking to see something original and beautiful disengage itself from our ceaseless fermentation and turmoil. You see I am willing to leave it a matter of instinct. God speed the day.[7]

The youngster, drunken with a perception of his own powers and possibilities, is nonetheless writing this letter under the lifelong shadow of "father's ideas." Consider the "ceaseless fermentation and turmoil," for example. In the father the turmoil is precisely the sign of the opportunity for "fusion and synthesis" on a fresh basis, the basis of "moral consciousness," which in turn must operate through an assimilation in the *aesthetic* mode. To be free of a "national stamp" is to be free of church and state, to work unconstrained by nature and society.[8] (We get a glimpse here of the solution of one of the most troubling anomalies in James: The meaning of business success, its *positive* meaning, may quite simply be that material abundance operates to *free* us from nature.[9]

We are likely to feel that James's use, in *Notes of a Son and Brother*, of the letters his cousin Minny Temple addressed to John Chipman Gray [10] is perhaps too confiding on his part; to feel that the somewhat desperate adolescent religiosity of the girl threatened with death is just religiosity and no more. But James assigns Minny's "sense for

[7] Quoted in Leon Edel, *Henry James*, pp. 264–265.
[8] For the elder James's treatment of the state and prospects of American civilization, see *Society*, pp. 84–86; *Logic*, pp. 201, 173n.; *Remains*, pp. 195, 198–199, 370.
[9] See "Property as a Symbol," *Lectures*.
[10] Leon Edel identifies Gray as Minny's correspondent (*Henry James*, p. 313).

verity of character and play of life in others" more weight
than we realize until we see how her sense of life is used
to characterize Milly Theale and Maggie Verver. Its nature
was of course far better represented in her talk than in her
letters, just as in the case of his father. In a passage from
Notes of a Son and Brother he describes Minny's curious
ascendancy, which, in the group he writes about, was felt
through her extraordinary and loving hospitality to the
forms and styles of those who surrounded her; but felt
also as a broader sympathy than we found in Gabriel Nash,
a sympathy for those who had not attained, and perhaps
never would attain, to an individual grace. James's "drama"
in the following quotation lies in the relation between
Minny and the four young men who on these occasions
surrounded her.

If drama we could indeed feel this as being, I hasten to add,
we owed it most of all to our just having such a heroine that
everything else inevitably came. Mary Temple was beautifully
and indescribably *that*—in the technical or logical as
distinguished from the pompous or romantic sense of the
word; wholly without effort or desire on her part—for never
was a girl less consciously or consentingly or vulgarly
dominant—everything that took place around her took place
as if primarily in relation to her and in her interest: that is
in the interest of drawing her out and displaying her the
more. This too without her in the least caring, as I say—in
the deep, the morally nostalgic indifferences that were the
most finally characteristic thing about her—whether such an
effect took place or not; she liked nothing in the world so
much as to see others fairly exhibited; not as they might
best please her by being, but as they might most fully reveal
themselves, their stuff and their truth: which was the only
thing that, after any first flutter for the superficial air or
grace in an acquaintance, could in the least fix her attention.
She had beyond any equally young creature I have known
a sense for verity of character and play of life in others, for
their acting out of their force or their weakness, whatever

either might be, at no matter what cost to herself; and it was this instinct that made her care so for life in general, just as it was her being thereby so engaged in that tangle that made her, as I have expressed it, ever the heroine of the scene. Life claimed her and used her and beset her—made her range in her groping, her naturally immature and unlighted way from end to end of the scale. No one felt more the charm of the actual—only the actual comprised for her kinds of reality (those to which her letters perhaps most of all testify), that she saw treated round her for the most part either as irrelevant or as unpleasant. She was absolutely afraid of nothing she might come to by living with enough sincerity and enough wonder; and I think it is because one was to see her launched on that adventure in such bedimmed, such almost tragically compromised conditions that one is caught by her title to the heroic and pathetic mark. It is always difficult for us after the fact not to see young things who were soon to be lost to us as already distinguished by their fate; this particular victim of it at all events might well have made the near witness ask within himself how her restlessness of spirit, the finest reckless impatience, was to be assuaged or "met" by the common lot. One somehow saw it nowhere about us as up to her terrible young standard of the interesting—even if to say this suggests an air of tension, a sharpness of importunity, than which nothing could have been less like her. The charming, irresistible fact was that one had never seen a creature with such lightness of forms, a lightness all her own, so inconsequently grave at the core, or an asker of endless questions with such apparent lapses of care.[11]

The elderly novelist, recalling those enchanted afternoons in the White Mountains of the summer of 1865, makes a poetic concretion of the elements of American hope, aspiration, and power which he had scattered through his letter to Perry in 1867. What is most striking about Minny as she appears in the reminiscences is her power, not her

[11] *Notes of a Son and Brother*, pp. 460–463.

pathos, her unmeasured demand on life, not the shortness of her span. The pathos, the short run, these are treated as they are in Milly and Maggie, who, like Minny, are somehow life incarnate.

If the reader has felt as James wants him to, he will find in the dramatic situation of each of these three something akin to tragedy. This is James's closest approach to a sense of the tragic, the power to imagine and project persons in whom, as in Oedipus and Hamlet, we lose what we have never had. Or, to put it as James does in this passage on Minny, the measure of whose demands on life, on *us*, is such that we cannot imagine how they could have been fulfilled, except by a diffusion of human greatness almost inconceivable. (That James did finally construct a world which might have filled Minny's cup, the world of *The Golden Bowl*, is thus a final proof of his incapacity for tragic vision.)

I am here concerned with the way in which Minny Temple became the priestess of "father's ideas" and in this fashion accompanied the young man to Europe on the momentous journey he made at the end of the sixties. My point is that the familiar group of his father's notions which found expression in the letter to Perry are represented over forty years later as having clustered around the image of Minny Temple. This is the meaning of the phrases in the letter to William on Minny's death; Minny has been "translated" from "this changing realm of fact to the steady realm of thought."[12] This "realm" is of course that implied by his father's "religion of consciousness," but it is also the region in which Minny was thereafter steadily available to the young writer as a representative of the sources of appearance. His father, the somewhat anomalous "artist in life," appears only in *The Tragic Muse*, but his father's niece, the novelist's cousin, became the spirit expressive of father's most general moral inten-

[12] F. O. Matthiessen, *Henry James: The Major Phase*, p. 48.

tion, fictionally available as a representative of the sources of appearance.

The novelist never tired of elaborating the hidden significance of the fact that his cousin's name was Temple. His father's favorite image of the human spirit was that of a house: Minny had indeed been the fittest house of the spirit he had known—in her he had come near the "sources"; in her graceful and courageous hospitality to every form of experience, in her concern with the finalities which other people were likely to see as "irrelevant or unpleasant," Minny was the "technical or logical" heroine, that is, the descendant of a god. She, like the elder James, could combine the most charitably catholic attention to the world with fidelity to generalities, and *her* "experiential authority" showed such "lightness of forms," and was yet so "grave at the core," that—the reader is led to surmise—she almost spoke for life itself.

The *Notes of a Son and Brother* treat Minny as she finally appeared. How does she first appear in the fiction? By way of preface to an account of a long story, *Travelling Companions*,[13] in which Minny Temple becomes a priestess of "father's ideas," here is a sentence or two from the long review, "The Novels of George Eliot," which the young man published in the *Atlantic* in 1866: "In morals her problems are still the old passive problems. . . . What moves her most is the idea of a conscience harassed by the memory of slighted obligations. Unless in the case of Savonarola, she has made no attempt to depict a conscience taking upon itself great and novel responsibilities."[14] And five years after Minny's death, in a review of Howells, published in 1875, he notes that Howells's young women satisfy James's own demand for moral adventurousness. In portraying "delicate, nervous, emancipated young

---

[13] *Travelling Companions*, pp. 1–51 (the first of seven stories in the volume).
[14] Henry James, *Views and Reviews*, ed. by Leroy Phillips, p. 36.

woman begotten of our institutions and our climate and equipped with an irritable moral consciousness," Howells had "outlined his field." [15]

The circumstances which bear on the writing of *Travelling Companions* are these: On March 8, 1870, while taking a cure at Great Malvern in England, Henry Junior wrote a letter in which he described his dislike of English women in this way: "I revolt from their dreary deathly want of—what shall I call it?—Clover Hooper has it—intellectual grace—Minny Temple has it—moral spontaneity." [16] (His father's chief value and his own are here spoken of as incarnate in Minny.) On the very day of his writing this letter (March 8) Minny died. One of the letters received from her during his European stay, which included his first delighted immersion in Italy, read in part as follows (Newport, June, 1869): "I shall miss you, my dear, but I am most happy to know that you are well and enjoying yourself. If you were not my cousin I would write and ask you to marry me and take me with you, but as it is, it wouldn't do. I will console myself, however, with the thought, that in that case you might not accept my offer, which would be much worse than it is now." [17]

It is most improbable that this proposal was taken literally by its author or the recipient. (It is inconceivable to me that James's imagination could even hold the idea of marriage or sexual intercourse for himself.) But Minny's playfulness was of a serious order. Orphaned, ill, remarkably independent and detached, she had been the subject of James's fantasy before her death came to crystallize all her meanings for him. Edel reports that the novelist had earlier written to William of a desire to regain his "natural lead" with Minny, that his part in their friendship might

---

[15] Quoted by Cornelia Pulsifer Kelley, *The Early Development of Henry James*, pp. 269–270.
[16] *Letters*, I, 26–27.
[17] Leon Edel, *Henry James*, pp. 314–315.

become more "active and masculine." In this letter his
invalidism, which on Edel's showing was largely psychoso-
matic, is used as a defense against what may be called the
threat of Minny's sexuality. Going to Europe had had a
double meaning for him. It had meant escaping his father's
cheery and oppressive assumption that his sons would
quickly marry and settle down;[18] it had also meant a desire
to assume the role of receptivity, to be passive to European
experience.

The gain of Italy, the loss of Minny, each had its contrary. He had been deeply fond of Minny, but her death
removed a threat to his conception of himself as a man.
His Italian experience also had a negative as well as a
positive meaning for him: Were he too passive to Italy, he
would lose the very opportunity he had celebrated in his
letter to Perry in 1867; the power to choose and to order
experience in the light of American "moral spontaneity." In
the event, Minny came to stand for the very thing that
he must use to control his experience of Italy, and of
Europe at large. Asserting his power to give form to
European experience became equivalent to asserting his
subordination to Minny's "spontaneity." The pattern was
complete. He could incorporate Minny's spirit within himself, and make his greed, his hunger for the picturesque,
subordinate to this inner imperative.

In *Travelling Companions* James tried for the first time
to "let these passions and foibles play themselves out." [19]
His story is the story of a young man making his first
journey through Italy, deeply absorbed in "the steady perception of the material present." He meets an American
girl and her father, and thereafter learns under the girl's
tutelage to value the art which speaks for life and sponta-

[18] Leon Edel, *Henry James*, pp. 156–157.
[19] This phrase is from the review of George Eliot (p. 24) cited
above. He reproaches the novelist for arresting the moral energies
apparent in her characters before they have run their course.

neity, and to deplore the attempt to make a capital of aesthetic impressions, without at the same time acknowledging that they represent the sources of appearance. This is familiar to us as the division between the two ways of taking experience. *Travelling Companions* is also an account of Henry James's "marriage" to Minny Temple.

In the letter written on the day of Minny's death, praising Clover Hooper and Minny, James writes: "Among the things I have recently read is father's *Marriage* paper in the *Atlantic*—with great enjoyment of its manner and approval of its matter." [20] In the elder James, as the quotations at the beginning of this chapter show, true marriage subordinates the masculine to the feminine. [21] In the article in the *Atlantic* he refers to marriage as the "germ cell" of society; without marriage we are but "atoms," disconnected from the "sole actual source and focus of the social sentiment." Such a marriage inverts the man's feeling about himself, as did the elder James's *vastation*. He becomes dependent: "This is what woman always represents to the imagination of man, a diviner self than his own; a more private, a more sacred and intimate self than that wherewith nature endows him. And this is the source of that passionate self-surrender he makes in marrying. . . ." The man who does not substitute his wife's self for his own is a "gross male Adam," who sets up a "concubinage," and thereby appropriates a representative of the divine love to his own base uses.

Travelling Companions symbolizes the division between the two ways of taking experience (taking it lovingly and creatively or taking it selfishly according to the prescriptions of public forms) in three distinct ways, all derived from the symbolism of the elder James. First, it employs the distinction between marriage and concubinage; second, that between the true self (conscience) and the false self

[20] *Letters*, I, 26–27; and "Is Marriage Holy?" (*Atlantic Monthly*, XXV, 1870, pp. 360–368).
[21] See *Substance*, p. 520.

(the Eve or selfhood); and third, the opposition between the letter and the spirit, or the portrait and the living truth. This third instance requires further explanation.

In *Lectures and Miscellanies* and the works which succeeded it, the elder James frequently describes scriptural law as giving us a merely negative indication as to what the divine man will be like. To take such a description for complete is to prize the "husk" above the actuality: "The letter aims to confer of itself the righteousness which only the spirit confers. It supposes that it promotes the spirit directly or positively, instead of negatively and indirectly, and hence becomes itself the very worst enemy its own original spirit acknowledges. In fact, the letter of a law, when once it looks upon itself as identical with the spirit, when once it looks upon itself as anything else but the rudest and most perishable husk of the spirit, is the *only* enemy the spirit knows." Spiritual evil consists in grasping some "outward natural representation" of the divine as a possession—trying to own God. In response to those who might succumb to this temptation, the elder James personifies the "law" and makes it say this: " 'Be not deceived therefore. . . . Do not imagine that you have a worthy or adequate portrait of the true man in this mere negative outline.' " [22]

After Brooke, the hero of *Travelling Companions*, has met and temporarily lost sight of Miss Evans, the heroine, he encounters a young Italian who describes himself as an artist. This young man tries to sell him a painting which he says is a Correggio. The artist's mother and sister are present when Brooke inspects the painting, and he is told that the sister, who is desperately ill, apparently with tuberculosis, had dreamed of a young man "from over the sea" who was seeking this very Madonna. Brooke finds a strong resemblance to Miss Evans in the picture. The young man of the dream had gone from church to church,

[22] *Lectures*, pp. 29, 34.

crying out, "Where, ah where, is my blessed Lady?" Disappointed in one church, he enters another, asking, "Where is my blessed Lady? I have come from over the sea, I have come to Italy to find her!" The girl, whom Brooke afterwards concludes to have been the victim of a "fatal wrong," tells the rest of her dream as follows.

"And then I fancied," said the young girl, "that I heard his voice pausing under my window at night. 'His blessed Lady is here,' I said, 'we must not let him lose her.' So I called my brother and bade him go forth in search of you. I dreamed that he brought you back. We made an altar with candles and lace and flowers, and on it we placed the little picture. The stranger had light hair, light eyes, a flowing beard like you. He kneeled down before the little Madonna and worshipped her. We left him at his devotions and went away. When we came back the candles on the altar were out: the Madonna was gone, too; but in its place there burned a bright pure light. It was a purse of gold."

The reader is left to imagine what "wrong" has afflicted the suffering girl—she has been jilted, ravished, abandoned, whatever we please, if we feel that she has been subjected to some injury from a man. We must also, however, think of her as a *European* woman, one who finds it natural to be subject, for she has had a dream in which the worship of an idol and its purchase for gold are taken for granted. Later, Miss Evans and her father, accompanied by Brooke, glimpse a young man in Florian's Café, who is said to resemble Brooke, an incident apparently without point, of which James writes, "I repeat the incident because I think it has a certain value in my recital." [23]

Brooke and his other self, the young man of the dream and of Florian's Café, are therefore juxtaposed with Miss Evans and her "portrait." The meaning of the juxtaposi-

[23] Passages quoted in this paragraph are in *Travelling Companions*, pp. 19, 25.

tion in the story is sufficiently stressed by Miss Evans'
remark to Brooke, after his tentative proposal: "It's not
with me that you're in love, but with that painted picture."
James in this way accuses himself of having taken Minny
Temple in the wrong way, and taken possession of Europe
in the wrong way; but by the time we reach the end of
the story Brooke has changed or inverted his perspective.
It is not as an appropriator but as a man under the dominion
of the feminine conscience that he marries Miss Evans at
the end of the story. Miss Evans has "denied" Brooke's
"Profane" love; she accepts his "Sacred" love.[24] This use
of the portrait to suggest spiritual greed and the linked use
of the true and the false selves is recurrent in James's later
work.

To reinforce my contention that the story is an an-
nouncement that he had compassed a "marriage" with
Minny's spirit, *The Sweetheart of M. Briseux*,[25] published
three years later, may be mentioned. In this story a self-
centered, adoringly mothered young man tries to paint
the girl he wishes to marry. The process reveals his
"narrow, personal, ineffectual self," of which he seeks to
make the girl a dependent ornament. The genuine painter
who happens by and paints a great portrait of the girl is
an "appealing messenger from the mysterious immensity of
life." When the story opens, years after these events, the
great portrait is being exhibited and there is a question as to
the identity of the model. One of the onlookers produces
his (and the world's) supposition: "Mon Dieu! a sweetheart of M. Briseux!—*Ces artistes!*" But it was not as a
subject woman but as a representative of the sources that
the girl had been painted, and never before or after had she
seen the artist. So James might have said that the vigorous,

---

24 *Travelling Companions*, pp. 31, 51.
25 In *Travelling Companions*, pp. 53–86. The phrases quoted below
are on pp. 83, 55. For the elder James's view of copyists, see *Lectures*,
pp. 115–117.

assertive men who gathered about Minny had been attracted by the portrait alone—but he had known the lady.[26]

James came to feel that assertion of himself involved subjecting himself to Minny's spirit that he might give it form. He had found a license to discard the embarrassing pressure to emulate his brother William.[27] He had begun to take control of his past by giving it emblematic form. The lady, the portrait, the creative self with its style, the other self, the house of life—these are the emblematic elements James was to use for the rest of his life.

He did not master their use all at once. Indeed, the death of Miss Evans' father in *Travelling Companions* and the fact that Brooke involves Miss Evans in a "compromising" situation afford evidence that James had not altogether abandoned the Oedipal struggle. The novel of the following year, *Watch and Ward*, and a number of works up to the year 1879, in which *Confidence* appeared, betray a continuing effort to imagine the scene on which he might cope with the threat posed by William's sexuality. These works, however, have a characteristic muddiness and confusion of motive. In them he was working against the grain. The "marriage" to Minny afforded him the imaginative disposition of his emotional resources which proved fruitful. It also made the figure of the young girl available as a dramatic hinge for the bootstrap myth, and thus put him increasingly in his father's role as a great explainer.

[26] For instances of characters who seize on an image to reflect themselves, see *The Sense of the Past*, XXVI, 177–178; the story *Glasses* (Macmillan, XXVII), in which Flora Saunt's blindness makes her a completely devoted worshiper of her own image; *The Liar* (XII), in which the protagonist destroys an image of himself; and *The Sacred Fount*, p. 56.

[27] Leon Edel, *Henry James*. One of the principal themes of the first volume of this biography is Henry's struggle to achieve a position in which he could cope with William (see "Jacob and Esau," pp. 241–251).

Abstractly considered, the portrait theme provides a moral sanction for an aesthetic principle. The aesthetically pictorial, taken alone, is the morally static or selfish. The artist must employ appearances, pictorial values, but if he is truly an artist, he will invariably subordinate them to realities, to dramatic values. This is in keeping with the elder James's emphasis on the consummatory moral impetus which drives us toward union with God and our fellows. Stasis, arrest, fixity, are evil. But there is no absolute evil except the attempt to appropriate a representative of conscience in the form of an image. To do this is to take the letter for the spirit, the portrait for the lady, to be an arch-criminal, such as Gilbert Osmond or Lord Mark.

James used the relation between pictorial and dramatic values to assert the moral primacy of the latter in the story called *The Real Thing*. The artist of the story is an illustrator whose pictures have reference to dramatic situations. The novel he has in hand involves society people, and he makes the mistake of hiring two poverty-stricken aristocrats as models. As such, they turn out to be intractable—limited, fixed, pictorial values. He replaces them with a stray young Italian and a Cockney girl who have style, an ability to project themselves in dramatic situations: a capacity flatly opposed to being an aristocrat, a licensed image of conformity. The act of representation is seen to be an unceasing invocation of that which gives form. It is an influx of the divine nature which creates the "ideal thing."

The point of the story is the distinction which, in the elder James, takes the form of the difference between "identity" and "individuality." [28] The world gives us an identity, but, as Gabriel Nash points out, we create our own individuality through our form or style. In the works of the novelist the distinction is often verbally rendered

[28] *Substance*, pp. 53–54, 141; *Secret*, p. 201.

as that between "reproduction" and "representation." [29] In *John Delavoy* (Macmillan, XXVII, esp. 363), the sister's *picture* of her brother is prized more than his writing; in *The Abasement of the Northmores* the writer explores the consequence of the fact that Lord Northmore had only an identity, whereas his friend and collaborator, Warren Hope, had actually had the individuality associated with creative power. *The Private Life* plays on this theme elaborately: Lord Mellifont is so very public a man, so thoroughly dependent on his "identity" in the public eye, that he disappears when no one is looking at him! *The Birthplace* deals at length with the demands of the administrators of Shakespeare's presumed birthplace that he be treated as a "personage," an identity, rather than as an artist knowable only through his form. On this, a single illustration will be more useful than the list of instances that could be compiled.

Mark Ambient in *The Author of Beltraffio* is James's most delightful instance of the worldly or greedy man turned artist. His attempt to invert reality and make "things" prior to consciousness is a transcendent miserliness. He is comically frank about what he does. "Perhaps I care too much for beauty—I don't know, I doubt if a poor devil *can*; I delight in it, I adore it, I think of it continually, I try to produce it, to reproduce it." (XVI, 46) Here James is careful to use "reproduce" rather than "represent," for what Ambient does is to appropriate nature's "firm and bright" forms. This demonic author is wholly unable to understand his demonic wife, who is as

[29] *A Small Boy and Others* (p. 113): "Strange enough the 'aesthetic' of artists who could desire but literally to reproduce." See also *The American Scene* (pp. 261–262), for the disparity between the "idea" and the work of art which is said to be its consequence. C. Hartley Grattan, in *The Three Jameses* (p. 331), gives a clear statement of the distinction the novelist makes between "reproduction" and "representation."

righteous as he is greedy. He tells the narrator that she ought to tolerate his search for beauty, since she is, or was, a beautiful object herself. "She's always afraid of it, always on her guard. And she's so pretty, too, herself! Don't you think she's lovely? She was at any rate when we married. At that time, I wasn't aware of the difference I speak of—I thought it all came to the same thing: in the end, as they say." (XVI, 43) It does come to the same thing in the end. For in the end greed and righteousness are but modes of appropriation. The beautiful Mrs. Ambient is amassing goodness just as surely as her husband is making a capital of the hard bright forms he pictures, or of the instances of human wickedness to be found in the history of fifteenth century Italy.

The struggle of these parents over the child Dolcino, whom the narrator sees as "an orphan or a changeling" (XVI, 12), is a struggle which can end in only one way, that is, in the destruction of the representative of their social selves. In this fashion the novelist is ready enough to recognize marriage as a going concern. The responsibility of parents to children is deeply felt. The parents must represent, however dimly, the love and wisdom which enveloped Adam when he was "a mere dimpled nursling of the skies," before Eve awoke him to selfishness.

The elder James's immediate application of this belief to family life is a little startling: "In marriage the man so makes himself over to the woman, so cordially endows her with all his substance, as to make a spiritual resurrection or glorification for him in his offspring logically inevitable. Thus it is the essentially objective nature of marriage, the fact that the parties to it are utterly disunited in themselves, and united only in their offspring, which makes it undefiled and honorable, or invests it with the social interest and prestige that distinguish human from brute prolification."[30]

[30] *Secret*, pp. 125–126.

This casts a somewhat lurid light on Henry Junior's celebration of his mother as utterly absorbed in her off-spring,[31] because it suggests that he is giving a description of his family life precisely analogous with his father's ideal, and with his father's description of the artist as utterly sunk in his work. For example: "In a perfect work of art accordingly the substance is wholly swallowed up in the form: what is spiritual in it completely glorifies or transfigures what is natural and material: so that out of two things so unequal and discordant *in se* as a sculptor's genius and a brute unconscious block of marble, a third thing is generated so Divinely perfect or at one with itself as to defy analysis, and forbid the wit of all mankind to discern what or how much belongs to the one parent, what or how much to the other." [32] Man and wife are related only through the little works of art they produce! God in creation is said to work in the same way. Through His total self-abnegation he produces a third thing: regenerate mankind. *Notes of a Son and Brother* describes a family of this very order. Our awareness of the great pressure that such an assumption of selflessness is likely to exert on children takes us far along the road to an understanding of the strains in the James family. The novelist may certainly be said to have devoted far too much energy to the fruitless attempt to repay his father.

In *What Maisie Knew* the novelist uses one of the emblems he shares with his father to describe Maisie's situation: "What was clear to any spectator was that the only link binding her to either parent was this lamentable fact of her being a ready vessel for bitterness, a deep little porcelain cup in which biting acids could be mixed." (XI, 5) Children are like angels if they are filled by love; devils

[31] *Notes of a Son and Brother*, pp. 176–180, esp. p. 179; and Ralph Barton Perry, *Thought and Character of William James*, I, 112. (The elder James's conception of his wife's part in their marriage.)
[32] *Substance*, p. 500.

if they are filled by hate. They are very like angels indeed, for an angel has no power to create or act spontaneously —he is not morally free. So the narrator of *The Author of Beltraffio* is moved to call Dolcino a "poor little devil," and is puzzled to know why he should have applied this term to "a living cherub" (XVI, 21). Dolcino and other children are both angelic and devilish, but in neither case are they responsible. It is their parents who are responsible —the children are simply emblems of the success with which the parents discharge their responsibility.[33]

The death of the child in this story is another instance of the portrait theme. The attempt of these parents to appropriate their child, the representative of all that is best in themselves, is an act of supreme spiritual greed. The mother who wears her child's portrait eventually makes him a dead image of himself. The subsequent death of the parents is likewise emblematically appropriate; they have condemned themselves to death through spiritual pride. The elder James describes death as "the state of a man in love with himself more than with God and his neighbor." [34]

The Figure in the Carpet, like *The Real Thing*, is a parable illustrating the relationship between reproduction and identity on the one hand and representation and spiritual individuality on the other. The artist of *The Real Thing* catches himself in time; his work has suffered, but he realizes at the end of the story the actual connection between the sources and style. Major and Mrs. Monarch have been frozen into the forms of a caste society. They take appearance for reality and have no connection with the "ideal thing," the sources. Such a mistake on the part of the artist is an inevitable prelude to self-discovery. *The Figure in the Carpet*, however, deals with a graver act of appropriation, with the ultimate evil.

[33] Note that the narrator compares Dolcino to a "work of art" (XVI, 21).
[34] *Nature of Evil*, p. 206.

In this story James employs many of the emblems suggestive of the attitudes of the appropriator. The great novelist's admirers edit a magazine called *The Middle;* one of them has written a novel called *Deep Down*, which is described as a great hole in a sandy desert. Their whole feeling about literature is that it gives them density and fixity, an opportunity to grab and keep experience, a knowledge of "the real thing." In this they recall Mark Ambient, whose aim the narrator of *The Author of Beltraffio* describes in this way: "To sink your shaft deep and polish the plate through which people look into it— that's what your work consists of. . . ." (XVI, 43) The figure shows that Ambient is not a person who *re*presents; he is an exhibitor of natural forms. Images of metal objects and jewels are recurrent in the essays in which James is discussing artists whom he suspects of wishing to reproduce the forms they see.[35] The figure of the "polished plate" suggests the poetic appropriateness of this: Such objects are *reflective* surfaces; they give us identity by showing us an image of ourselves. To be in love with oneself is to wish to see *oneself* reflected in the world rather than God. Note that Ambient reads a periodical called *The Observer* (XVI, 39); and that the periodical in *John Delavoy* which wants to print the artist's picture, rather than an account of his actual work, is named *The Cynosure* (Macmillan, XXVII, 400). These things are the reading matter of those who have no "faith in the power of the moral to offer a surface," who want the world to reflect *them*, or to be heavy in *their* purses. Mrs. Gereth in *The Spoils of Poynton* may be used to suggest how one gains an identity through possessions of this delusive sort: ". . . it took all the light of her treasures to make her concrete and distinct." (Macmillan, XV, 129)

Instances multiply here. Just to suggest how the emblematic pattern proliferates, consider Mark Ambient's name.

[35] *Essays in London,* pp. 138–139, 141, 143, 147, 156.

Strether of *The Ambassadors* attends the theater with
Maria Gostrey and is confronted with a world of "types"
in the English audience, whereas in Woollett there had
been only two, the male and the female: "Here, on the
other hand, apart from the personal and sexual range—
which might be greater or less—a series of strong stamps
had been applied, as it were, from without; stamps that
his observation played with as, before a glass case on a
table, it might have passed from medal to medal and from
copper to gold." (XXI, 53) We note that the name
"Mark," which is employed with a similar range of meanings in *The Wings of the Dove*, carries several significa-
tions: metal, form imposed from *without*, coin, identity,
hardness, and so on. Moreover, when we add the name
"Ambient," we get a sort of runic sentence: "He who
encompasses things to give them an identity which will
reflect him," is one possible translation, not in all proba-
bility the only one, but simply the most apparent.

The curiosity which animates the critics in *The Figure
in the Carpet* is one of the human emotions which James
finds most despicable. We find it excoriated, for example,
in *The Reverberator*, *The Aspern Papers*, and *Flicker-
bridge*. The desire to appropriate the artist's form, quite
detached from the life that informs it, is an instance of the
awful spiritual greed of the portrait theme. The narrator
of *The Aspern Papers* says: "That was what the old
woman represented—esoteric knowledge; and this was the
idea with which my critical heart used to thrill." (XIII, 44)
The attempt to appropriate Jeffrey Aspern in the form of
his image, rather than to subject oneself to the still living
reality of his work, is made by a man spiritually dead; but
his efforts are countered by a creature who has an impulse
to grasp images of life even stronger than the critic's, and
he gets his deserts—it is dog eat dog.

The critics in *The Figure in the Carpet*, however, have
before them an authentically great novelist, whose inten-

tion they cannot discover because they have no power to love. Vereker enjoys the spectacle of their frustration: "Our density was a thing too perfect in its way to touch." (XV, 241) The particular plight of these critics is indicated figuratively. The narrator of the story has noted that he and his fellows are confined to "literary circles": "I have sufficiently intimated that it was only in such circles we were all constructed to revolve." (XV, 272) He concludes his account with this characterization of himself and his companion in the search for the "figure": "I may say that today as victims of unappeased desire there isn't a pin to choose between us." (XV,277) Dante's Limbo, where without hope one lives in desire, is the proper abode of such creatures, whom the great novelist, Hugh Vereker, describes as "little demons of subtlety" (XV, 232, 243). Such Virgilian intelligences, acquisitive of knowledge and incapable of love, are not infrequent in James. The end of this story furnishes still another example of the portrait theme. Corvick, whose name suggests a bird acquisitive of bright and shining objects, is said to have found the "figure." What he has found is an image, or inversion, which reflects his greedy self. His death and the death of his wife promptly ensue, and these are emblematic deaths.

It is therefore true, as most critics have concluded, that *The Figure in the Carpet* gives no clue as to *what* the "figure" was. The point it enforces is simply that the artist is a celebrant; he loves the image as it reflects life, not as it reflects his "narrow, personal, ineffectual self." [36] As the elder James somewhere puts it, such spiritual greed has the effect of forcing God and our fellows "to stand in a purely sensible or outward and subjective relation to us."

To complement my examination of the portrait theme in this group of stories which are also parables, *The Real Thing, The Author of Beltraffio,* and *The Figure in the Carpet,* I turn back to certain early stories in which this

[36] *Travelling Companions,* p. 83.

theme is first used to exemplify the right and wrong modes' of taking European experience.

It appeared above that Brooke of *Travelling Companions* went aesthetically and morally astray when he pursued the "picturesque" without the guidance of Charlotte Evans. Even in the rather uncertain and shaky frame of this story, however, James does not leave us with the impression that "the steady perception of the material present" deserves categorical condemnation. He simply suggests that it has a dangerous incompleteness—it is, or may become, greedy. This theme is pursued in *At Isella* and *Adina*,[37] stories of the seventies which are also laid in Italy. At first blush, this attitude toward Italian experience looks like a puritan response to multiplied opportunities for enjoyment. It is more complex than this, as the following passage from *Travelling Companions*—a part of the account of Brooke's stay in Rome—will show.

But I remember with especial delight certain long lonely rides on the Campagna. The weather was perfect. Nature seemed only to slumber, ready to wake far on the hither side of wintry death. From time to time, after a passionate gallop, I would pull up my horse on the slope of some pregnant mound and embrace with the ecstasy of quickened senses the tragical beauty of the scene; strain my ear to the soft low silence, pity the dark dishonored plain, watch the heavens come rolling down in tides of light, and breaking in waves of fire against the massive stillness of temples and tombs. The aspect of all this sunny solitude and haunted vacancy used to fill me with a mingled sense of exaltation and dread. There were moments when my fancy swept that vast funereal desert with passionate curiosity and desire, moments when it felt only its potent sweetness and its high historic charm. But there were other times when the air seemed so heavy with the exhalation of unburied death, so bright with sheeted ghosts, that I turned short about and galloped back to the city.[38]

[37] In *Travelling Companions*, pp. 125–156, 223–269.
[38] *Travelling Companions*, pp. 47–48.

Following this passage, Brooke meets Charlotte once again and persuades her to marry him. Although the meaning of his central recognition is somewhat blurred by the fact that Charlotte has been orphaned in the interval, and is therefore lonely and frightened, her moral authority has actually been enhanced by Brooke's experience of Rome. Marrying Charlotte and accepting his mingled sense of "exaltation and dread" are resolutions which complement one another. The passage quoted, in which the physical movements of the "passionate gallop" are a reinforcement of James's description of his movements of advance and recoil from the meanings of the Campagna itself, is close to being an account of his "marriage" to Europe. The sense of "exaltation and dread" experienced by someone who is taking possession of a wealth of felt values is a theme of the utmost importance, both early and late.

James's feelings about the Campagna epitomize as well as anything can his sense of the challenge of European experience. His first fictional attempt to render his mingled sense of Europe had, however, preceded the journey into Italy of 1869. *Gabrielle de Bergerac*, which was published in that year, is laid in France. Mlle de Bergerac and her lover Coquelin (whom James named after his accomplished schoolfellow, the actor) spend a day picnicking at the Castle of Fossy, on which Coquelin delivers a little discourse: "The truth is, this old feudal fortress is a decidedly melancholy spot. It's haunted with the ghosts of the past. It smells of tragedies, sorrows, and cruelties . . . it's like the history of that abominable past of which it's a relic. At the first glance we see nothing but the great proportions, the show and the splendor; but when we come to explore, we detect a vast underground world of iniquity and suffering. Only half this castle is above the soil; the rest is dungeons and vaults and *oubliettes*." [39]

In *Travelling Companions* the discovery of the dual

[39] *Gabrielle de Bergerac*, pp. 100–101.

meaning of the past is more clearly distinguished from the attitudes found in *Innocents Abroad*. Edel refers to a letter in which James says he will not lay any more stories in the past, which indicates that even in these years he valued the past as an index to present possibilities rather than as a scene. The past tells us what we may do or become. It serves him as the figure of the "house" served his father, of whose houses we are strongly reminded by the Castle of Fossy. There are many passages in the elder James in which the beautiful house of the spirit is said to be erected on a necessarily iniquitous foundation.[40] The duality of our response to the past may be described as an awareness that the great and beautiful forms it produced are drenched in blood—our very knowledge of them gives us a sense of guilt.

Certain other passages will make this plainer. First, the Campagna itself becomes a kind of shorthand symbol for an equivocal and complex response to Europe. In *Watch and Ward* (1871) Hubert says of Rome: "Ah, as I sat there, how the Campagna used to take up the tale and respond to the printed page! If I know anything of the lesson of history . . . I learned it in that enchanted air." (Macmillan, XXIV, 95) Almost twenty years later (in *The Solution*) someone observes: "The Campagna lay below us like a haunted sea (if you can imagine that— the ghosts of dead centuries walking on the deep). . . ." (Macmillan, XXVI, 320) In *The American Scene* (1907) James refers to the view of the Capitol and the "yellow Potomac" which, "seen at a distance . . . varies but by a shade from the sense—yes, absolutely the divine Campagna sense—of St. Peter's and the like-coloured Tiber." [41] This carries us back once more to the first ecstatic letter from Rome in 1869: "I've seen the Tiber hurrying along, as

---

[40] *Lectures*, p. 28; *Substance*, p. 389. (Additional instances: *Lectures*, pp. 377, 413; *Substance*, pp. 382, 412; *Remains*, pp. 374–375.)
[41] *The American Scene*, p. 347.

swift and dirty as history." [42] In *A Small Boy and Others* (1913) James quotes a cousin's lines on the Campagna: ". . . the mighty past around us lived and breathed again."

The reference to a haunted *vacancy* is often generalized, as in *The Portrait of a Lady*, where James speaks of "the mighty plain" and a "dusky uncertain tract." And Isabel reflects: "To live in such a place was, for Isabel, to hold to her ear all day a shell of the sea of the past. This vague eternal rumour kept her imagination awake." (III, 355) In *The Author of Beltraffio* the young narrator is attracted to Ambient partly by his ability to convey "the look of certain lonely grass-grown places which, in the past, had echoed with life" (XVI, 5). The houses we shall encounter in the next chapter are, though vacant, "reverberant" of the past. In *The Princess Casamassima*, in which the house of life is throughout the scene, the extremes whose interplay produces the "rumour" or reverberation are explicitly present. Hyacinth finds himself in a "beautiful horrible world" (VI, 125). A passage on Paris runs in part, "the most brilliant city in the world was also the most blood-stained." Ralph Pendrel in *The Sense of the Past* feels a "sacred terror" which leads us back to Brooke's "exaltation and dread" once more.[43]

The meaning of Brooke's mingled emotion is more clearly rendered in other early stories. One of the earliest of James's attempts to realize this terror in objective action is *The Last of the Valerii*. Another is *Adina*, also published in 1874. In this story Sam Scrope rides, like Brooke, across

[42] *Letters*, I, 25.

[43] Isabel Archer is given the most feminine response to the Italian past: "The sense of the terrible human past was heavy to her. . . ." (III, 413.) She has what in *Roderick Hudson* is called "the historic consciousness," a very different thing from Osmond's collector's sense of the past. Merton Densher and Kate Croy moving toward a crucial encounter across the piazza at Venice, are brushed by the same wing, "the bright historic air . . . begot in the heart of each a fear" (XX, 193).

the Campagna. He is accompanied by the narrator. The pair encounter a sleeping Italian youth whose manly grace awakens the "Byronism" of the teller of the story. Scrope, who is himself ugly, is also a classicist and a collector—one of the first of a long line in James. He cares nothing about the youth, but his eye is caught by what looks like a carved gem clutched in the sleeper's hand. After some rather shrewd bargaining, Scrope obtains the stone for eleven *scudi*. The stone turns out to be of incalculable worth. The narrator later concludes that his deepest motive in cheating the youngster, Angelo, was a kind of jealousy of Italy—"the indefinable gracefulness of nature and man murmured forever in his ears that he was an angular cynic." This feeling "prompted him now to regale himself, once for all, with the sense of an advantage wrested, if not by fair means, then by foul, from some sentient form of irritating Italian felicity."[44] His innocence blasted by Scrope's action, Angelo comes, like Hawthorne's faun, to a knowledge of evil and a desire for revenge. In the end he captures Scrope's fiancée, Adina Waddington, and Scrope tosses his prize, an intaglio bearing the likeness of the Emperor Tiberius, into the Tiber.

Whether this is another and rather literal instance of the portrait theme—Tiberius is known for his stinginess—is less important than an issue on which the story speaks more clearly: the relation between those who can love, and are therefore proper begetters and possessors of works of art, and those who, like Sam Scrope or Gilbert Osmond, have no fount of life in them, and attempt to grasp what others have made.

This story gives us an insight into the germs of James's sense of the past. It is far removed from Hawthorne's feeling that the evil men do lives after them—a view which involves the assertion that we are not fully responsible, and denies the possibility of a great community of those who

[44] In *Travelling Companions*, p. 233.

are conscious. The question in James seems to be: How do we discover the evil that is in us, and are we capable of recognizing it for what it is? This question recapitulates the question as to the nature of the fear that the past inspires. Sam Scrope appears to lack a kind of piety marked by fear, as does the narrator of *The Aspern Papers*. The fear is not of the past except as the past may be conceived as one's own; it is a fear of oneself, of what one has been or may become. It is the fear which beset the elder James in the dining room. The past is a wonderful and terrible index of our possibilities. It is not that the selfish see one world, whereas we see another, but that the actual may be taken in two ways. In *Adina*, Adina Waddington is regarded in two ways—as something to be owned, like a portrait or a jewel, and as a person, a form representative of life. The story enforces a parellel between Scrope's desire to possess Adina and his desire to possess the intaglio. Both are to be kept from the rest of the world. The fear he lacks is the fear of himself as a possessor. The desire to possess the past is a peculiarly dark wickedness. James uses the more immediate dramatic situation in which a man wants to lock up a beautiful living creature to exemplify the meaning of doing the same thing to works of art. Works of art are produced by invokers and encouragers of life, and they have this function themselves. They suggest, not stasis, but change; in their wonderful variety they justify variety. There are never enough of them in the public eye or the public heart to do justice to life's infinite possibilities. Adina Waddington is a kind of lay figure dragged in to make this point, which is so important to James as an artist, an American, and his father's son.[45] We

[45] Because she is herself rather passive, and is contentedly yoked to an unregenerate Italian, Adina Waddington is not a notably "American" girl, nor does her marriage to the vengeful Angelo suggest very directly an inversion of the marriage Scrope had sought to bring about.

must not regard the art of Europe, the manners of Europe, its heroic history, as something we can rifle; if we do, we will destroy ourselves. *Scrope* is an anagram of *corpse* because the character is morally dead—more in love with himself than with God and his neighbor.

We may regard Scrope as characteristic of one broad response to Europe, and Brooke of another. James has found a way (though in neither case a very persuasive way) of making this moral judgment *offer a surface*. The aesthetic standard to which his moral principles committed him was very high, and it is not satisfied in these stories. This matter will come up again and again. To make a point about the way in which his characters have discharged their responsibility to life, James must completely submerge the point in the story—the form is all, and there ought not to be any other road to apprehension of it. So a bad, a skimpy, or an incompletely rendered story is an offense against art *and* life. On the other hand, James's readers proved so very resistant to his most general intentions that he often takes teasing risks—puts up signposts of emblematic reference toward which he has an ambivalent attitude. He both wants and does not want to be found out.

Brooke and Scrope represent two attitudes, not toward Europe alone, but toward the meaning of marriage as well. These associated complexes of meaning were to persist in his work. But during the seventies he did not completely disengage them from other themes. For instance, *A Passionate Pilgrim* is so rambling and rhapsodic, plays with so many conventional motifs (like that of the long separated branches of the same family), that it suggests a considerable confusion in James's own mind as to what was to be done with Europe. The social question, the question of Europe's political inequities and class discrimination which had appeared in *Gabrielle de Bergerac*, is used in *A Passionate Pilgrim* once more. James later came to realize that this was not a question to handle directly—his art is not compatible with such generalities.

Although the portrait theme, so schematically employed in *Travelling Companions*, is mixed during the seventies with other elements which do not come from the same imaginative center (the long drawn-out struggle between rivals in *Watch and Ward* and *Confidence* may be cited), James did use it without these intrusive elements thereafter, as my analysis of *The Author of Beltraffio* has shown. And the two couples who are inversions of one another, the portrait, and the meaning—the elder Jamesian meaning—of marriage, are finally treated in *The Wings of the Dove*. James's first and somewhat incoherent response to Minny Temple's death and Italy employs the same emblems for father's ideas which his novel of thirty-odd years later employs. We shall even encounter Lord Mark sitting in Florian's Café, and Densher will be instructed by the sight, as Brooke had been so long before, of the danger of seizing Milly as a possession, a portrait, and will become afraid of himself.

On the basis of these stories of the seventies and eighties, James's use of his emblems in the early period may be summarized. The conclusion that Europe is *the* scene of experience is confirmed. The division between the two ways of taking experience is treated as the difference between taking the young American girl and the rush of European sensations as possessions, and taking them as representations of life. In the former case the nature of the evil is a kind of selfishness which takes the means for the end; that is, the power to live, love, feel, understand, and multiply the variety of one's connections with the world, is inverted. The transgressor tries to arrest love by confining it and turning it back on himself. He thus denies the duality of the past and the promise of life represented by the girl.

The futility of this evil, the way in which it plunges

its votary ever deeper into sin, is analogous to Dante's conception of what happens in the very pit of hell. The beating of Satan's wings gives rise to a freezing breeze, and the ice more and more constrains the sinners who are imprisoned in this circle. In James the attempts of sinners to seize on the pictorial and thus get something for themselves make them ever more like one another and remove them ever further from the sources. Those who love life attain to variety; those who do not become a mass, not simply in numbers but in spirit. They have the mere identity which the elder James attributes to the minerals, the hard, resistant, heavy stuff of nature.[46]

To tie together these feelings and perceptions, James used the portrait of the young girl, into the meaning of which there entered for Brooke all the considerations I have enumerated. The way in which Brooke takes experience is indicated by his two successive attitudes toward the portrait. First, it is to be possessed as he wants to possess the girl—without knowledge of what she represents, as if she were a mirror in which he could admire himself. When this desire passes, a whole cluster of feelings is inverted. Giotto is now to be prized above all other painters because he, like Charlotte Evans, is not tied by questions of class or technique or patronage to some limited or limiting view of the marriage of particularity with universality. It was proper, necessary, and a sign of grace that Brooke, riding on the Campagna, should feel both exaltation and dread.

Whenever we establish a relation which has the finality of marriage—or in James's own case, here covertly employed, the finality of transplantation to Europe (XIII, xix)—we must feel both its infinite possibilities and a dread that something in ourselves, in mankind, something of which history is full, our own greed and self-righteousness, will serve to despoil us of the wealth of human meanings we have that instant embraced. The Other Self confronts

[46] *Substance*, p. 430.

us and we tremble. The Other Self is seen by those who have *not* taken life in the form of a portrait—to see it is the sign of grace. The fair young man Brooke sees in Florian's Café is in fact the devil—our own inward evil— and to escape him we must recognize him.

VI The House of Life

TO WILLIAM JAMES, THE PSYCHOLOGIST, HIS FATHER'S description of the psyche must have seemed archaic, since it denied the efficacy of the moral will and described men as riven by conflict. In the 1950's, William's own position, though it seems admirable in him, is farther removed from our conception of psychology than is the account of personality found in the elder James and employed by the novelist. William's hard-won assurance that moral order is being established here and now, by namable persons and in the very world of everyday experience, still provides us with moral refreshment; but for an interpretation of human personality as a set of relations between forces—for a description of men as "events" or psychic dynamisms—we must turn to the two Henry Jameses.

Man, as the elder Henry James describes him, moves between opposing poles in his own psyche; his capacity for brotherly love is in uneasy equilibrium with his capacity for self-love. What this meant to the novelist we must now discover. It has been suggested in the distinction between Sam Scrope's love for Adina and Brooke's love for Charlotte Evans. The one love is exclusive; the other is inclusive. Selfhood isolates us in the manner suggested by *The Tragic Muse:* "If the affection that isolates and simplifies its object may be distinguished from the affection that seeks communications and contacts for it, Julia Dallow's was quite of the encircling, not to say the narrowing sort." (VII, 148) Between these two loves man must move.

In the elder James we find it asserted that human nature *is* this relation, a relation between our dove and serpent natures. Life is therefore dramatic in its essence, if we limit the possibilities of drama as the morality play does. Both father and son are in sympathy with Augustine's saying, "Man is a great deep." Prince Amerigo says, toward the end of *The Golden Bowl*, "Everything's terrible, *cara* —in the heart of man." (XXIV, 349) His insight is the final assurance of his regeneration. Tony Bream of *The Other House* recalls that even before the murder of his child he "grew afraid." Jean Martle asks, "Afraid of what?" Tony replies, "Afraid of everything. You don't know—but we're abysses. At least I'm one!" [1] His fear is the ultimate fear, the fear of the Other Self. But we cannot, simply by feeling this fear, dispose of the conflict between the dove and the serpent. A quotation from the elder James, who is sometimes referred to as a giddy optimist, is in place here.

The natural inheritance of every one who is capable of spiritual life, is an unsubdued forest where the wolf howls and every obscene bird of night chatters; so that his very manhood is contingent upon his subduing this inheritance to light and air, and making it yield, instead of its wild and poisonous undergrowths, every fruit good for food. Every man who has reached even his intellectual teens begins to suspect this; begins to suspect that life is no farce; that it is not genteel comedy even; that it flowers and fructifies on the contrary out of the profoundest tragic depths. All that is distinctive in human culture betrays an ever present conflict between the inner and outer life, between the private and public soul, and exhibits in itself that conflict reconciled. Whatsoever is noblest in human character, best in human

---

[1] *The Other House*, p. 373.

action, most permanent in human achievement, most renowned in art, tells only of obstacles overcome, of difficulties toilsomely vanquished, in short of hell patiently subjugated to heaven, or evil reconciled to good, in some higher natural and therefore positive quantity which men would never have otherwise divined.[2]

A man who has, like Emerson as the elder James conceives of him, "the purely natural innocence of the dove" is incomplete. A man who swings to either extreme without going through the necessary conflict "may make thenceforth a very good dove or a very good serpent, but no longer a *man* containing in himself the stupendous contrarieties of heaven and hell, or the exactly equal possibilities of the brightest spiritual day, and the murkiest most menacing spiritual night."[3] The elder James was not much concerned about angels or devils as such, but only about their conflict within us. It is this fact that made possible the novelist's covert use of his father's opposed forces. We become admirable or awful creatures by the use we make of our experience, not by the intervention of some wholly foreign power.

He who does take the portrait for the lady, he who construes nature as subject to his greed instead of perceiving it as a representation of his own nature, his possible heights and depths, does not fear his other self; for he has been assimilated to it and lives under its dominion. But such figures cannot play central roles in fiction. Far more important is the character who is afraid of himself. This is the heart of the moral life. The novelist's uses of this inner conflict are numerous, for it is indispensable to his great theme, redemption. All the adventures of the morally

[2] *Substance*, p. 75. Of course, anyone who envisages the world as a totality with the irresistible love on his side is a cosmic optimist. The point is that the elder James saw life as characterized from day to day by bitter internal conflict—not that he believed that its ultimate end is bitter or meaningless.

[3] *Substance*, p. 157.

spontaneous person may be represented as encounters with the other self in the house of life.

The ambivalence James gave to the American's response to Europe has been traced to the mingled fear and delight he feels in the presence of Europe's cultural achievement and the evidence of its terrible cost in wickedness and suffering. The novelist's use of the "house of life" as a poetic concretion of this situation is best introduced by a famous passage from *A Small Boy and Others*. James is recalling his first visits to the Louvre as a child: "The beginning in short was with Géricault and David, but it went on and on and slowly spread; so that one's stretched, one's even strained perceptions, one's discoveries and extensions piece by piece come back, on the great premises, almost as so many explorations of the house of life, so many circlings and hoverings round the image of the world." James's account of the Galerie d'Apollon and of the nightmare of which it was the scene, I quote in full because it is crucial for an understanding of his symbolism. He has been speaking of a dawning sense of the "forms" of style.

It was as if they had gathered there into a vast deafening chorus; I shall never forget how—speaking, that is, for my own sense—they filled those vast halls with the influence rather of some complicated sound, diffused and reverberant, than of such visibilities as one could directly deal with. To distinguish among these, in the charged and coloured and confounding air, was difficult—it discouraged and defied; which was doubtless why my impression originally best entertained was that of those magnificent parts of the great gallery simply not inviting us to distinguish. They only arched over us in the wonder of their endless golden riot and relief, figured and flourished in perpetual revolution, breaking into great high-hung circles and symmetries of squandered picture, opening into deep outward embrasures that threw off the rest of monumental Paris somehow as a told story, a sort of

wrought effect or bold ambiguity for a vista, and yet held it
there, at every point, as a vast bright gage, even at moments
a felt adventure, of experience. This comes to saying that in
those beginnings I felt myself most happily cross that bridge
over to Style constituted by the wondrous Galerie d'Apollon,
drawn out for me as a long but assured initiation and seeming
to form with its supreme coved ceiling and inordinately
shining parquet a prodigious tube or tunnel through which I
inhaled little by little, that is again and again, a general sense
of *glory*. The glory meant ever so many things at once, not
only beauty and art and supreme design, but history and fame
and power, the world in fine raised to the richest and noblest
expression. The world there was at the same time, by an odd
extension or intensification, the local present fact, to my
small imagination, of the Second Empire, which was (for my
notified consciousness) new and queer and perhaps even
wrong, but on the spot so amply radiant and elegant that it
took to itself, took under its protection with a splendour of
insolence, the state and ancientry of the whole scene, profiting
thus, to one's dim historic vision, confusedly though it might
be, by the unparalleled luxury and variety of its heritage. But
who shall count the sources at which an intense young fancy
(when a young fancy *is* intense) capriciously, absurdly
drinks?—so that the effect is, in twenty connections, that of a
love-philtre or fear-philtre which fixes for the senses their
supreme symbol of the fair or the strange. The Galerie
d'Apollon became for years what I can only term a splendid
scene of things, even of the quite irrelevant or, as might be,
almost unworthy; and I recall to this hour, with the last
vividness, what a precious part it played for me, and exactly
by that continuity of honour, on my awaking, in a summer
dawn many years later, to the fortunate, the instantaneous
recovery and capture of the most appalling yet most admirable
nightmare of my life. The climax of this extraordinary
experience—which stands alone for me as a dream-adventure
founded in the deepest, quickest, clearest act of cogitation
and comparison, act indeed of life-saving energy, as well as in
unutterable fear—was the sudden pursuit, through an open

door, along a huge high saloon, of a just dimly-described
figure that retreated in terror before my rush and dash (a
glare of inspired reaction from irresistible but shameful
dread,) out of the room I had a moment before been
desperately, and all the more abjectly, defending by the push
of my shoulder against hard pressure on lock and bar from
the other side. The lucidity, not to say the sublimity, of the
crisis had consisted of the great thought that I, in my appalled
state, was probably still more appalling than the awful agent,
creature or presence, whatever he was, whom I had guessed,
in the suddenest wild start from sleep, the sleep within my
sleep, to be making for my place of rest. The triumph of my
impulse, perceived in a flash as I acted on it by myself at a
bound, forcing the door outward, was the grand thing, but
the great point of the whole was the wonder of my final
recognition. Routed, dismayed, the tables turned upon him by
my so surpassing him for straight aggression and dire intention
my visitant was already but a diminished spot in the long
perspective, the tremendous, glorious hall, as I say, over the
far-gleaming floor of which, cleared for the occasion of its
great line of priceless vitrines down the middle, he sped for
his life, while a great storm of thunder and lightning played
through the deep embrasures of high windows at the right.
The lightning that revealed the retreat revealed also the
wondrous place and, by the same amazing play, my young
imaginative life in it of long before, the sense of which, deep
within me, had kept it whole, preserved it to this thrilling use;
for what in the world were the deep embrasures and the so
polished floor but those of the Galerie d'Apollon of my
childhood? The "scene of something" I had vaguely then
felt it? Well I might, since it was to be the scene of that
immense hallucination.[4]

[4] The sentences from *A Small Boy and Others* quoted in my text by
way of introduction are on p. 351; the long passage runs from p. 345
to p. 349. This passage has been discussed at length by Lionel Trilling, in *The Liberal Imagination*, pp. 80–86; and by F. W. Dupee, in
"The Dream of the Louvre," *Henry James*, pp. 3–35; and also by
Leon Edel, in *The Untried Years*, pp. 67–80. The expression "house
of life" is also found on p. 118 of *A Small Boy and Others*, and in
XIV, 409.

What here appears as James's own experience in a dream had been a recurrent theme in his fiction since 1870. The "exaltation and dread" felt by Brooke on the Campagna have become "a love-philtre or a fear-philtre, which fixes for the senses their supreme symbol of the fair or the strange." The fair young man who sat in Florian's Café, and appeared as the purchaser of the portrait in the dream of the girl stricken with tuberculosis, has become an opponent, who must be expelled from the house of life. Moreover, the "damned shape" encountered by his father in the dining room, the creature from which his father had fled, has here been routed—routed by a man possessed of a style.[5] The meaning of James's remark that only an American can become a European is given poetic precision in this passage. "The American steps ashore in Europe and says in effect: 'Look what I have gone and done!' "[6]

To assume quite deliberately, as only the American can, the full burden of the mixed heritage of Europe is to confront at the same time one's own mixed character—here, written large, are man's wonderful possibilities, and his crimes, his wastefulness, and his sorrows. All the emblems fit this situation: dove against serpent; marriage against concubinage; the conscience against the other self; Minny Temple's genuine universality—love for all—against the "church," the false universal—spiritual greed. And the mediating term which can reconcile all these is "Style." Art

[5] Leon Edel, in *The Untried Years*, uses this passage chiefly to establish two things: the depth and importance of the novelist's rivalry with William James and his identification of his literary powers "with the pomp of Imperial power." Mr. Edel's case for the dream as representative of sibling rivalry is a good one, but he has neglected the aspect of the dream emphasized by the present writer, and by Professor Trilling (*The Liberal Imagination*, pp. 80–86), that is, the guilt mingled with the ecstasy which James felt on taking possession, through his style, of Europe.

[6] "Henry James and the New Jerusalem" (*Kenyon Review*, VIII, 1946), p. 546.

alone has the power to subdue the splendor *and* the iniquity of the Second Empire to the uses of the spirit.[7]

Since its emblems occur in the father's work and in earlier and subsequent work of the novelist, we may read the dream as a parable. A child, who is, in the elder James's phrase, a "dimpled nursling of the skies," whose experience of the world is "diffused and reverberant"—is the experience of "a general sense of *glory*," that is, of the marvelous fullness of what love and wisdom have made—awakens "many years later" to a sense of the mixture in himself of the desire to possess the world and the desire to celebrate it. The description of the gallery is a description of the state of innocence; the description of the nightmare is a description of regeneration—the triumphant explusion of the other self. What lies between these stages is the period of "the middle years."

The fact that the act of celebration involves renouncing material acquisition, the desire for personal recognition, and an active sexuality has not been clear to James's readers, and some have affirmed his creative power and at the same time deplored his use of it to describe people who renounce these things. The renunciations of James's characters are like his own: they are made in behalf of the love "that seeks communications and contacts" so that consciousness may be widened. If this attitude seems too self-deprecatory to be biographically plausible, this is simply because we are not aware of the opportunities for covert self-glorification the two Henry Jameses found in it. They had an abundant satisfaction in their role. To compel others to experience life as one conceives it is the greatest imaginable human power.

In the set of correspondences which father and son employed, a man *is* a "house of life," in which the struggle

[7] This statement of what the artist can do through style parallels the elder James's statement of Christ's accomplishment. Christ is said to be "incapable of *realizing Himself except in others*" (*Secret*, p. 334).

with the other self is carried on. A regenerate man houses the world—or, as the elder James liked to put it, all nature and all history are to be brought within the compass of the human form. In an essay on the first World War his son writes: "If it would have been hard really to give the measure of one's dismay at the awful proposition of a world squeezed together in the huge Prussian fist and with the variety and spontaneity of its parts oozing in a steady trickle, like the sacred blood of sacrifice, between those hideous knuckly fingers, so, none the less, every reason with which our preference for a better condition and a nobler fate could possibly bristle kept battering at my heart, kept, in fact, pushing into it, after the fashion of a crowd of the alarmed faithful at the door of a church. The effect was literally, yes, as of the occasion of some great religious service, with prostrations and exaltations, the light of a thousand candles and the sound of soaring choirs —all of which figured one's individual inward state as determined by the menace." [8]

Earlier in the same essay, James says that his "house of the spirit" required enlargement because of the war across the Channel, quite as if the variety and spontaneity of the French had found shelter in his comprehending heart.[9] What no reader of his novels has discovered in Hugh Vere-ker, the great novelist of *The Figure in the Carpet*, is "the organ of life" (XV, 234), or heart, which in *The Bostonians* is figured as a "mansion" (Macmillan, IX, 58).[10] His

[8] *Within the Rim and Other Essays*, pp. 29–30.
[9] *Within the Rim and Other Essays*, pp. 19–20.
[10] The rather puzzling name "Nash," which James bestowed on his father's representative in *The Tragic Muse*, may perhaps be explained as a recollection of one of the books of his childhood. Leon Edel notes that as a youngster he had pored over Joseph Nash's *Mansions of England in the Olden Time* (*The Untried Years*, p. 91). We may surmise that the association of this title with his father's attempt to compel the "European" to exemplify the "American," to compel the world to exhibit the spirit (which the novelist had carried forward), has coalesced in his mind with the Biblical verse, "In my

father's own "temple," the scene on which he elaborated
his ideas, is described in *Notes of a Son and Brother*.[11] In
the play called *The High Bid*, which James made out of
Covering End, the English heir is taught how to occupy
his house by an American woman, who says of it: "This
is the Temple." [12] We shall of course find that James did
not keep one house for morals and another for art; the
"house of fiction" has countless windows (III, x), just as
Miriam Rooth is "like a room with windows" (VIII, 209).
The point is always that what animates the house and, so to
speak, opens its infinite variety of windows is the artist's
great love of the image of life as a reflection of its spirit.
In this form these emblems are the small change of James's
achievement; what we must look for is their use *in conjunction* with one another. These emblems, like the principles from which they derive in the elder James, are co-
ordinates of the interplay of consciousness; they do not
"stand for" people except as they indicate phases of the
moral life or the extreme limits of moral motion. Milly
Theale, lying ill in her palace during the storm, and Gilbert
Osmond, left alone by Isabel in the Palazzo Roccanera,
have reached such ideal limits—we can know them only as
others are affected by them.[13] Before introducing some instances of the related use of the girl (as conscience), the
other self, and the house, I shall cite some examples of the
elder James's figurative use of houses.

---

father's house there are many mansions." "Gabriel Nash" as a runic
phrase then becomes: "He who announces the achievement of unity
through variety"—since the house has many mansions.
[11] Pp. 159, 160, 169. A "house" may represent a heart ruled by lust or
greed, for example, Mrs. Lowder's house and Densher's flat in *The
Wings of the Dove*, and Poynton in *The Spoils of Poynton*.
[12] *Complete Plays*, p. 582.
[13] The most useful critical formulations of the primacy of structure
over character in the later novels are Francis Fergusson's "The
Drama in the Golden Bowl" (*Hound and Horn*, VI, 1934, pp. 407–
413); and Austin Warren's "Myth and Dialectic in the Later Novels"
(*Kenyon Review*, V, 1943, pp. 551–568).

In the first of these, righteousness is declared provisional, the mere scullery maid of art. "The moral force was never anything but a scaffolding for God's spiritual house in the soul; it was never designed to give permanent substance but only temporary form to God's finished work in human nature; and when accordingly it ceases to look upon itself in this subordinate plight, and insists upon being treated not as the scaffolding but as the house, not as the mould but as the substance to be moulded, not as the matrix but as the gem, in short not as an accessory but as a principal, it loses even this justification and becomes a positive nuisance. The social sentiment, the sense of living organic unity among men, is accordingly fast absorbing it or taking it up into its own higher circulation, whence it will be reproduced in every regenerate aesthetic form." [14]

In the second example, it is the architect, who transmutes the things of sense into a representation of consciousness, with whom James is concerned. "No one looking at a house and estimating its distinctive character or individuality, regards or even sees the bricks and mortar implied in its structure. These things, unless the architect has been a noodle, are forever covered up from sight, only to reveal themselves again when the edifice shall have tumbled into dilapidation. Every house accordingly that deserves the name stands forth to the beholder a pure form of heavenly Art, beckoning onward and upward the soul."

Many of the elder James's uses of the house as a figure relate to the soul's dwelling: "Our hitherto neglected body shall become the only visible and acknowledged temple of God." Or they relate to the stories of the house as representative of stages in human or providential history —"Nature is in truth but the basement or culinary story of the Divine edifice; and when we make her primary, or allow her to dominate the house, we of course degrade the

[14] *Substance*, p. 13. The next two quoted passages are on pp. 296–297 and p. 250.

drawing and bedroom floors, filling them with sounds and
odors fatal to every cultivated sense." [15] Angels, though
there is no merit in them because God constrains them to
be good, may be thought of as inhabiting an upper story
"in that house of mystical *revelation* to which the church
on earth has served as needful but unhandsome basement.
. . ."

These figures, however, have less interest here than
those which represent us as in conflict in the house of life.
The emphasis in the following comparison on the likeness of
evil to excrement is not uncommon in the elder James: [16]
"Man's nature, whatever the splendors of Divine power
incident to it, is after all nothing but a vehicle of transcendent spiritual blessing to the man himself; whereas the
brute nature knows no such spiritual subserviency. And
when accordingly the subject of the higher nature persistently identifies himself with the lower, he is sure to
find in his way every sharp regret and bitter humiliation
which may tend to frighten him back into his place. Otherwise he would be like a noble house ruined by bad drainage." [17]

In speaking of the period of his vastation, the elder
James describes himself as having conformed to all the
church demanded of him, yet remaining "uneasy"—since,
as we have learned, he had yet to discover his selfhood and
confront it. "The house of my soul had been swept of its
evils, but it still remained desolate of goods." The most
striking of these passages refers (in the course of a rather
jocular discussion of the way in which people were fritter-
ing away their time on the vulgar spirits produced by
mediums) to the climax and conclusion of the vastation.
Before this event he had been prone to an extremity of self-
reproach. This sense of guilt was dispelled by Sweden-

[15] *Logic*, p. 202.
[16] See *Nature of Evil*, p. 210.
[17] *Society*, p. 155.

borg, from whom he learned that it came "from certain ghostly busy-bodies intent upon reducing the human mind to their subjection, and availing themselves for this purpose of every sensuous and fallacious idea we entertain of God, and of every disagreeable memory we retain of our own conduct." The mode of getting rid of this guilt is to see that our "moral" self is other, is alien: "The first step toward my acknowledging the evil of my doings, is my perception of its being a foreign influx or importation." His figure for his dilemma is the one I wish to emphasize because it takes us back to his son's passage on the Galerie d'Apollon: "Hence I had little doubt that the fact might be as Swedenborg alleged, and that I had been all along nourishing, by means of certain falsities in my intellect, a brood of ghostly loafers who had at last very nearly turned me out of house and home." [18]

Some evidence will be given later on that the novelist was conversant with the principle illustrated by the three levels of the house: the basement as the sensuous or natural level; the first floor as the realm of the rational or scientific; and the second as that which includes the significance of the other two, the spiritual or conscious. The elder James found the house illustrative in part *because* it had drains —we receive a spiritual influx above stairs, and discharge moralistic and sensuous "falsities" through the sewers. The process is never intermitted until we are thoroughly regenerate. If we turn to the Galerie d'Apollon passage, we find that this representation of the experiencer as a conduit is hinted at. The gallery with its rounded ceiling becomes a "tube or tunnel through which I inhaled little by little, that is again and again, a general sense of *glory*." This last word has a technical meaning for Swedenborg and the elder James; it is a term for the union of wisdom and love,

[18] The four passages quoted above are in *Lectures*, pp. 412–413. The first is the earliest reference (1852) to the vastation that I have found in James's published work.

our soul's parents. When we juxtapose the notion of influx through the tube with the expulsion of the "awful agent" by one who feels "shameful dread," the image of a man as a pipe, liable to obstructions which hinder the influx of spirit (or, to revert to the elder James's figure, "a noble house ruined by bad drainage"), we have the first of a series of references to man as a pipe which I shall deal with below.[19]

Passages reminiscent of the elder James's "ghostly loafers" are not hard to find. Austin Warren has emphasized Maggie's encounter with evil, which is "like some bad-faced stranger surprised in one of the thick-carpeted corridors of a house of quiet on a Sunday afternoon."[20] But to construct a representative or ideal case of James's use of the encounter with the other self in the house of life, I shall juxtapose *The Beast in the Jungle*, *The Jolly Corner*, and *The Sense of the Past* with the passage on the Galerie d'Apollon. James himself never undertook exegesis; that, after all, had been done by his father, done so insistently and so repeatedly (as in the case of Gabriel Nash) that the great point had been obscured. The great point was that one's sense of life should appear only in one's form.

The stories and the unfinished novel listed above relate to one another, not simply in their employment of the same emblems, but in turns of speech and effects of atmos-

[19] The association of constipation with the incapacity to give love, and with self-righteousness, seem psychosomatically sound. A further association between the son's passage on the great gallery and the elder James's description of the state of his soul is to be found in the fact that during the father's "vastation" (the period in which his beliefs had been laid waste, and he had been voided) his house of the soul is described as "swept of its evils," while remaining "desolate of goods." In the son's "houses," described below, and in the great gallery as it appeared in the dream, furnishings have also been removed.

[20] Austin Warren, "Myth and Dialectic in the Later Novels" (*Kenyon Review*, V. 1943), p. 564.

phere as well. *The Jolly Corner* has been treated as a venture in the supernatural, and an unwitting betrayal of James's own psychic wounds, but it is something much more important than a remnant of uncontrolled experience or a mere fictional device. It is a parable which employs James's "ideal limits" of moral and aesthetic motion as characters. The story has to do with the return of an American expatriate. James's own overt commentary on "alternative visions in respect to the American absentee" is to be found in his biography of William Wetmore Story,[21] the American expatriate, who was a sculptor and at times a poet as well: "It becomes interesting, in the light of so distinct an example, to extract from the case—the case of the permanent absentee or exile—the general lesson that may seem to us latent in it. This moral seems to be that somehow, in the long-run, Story *paid*—paid for having sought his development even among the circumstances that at the time of his choice appeared not alone the only propitious, but the only possible." The "worst" such case is that of those who "have found themselves (sometimes quite unconsciously, but sometimes sorely suspecting) the prey of mere beguilement. That really rises before us as the formula of Story's Roman years, making us—unless we yield, in the view, too much to wanton fancy—figure his career as a sort of beautiful sacrifice to a noble mistake. I cannot, in truth, otherwise describe the mistake than as that of the frank consent to be beguiled."

The theme of *Travelling Companions*, the danger of a "steady absorption in the material present," is restated in what follows. Story's *"relation"* to his subjects had been wrong; he had submerged himself: "Subjects float by, in Italy, as the fish in the sea may be supposed to float by a merman, who doubtless puts out a hand from time to time to grasp, for curiosity, some particularly iridescent speci-

[21] *William Wetmore Story and His Friends.* Quotations are drawn from pp. 222–227.

men." The emblematic reference here is precise: Those who live under water are absorbed in the pictorial. Their situation parallels that of the seekers after the "real thing" in *The Author of Beltraffio* and *The Figure in the Carpet*. One descends from the "sources" to the river, from the river to the sea. These passages constitute a gentle indictment of James's friend, who had gone astray both morally and aesthetically. Story would have been a better poet and sculptor "in—let me tell the whole truth—Boston by the Charles, or even in London by the Thames, than in Rome, in Florence, or most of all, in the shuttered noon of the Sienese day itself." Story had found what James here refers to (just as in *Travelling Companions*) as the "picturesque," but he had removed himself from the "sources," had lived, in effect, under water.

The story of Spencer Brydon in *The Jolly Corner* is the story of a man who, having taken in his youth the apparently bold and free step of casting off his family and his peculiar heritage, finds after a third of a century that he has avoided both himself and the promise of life—has left behind both those talents which were peculiarly his and the love which Alice Staverton had offered his blinded youth. The story begins close to the point at which *The Beast in the Jungle* ends, for the beast is about to spring; the awful other self is finally to appear. Brydon, unlike Marcher, has at the end of the story "turned the tables" (the phrase employed in the Galerie d'Apollon passage is "the tables turned upon him") and effectually routed his other self by perceiving and asserting its otherness.[22] That he does

22 Two sentences are worth quoting for their correspondence with James's description of his nightmare: "People enough, first and last, had been in terror of apparitions, but who had ever before so turned the tables and become himself, in the apparitional world, an incalculable terror? He might have found this sublime had he quite dared to think of it; but he didn't too much insist, truly, on that side of his privilege." And in the gallery passage: "The lucidity, not to say the sublimity, of the crisis had consisted of the great thought that I, in

so on a scene which had served him, as the great gallery had served the infant James, "for the growth of an early conception of style" (XVII, 455), is a sufficient indication of the fact that in the "jolly corner" we encounter another "house of life," not, in this instance, European.

There is a robust and practical element in the moral principles of the two Henry Jameses which the characters of Brydon and Marcher illustrate. Both had refused to incur the guilt of experience—that plunge into the possibilities of our nature which inspires both exaltation and dread. Brydon says of his friends that they thought of him as living a life devoted to "sensation," a life comparable to Story's immersion in what James calls the "golden air" of Italy. This refusal to acknowledge one's implication in our common guilt is held to be a denial of one's own guilt. Brydon's life, like Story's, has been a greedy one. In the story Brydon makes use for the very first time of his capacity; he becomes the actual overseer of the repairs to his property. The man who has had the habit of destroying important letters unopened, the man who cannot conceive that Alice Staverton should expect anyone to "live" in New York, has been belatedly awakened to his own possibilities. What would his "Form" have been? He asks this question in what may be called the classic Jamesian moral situation: the situation of the man who encounters his other self in the house of life under the aegis of fostering love and thereby discovers his form or style. This is reminiscent of *The Birthplace*, although we are not led to respect Brydon in the degree that we respect the keeper of Shakespeare's "birthplace" at the end of that story.

We have fallen into James's trap in reading this story as that of a man who discovers what he *would have been.*

---

my appalled state, was probably still more appalling than the awful agent, creature or presence. . . ." For another use of the apparition on which the tables are turned (in *The Sense of the Past*), see *Notebooks*, pp. 367–368.

What Spencer Brydon really discovers is what he *has been*.
It is this discovery that enables him to recognize Alice
Staverton's love. This is one of James's pretty inversions
or equivalences—there is no moral distinction between the
greed of the American expatriate and that of the American
millionaire. And, James surmises, had William Wetmore
Story lived in Boston, he might have become a real poet!

Spencer Brydon, however, is extricated. He undergoes
what the elder James had referred to in his own case as
"My Moral Death and Burial." He confronts the awful
creature, "to advance upon which was the condition for
him either of liberation or of supreme defeat." The man
he sees is presented with more "shade and salience" than
any "portrait" could have given him. Brydon's whole
being revolts; he asserts the total *otherness* of the creature
in evening dress with his two amputated fingers—and dies
to selfhood. (The reader will find this a useful instance of
the portrait theme. To accept this presentment as one's
self is to be damned; when Alice Staverton encounters this
creature in her dream of the same hour, she in effect replaces him. What has become *other* for Brydon does so at
the moment he is prepared to accept Alice Staverton's
version of life and reject the one he has so long cherished.)
His "early conception of style" had been nothing less than a
love of the images of life for the sake of life itself which
had been represented by the persons whose love had filled
the house.

The detail to which this "conception of style" refers, the
black and white marble squares of the entrance hall, is also
to be found in the empty house in *The Sense of the Past*.
The sound of the steel point of his stick on these squares
awakens echoes of the life which had filled the house for
him as a child. "This effect was the dim reverberating
tinkle as of some far-off bell hung who should say where?
—in the depths of the house, of the past, of that mystical
other world that might have flourished for him had he

not, for weal or woe abandoned it." Pendrel's house in *The Sense of the Past* is "a museum of held reverberations still more than of kept specimens." The experience of Henry James as a "small boy" had been of the "diffused and reverberant" forms of the great gallery. What these three great houses have in common is James's most inclusive emblem for the archetypal human situation: Man first attempts to take possession of the house of life, but finally learns that it is his task to celebrate it. What he celebrates is not particular forms, but the current of life which creates form, the "reverberant" flux of creation itself, which resounds as it does in Isabel Archer's imagination, like a sea-shell, or, as in Brooke's case, makes the air of the Campagna "bright with sheeted ghosts."

The passage in which Brydon awakes to his "inheritance," an awakening which he later defines by saying to Alice Staverton, "Yes—I can only have died," is interesting for its associations with the passage on the Galerie d'Apollon and, in particular, with the elder James's figure of man as a kind of conduit. The "grey passage" in what follows is suggestive of the period of the "middle years," as is Brydon's further remark to Alice Staverton, "You brought me literally to life." ("Death," the reader will recall, is the state of those more in love with themselves than with God and their neighbors.)

He had come back, yes—come back from further away than any man but himself had ever travelled; but it was strange how with this sense what he had come back *to* seemed really the great thing, and as if his prodigious journey had been all for the sake of it. Slowly but surely his consciousness grew, his vision of his state thus completing itself: he had been miraculously *carried* back—lifted and carefully borne as from where he had been picked up, the uttermost end of an interminable grey passage. Even with this he was suffered to rest, and what had now brought him to knowledge was the break in the long mild motion.

7

It had brought him to knowledge, to knowledge—yes, this was the beauty of his state; which came to resemble more and more that of a man who has gone to sleep on some news of a great inheritance, and then, after dreaming it away, after profaning it with matters strange to it, has waked up again to serenity of certitude and has only to lie and watch it grow. This was the drift of his patience—that he had only to let it shine on him. He must, moreover, with intermissions, still have been lifted and borne; since why and how else should he have known himself, later on, with the afternoon glow intenser, no longer at the foot of his stairs—situated as these now seemed at that dark other end of his tunnel—but on a deep window-bench of his high saloon, over which had been spread, couch-fashion, a mantle of soft stuff lined with grey fur that was familiar to his eyes and that one of his hands kept fondly feeling as for its pledge of truth. (XVII, 478–479)

At one end of the "interminable grey passage" there had stood the other self. Now *"carried* back" from "the dark other end of his tunnel," he finds himself possessed of a wonderful fullness of "knowledge." Directly, this is of Alice Staverton's love, an "inheritance" no less than infinite. But we are reminded of the "general sense of *glory"* offered by the "tube or tunnel," at one end of which the "awful agent" had stood. Love has borne Brydon back a third of a century and given him an actual second chance; not a supernatural glimpse of what he might have been, but a chance to become what his inordinately extended "middle years" had not made him—the inheritor of the house of life, delightedly dependent on fostering love.

The publication date of *The Jolly Corner* is 1908. *A Small Boy and Others* was published in 1913. James's use of his dream of the Galerie d'Apollon is thus dated back some years. Far from being an account of uncontrolled experience, *The Jolly Corner* renders in ostensibly supernatural form the dream which had marked for him the termination of his "middle years." Moreover, the protagonist in the story is not an artist, but a dilettante, a redeemed appropriator, who stands, morally speaking, much closer to William Wetmore Story than he does to Henry James, who has so contrived the situation that the real sinner is the expatriate, not the American he might have been. Alice Staverton ties the knot by telling Brydon that *she* had seen and "accepted" his other self, and this instance provides our first full illustration of what the girl (or, in this case, middle-aged woman) who becomes a man's conscience does for him. Her acceptance of his human limitation is in no way censorious. Nor is it coercive. The struggle within Brydon, which James so often renders as the struggle within the house of life, is conceived as Brydon's own effort, in which his conscience undergoes a kind of crucifixion; bears, that is, the fury of the dispossessed selfhood and eventually tames this lowest element of human nature to divine uses. Later on, we shall examine a number of figures employed by James to suggest this "marriage" of the human and the divine in our nature. It is important to note here that the creatures so often called "beasts," and so often reminiscent of Blake's "tigers of wrath," have a part and a place in human destiny.

The key to the difference between the situation of Marcher in *The Beast in the Jungle* and Brydon in *The Jolly Corner* is that Marcher waits all his life for the "beast" to spring, while Brydon, using images drawn from big game hunting to describe the process, actually brings his other self to bay. The fact that he requires Alice Staverton's assistance, while the man of James's great dream does not, will be explained in the next chapter as a function of the difference between artists and lesser men. *The Beast in the Jungle* does not have the helpful emblematic completeness of *The Jolly Corner*. Marcher's realization of the nature of the "beast" comes too late: May Bartram is dead, and can no longer assume the place of the selfhood which had so firmly ruled him that he could not glimpse the meaning of her offered love. We can, however, associate *The Sense of the Past* with *The Jolly Corner* with respect to emblematic significance.

In his notes for this unfinished novel James considers and rejects the possibility of having "sweet Nan" confront Pendrel's other self, the man of the 1820's, whose place in the past he takes. In this particular, the parallel with *The Jolly Corner* fails. But Nan is representative, as Alice Staverton had so long and so patiently been, of the promise of life; Pendrel seeks to get experience of the past in the appropriator's mode; the scene is the house of life; and finally he is rescued in some unspecified way by "sweet Nan," presumably with the aid of Aurora Coyne, whom he is to marry when he returns to the twentieth century. This eighteenth century scene is peopled by persons Pendrel has a way of taking for portraits, images of the past. The surprise James has contrived for him is simply that history has given him no intimation of Nan's existence (or rather, the fact that she existed in 1820), because, being "modern," a representative of the promise of life, she is not datable, not seizable, and to come under her sway is to be freed from greed. She is therefore the last of the avatars of Minny Temple.

James's choice of a particular set of emblems or symbolic constants (described in this chapter) to contain and define his action is the clearest sign we have of his attitude toward life. His American faith is the vessel of his power.

VII News of Life

MANY OF JAMES'S READERS, IF ASKED WHICH OF HIS WORKS
have most to say about the uncertainties and complexities
of the moral life, would doubtless name *The Portrait of a
Lady* (1881) and *The Princess Casamassima* (1885). These
two novels and *The Bostonians* provide ample illustration
of the effect of James's moral outlook on subjects offering
more variety and density than those of his other novels. I
consider *The Bostonians* an *open* novel because it renders a
whole series of worlds of which the reader may be presumed to have heard: the South, Boston and New England
reformers, the world of journalism, New York society,
Harvard and Cambridge, a shore resort, and so forth. Such
sources of appearance as these were employed by Balzac,
and this is the only major James novel which may be
directly compared with Balzac's work.

These three novels of the eighties show that this decade
was James's boldest and bravest, the period of which we
may say (as James does of the hero of *The Princess Casamassima*), "he had more news of life . . . than he knew
what to do with . . ." (V, 159). Never again was James
to feel free to treat a big subject so much on its own terms,
and so little on those his father's vision had prescribed for
him.

Although he found a quasi-dramatic form effective against his growing tendency to render things emblematically, the novels of the nineties in which he used this defense (*What Maisie Knew* and *The Awkward Age*) are, by comparison with those of the eighties, constricted and airless. And in the last three completed novels, *The Ambassadors, The Wings of the Dove,* and *The Golden Bowl,* the elder James does not appear simply as a limiting influence; he becomes a defining framework. These novels are as explicable morally as so many morality plays. They offer no "news of life" which is not completely congruous with James's American and paternal heritage.

The Portrait of a Lady and *The Princess Casamassima* are, for different reasons, challenges to any of James's ideas. The first affords his most brilliant presentation of an individual life; and the second makes the fullest and most various uses of the European scene James ever attempted. He tried in each case to exploit a particular mode of achieving novelistic density, and it is a partial measure of his success that these two novels offer more chances for comparison with the fiction of his predecessors and contemporaries than the rest of his major novels. Such studies have been made by F. R. Leavis and Lionel Trilling. Unlike *The Bostonians, The Portrait of a Lady* and *The Princess* are clearly written in a mixed mode: James's emblematic convention organizes them in part, but only in part; for the rest, a variety of competing and not altogether congruous principles are at work.

The question proposed here is this: How do James's "ideas," in their emblematic form, enter into these works, and to what effect? Particularly, how is his vision limited or defined by the emblems described in the preceding chapter? It will be apparent in what follows that James's powers and his limitations are so interlinked that we must acknowledge that although the ideas are necessary conditions of these two novels, they confuse and distort the subjects James chose to treat.

In both books we may take as a starting point one of the reflections of its central figure. Hyacinth Robinson asks: "How can one appear what one is when one is a mixture?"[1] And Isabel Archer, considering the dangers of inconsistent conduct, decides that "her life should always be in harmony with the most pleasing impression she should produce; she would be what she appeared, and she would appear what she was" (III, 69). The connection between the situations of these characters which these quotations suggest is a valid one. Both novels have to do with attempts to contrive an appearance which will reflect inner reality. But the perception with which Hyacinth begins his career is the one which closes Isabel's—we first discover him in the house of life confronted by his antithetical nature, whereas the whole of the novel which centers about Isabel barely suffices to place her there, and to make her ask herself whether Mme Merle can be "wicked" (IV, 329). Since "Madame Merle had married her . . ." (IV, 327), and she herself had collaborated in the process, some element in herself must correspond to Mme Merle's wickedness. Emblematically, these novels treat successive stages in our lives. In the first we fail to see that we are "mixed" until our greed presents us with an image of ourselves which reveals the other self; in the second we undertake to celebrate rather than to appropriate the contents of the house of life.[2] Given these conclusions, let us briefly recapitulate Isabel's career to see how they may be justified.

We first meet her sitting before the locked outer door of the room known as the "office" in her Albany home.

[1] See also V, 86, 171–172.

[2] For James's own consideration of the "unfinished" character of *The Portrait of a Lady*, see *Notebooks*, pp. 15–19; and F. O. Matthiessen, *The Major Phase*, pp. 173–186. I think it not improbable that James conceived of Hyacinth as a logical successor to Isabel insofar as his awareness of the European world is concerned.

Beyond this door she prefigures "a region of delight or of terror." What she later says of herself at Gardencourt bears out the subtle shading here; the suggestion that the alternatives are exclusive. At Gardencourt, Isabel wonders whether after a childhood so generally pleasant she does not require a certain amount of education through suffering. James reveals in a number of places Isabel's desire to *see* life, without either judging or suffering. This same impulse is seen many times in the desire for the picturesque in James's American travelers—and of course this guilt is common to us all. It is through this delight that terror comes; that we perceive the need of transcending our selfish self and our social self, and arriving at the particular style which frees us from selfhood.

Isabel's experience of terror is long delayed, however. She is in search of that constellation of impressions which will answer to her crystallized desire to be great. Those who seek this image are bound to find it. James makes this very clear by his use of Mme Merle. This lady is not, as Ralph Touchett says, "worldly"; she is "the great round world itself." She is Isabel's fate because Isabel is seeking an account of the world which will minister to her, which will reflect her, as if it were indeed her portrait. "The world" in this emblematic sense is eager to minister to this desire, and Isabel offers in exchange, not simply her beautiful person, her charming spontaneity, but, with Ralph's help, a fortune as well.

This emphasis on Isabel's greed runs quite contrary to our image of her as "spreading her wings," as holding high the torch of possibility, of readiness for moral adventure. Here the doubleness which James later employs to handle the figure of Milly Theale is constantly at work. It is a way of summing up his technical problem in *The Portrait* to say that he must at one and the same time give us this sense of Isabel, which is Ralph's and her own, and also make us aware that her frozen desire must find a frozen complement—that the aim of being "exquisite"[3] which the black Osmond quite honestly proffers is completely congruent with Isabel's own aim as a young woman. The point is that only the self-absorbed person can be trapped by the self-absorbed person; and the imagination of greatness can never be the imagination of one's own greatness. Isabel makes a disastrous marriage because she fails to discover "Europe," fails to have the experience of "exaltation and dread" which Brooke has on the Campagna. Isabel evades that relation with something quite "other" which makes for real adventure; with, for example, the steely will of Goodwood, or the fascinating complex of inherited and imposed responsibilities which Warburton's wife would face. Such a relation would, she fears, shatter her image of herself, the portrait of which she is covetous. Down the path indicated by Mme Merle she finds, as she believes, something wholly appropriate to herself, a cup without a flaw into which she can pour her love.

Osmond's proposal makes possible the opening of a long-closed door: "The tears came into her eyes: this time they obeyed the sharpness of the pang that suggested to her somehow the slipping of a fine bolt—backward, forward, she couldn't have said which." (IV, 18) It has been Isabel's notion of happiness that she should realize one of the dreams of her youth; she has done so, the door of the "office" has opened, but, as the figure intimates, she may have made her way into a place of confinement rather than effected her release.

James's use of "portrait" in his title has a double significance. His "lady" makes the mistake which mankind generically makes. She tries to make the world reflect her, instead of perceiving that it reflects the sources of being.

---

[3] "They [Isabel and Osmond] had attempted only one thing, but that one thing was to have been exquisite. Once they missed it nothing else would do; there was no conceivable substitute for that success" (IV, 247).

At the end of the novel Isabel sets about correcting this error, as we all must. But Osmond's appropriation of Isabel *as* a portrait is an ultimate sin; he tries to make the young American girl, representative of the promise of life, reflect him. He appropriates what might become his conscience. This is not marriage, but concubinage. Isabel's greed is worldly, and corrigible; Osmond's is spiritual, and it damns him. The group of related emblems described in the preceding chapter may of course be applied here. Osmond (whose name suggests something fixed and dead, bony or of the earth) stands at one of the limits of moral motion. When Isabel comes to fear herself, her fear will be of what he represents, absolute or spiritual greed. Having declared at the outset, "I only want to see for myself," she sees Osmond as an image which answers *her* sense of *her* claims on the world. She marries the man who *thinks* he is the first gentleman in Europe. In this way she creates the "blasted circle" (IV, 203) round which she walks, and comes to the realization classic among James's central characters: "I'm afraid," she tells Ralph during their last meeting in Rome, "Afraid of myself." (IV, 306) While she has become afraid, Osmond has become ever more exigent; he holds her on a tighter and tighter rein, since he needs her to reflect him. His prime desire is to "preserve appearances" (IV, 357).

This phrase has for James a weight, a force, which is hard to exaggerate. Those who try to "preserve appearances" at such a cost are trying to preserve false institutional forms which are in deadly opposition to moral spontaneity and the forms to which it gives rise. They represent what the elder James called the "church," an organized inversion of love and truth. Isabel's return to Rome, the house of life in which she has encountered her other self, is emblematically consistent, although it may seem to the reader of the novel to depend too much on an exaggerated idea of the sanctity of marriage, or an exaggerated estimate of Isabel's ability to help Pansy Osmond, who, as the novel presents her, is in a hopeless position.

The novel closes at the moment when Isabel has her foot on the threshold of the adult world. She knows what Maisie knows at the end of the novel in which she figures. She recognizes that one must fear one's own impulses.[4] And something more: All the aesthetic values, all the "old things," the whole burden of the human past which she and Osmond have collaborated in seizing, have now to be reseen, not as possessions, but as evidence of the divine and devilish, of the mixed character of man. She is in the state of the American setting foot in Europe only to exclaim: "Look what I have gone and done!"

Ending the novel here, James leaves on the reader's hands the question of what ultimately happens to Isabel. When she goes back to Pansy, she does not go back to the possibility of action. Pansy is and will remain a hopeless sacrifice to Osmond's respect for "appearances."[5] It is best that she become a nun, for the only alternative is that she be appropriated. Even the elder James is ready to recognize the function of nunneries in Europe. They may save subject women from appropriation.

Since Pansy cannot be helped by Isabel, Isabel's return is a return to the struggle with herself, to the contention with that group of impulses in her of which Osmond is the ultimate expression. James has substituted an emblematic conclusion for a dramatic one. His notebooks suggest that he found this satisfactory, but the book clearly seems more rounded off to him than it can to the uninitiated reader.

[4] "She [Maisie] was afraid of herself." (XI, 338; see also pp. 326 and 342.)
[5] See IV, 28, on Pansy's desire to marry her father; and *The Ambassadors*, XXII, 155, for Jeanne de Vionnet's inordinate desire to please Chad Newsome. James's point is explicitly made by D. H. Lawrence; see F. R. Leavis, "The Novel as Dramatic Poem (VII): *The Rainbow*" (*Scrutiny*, XIX, 1952, pp. 16–19).

The clue to James's moral and symbolic intention at the end of the book is apparent in his description of Isabel's journey northward to see Ralph Touchett, who is dying. Her love for him has led her to make the journey; her awareness of his love for her has been reinforced by Mme Merle's final thrust: Ralph has endowed Isabel with her fortune, Mme Merle tells her. But, just as in the case of Milly Theale and Densher, Ralph's love will be her real inheritance, not the seventy thousand pounds. As she rides, she puts together many memories. The past begins to compose itself into a structure: "The truth of things, their mutual relations, their meaning, and for the most part their horror, rose before her with a kind of architectural vastness." (IV, 391) Even this awareness leaves her passive; she is not ready to do battle with her self.

Nothing seemed of use to her to-day. All purpose, all intention, was suspended; all desire too save the single desire to reach her much-embracing refuge. Gardencourt had been her starting-point, and to those muffled chambers it was at least a temporary solution to return. She had gone forth in her strength; she would come back in her weakness, and if the place had been a rest to her before, it would be a sanctuary now. She envied Ralph his dying, for if one were thinking of rest that was the most perfect of all. To cease utterly, to give it all up and not know anything more—the idea was as sweet as the vision of a cool bath in a marble tank, in a darkened chamber, in a hot land.
She had moments indeed in her journey from Rome which were almost as good as being dead. She sat in her corner, so motionless so passive, simply with the sense of being carried, so detached from hope and regret, that she recalled to herself one of those Etruscan figures crouched upon the receptacle of their ashes. (IV, 391)

Isabel, with her "sense of being carried" from the scene of her encounter with herself in Rome to her "starting-point," which is now a "sanctuary," reminds us strongly of

Brydon in *The Jolly Corner*. She is traversing the path
between the same extremes, undergoing a kind of death as
she does so. Gardencourt and its fostering love, the Palazzo
Roccanera and its image of her selfishness, are in her case
the extremities of the "tube or tunnel" of the Galerie
d'Apollon passage. James is at pains to establish her
inability, at this stage in her life, to realize fully the meaning of her movement between these extremes.

Deep in her soul—deeper than any appetite for renunciation—
was the sense that life would be her business for a long time
to come. And at moments there was something inspiring,
almost enlivening, in the conviction. It was a proof of
strength—it was a proof she should some day be happy again.
It couldn't be she was to live only to suffer; she was still
young, after all, and a great many things might happen to
her yet. To live only to suffer—only to feel the injury of life
repeated and enlarged—it seemed to her that she was too
valuable, too capable for that. Then she wondered if it were
vain and stupid to think so well of herself. When had it ever
been a guarantee to be valuable? Wasn't all history full of
the destruction of precious things? Wasn't it much more
probable that if one were fine one would suffer? It involved
then perhaps an admission that one had a certain grossness; but
Isabel recognised, as it passed before her eyes, the quick vague
shadow of a long future. She should never escape; she should
last to the end. Then the middle years wrapped her about
again and the grey curtain of her indifference closed her in.
(IV, 392–393)

Isabel's flickering perception of a "certain grossness" in
her composition is not a sufficient recognition of the
extremes between which mankind moves. Not until the
"middle years" have ended is a full recognition of these
extremes possible. The important emblematic concept of
the "middle years" may be introduced by a quotation from
the elder James. His theme here is the familiar one of the
need to get over our selfish conviction that appearances

are absolute, and may be owned or used to give us moral ascendancy over others: "Thus, reason emancipated from sense, or what is the same thing enlightened by revelation, disowns our *a priori* reasoning, and pronounces nature an altogether subjective divine work enforced in the exclusive interest of man's spiritual evolution; just as the moral control I exert over myself is a subjective work on my part enforced by my objective regard for society, or my sense of human fellowship; just as an artist's education and discipline—which often are nothing more than his physical and intellectual penury and moral compression—are a needful subjective preparation for his subsequent objective or aesthetic expansion." [6]

The character of childhood as the Henry Jameses conceived of it is a period of innocence in which our "general sense of *glory*" is simply a sense of what our parents, love and wisdom, have provided. There follows a period in which we incur the guilt of appropriating goods and status, or, to put it more generally, as the elder James does above, a period in which we prepare ourselves for "objective expansion." This involves creating a form which is a worthy vessel of the divine love to replace the provisional or "subjective" form. James the novelist frequently uses the term "middle years" to describe a period precisely analogous to what the elder James calls the artist's "subjective preparation." These were the years in which James himself was subject to the provisional delusion that the world can give us a satisfying image of ourselves. In an account in *The Middle Years* of a meeting with certain English celebrities he writes: "My identity for myself was all in my sensibility to their own exhibition." [7]

The "middle years," which James often describes as "grey" (Brydon of *The Jolly Corner* is carried through

[6] *Secret*, p. 129.
[7] See Ferner Nuhn's chapter on James in *The Wind Blew From the East*, p. 105.

"an interminable grey passage"), are of their nature obscured by struggle in the world. The attempt to create an
identity for oneself out of forms which are not one's own
is a long and discouraging process, inspiring feelings of
guilt which it has no power to allay. But this process may
lead to the great climax of the dream of the Galerie
d'Apollon: the acquisition of a form or style powerful
enough to banish all guilt. Adam Verver, in considering
his "middle time," concludes that "the years of darkness
had been needed to render possible the years of light"
(XXIII, 144). Such a happy conclusion is not foreordained,
however, since Strether's "grey middle desert" is not the
prelude to a triumph.[8] The artist of the short story called
The Middle Years comes to accept the loss of his selfhood;
he dies into his work, into creation, and his physical end is
emblematically a death to selfhood. Nonetheless, there is
pathos in his demand for another chance; we listen with
sympathy to the outraged cries of the very nearly stifled
selfhood demanding a further opportunity to range a world
of admirers about its proud identity.

James's use of the term "middle years" to describe the
period on which Isabel Archer is entering is an assurance
that her life is beginning, not ending. Just at this point,
though, there is an imaginative check. We have been given
no intimation of the possible creative result which lies
ahead. What is Isabel going to do? James has scrambled his
moral elements in an odd way.

When we consider the young man of *Travelling Companions*, or Merton Densher of *The Wings of the Dove*, or
Prince Amerigo of *The Golden Bowl*, we find that each is
exposed to the moral danger of seizing the promise of life
in the form of a portrait, a possession, but that it is open to
them to subordinate themselves to their spiritual superior:

[8] *The Ambassadors*, XXI, 52. See also XXI, 87, for the phrase "the
great desert of the years." For Nick Dormer's "twilight of the soul,"
see VIII, 267.

the spontaneous American girl. It is a question of choosing between the two loves, the two ways of taking experience. These young men are posted, in their variously interesting and absorbing ways, between the portrait and the lady. The question is, What will be the direction of their moral motion? Or, to vary the emblems as James does, Will Densher and Amerigo choose the encircling love of Kate and Charlotte, which gives them identity in their own eyes and those of the world, or will they accept the heavy burden of creating an individuality fit to hold the love which multiplies communications and contacts? [9] In these two cases the emblematic elements are discriminable as leading impulses in particular characters, and it is intelligible to say that morally, the action of the novel takes place *within* a character who represents mankind, as do Amerigo and Densher. This mode of rendering a moral career does not, however, help us to classify Isabel's emblematic situation. Certain stories about artists furnish more useful analogues.

In *John Delavoy*, in *The Birthplace*, and in *The Real Right Thing* we may find instances in which a conflict of the sort Densher and Amerigo undergo is represented by one character, just as James's account of the Galerie d'Apollon, and of the nightmare of which it was the scene, sums up the whole of man's struggle in the house of life. In these three stories, in *The Tragic Muse*, and in other instances too numerous to name, the moral point is someone's realization of the difference between the form which passes current in the world, an identity, and the form which is associated with creation, spiritual individuality or style. We find Nick Dormer stating his perception of the difference between representing a constituency and representing life in this way: "Art was *doing*—it came back to that—which politics in most cases weren't." (VIII, 267) Of John Delavoy it is said: "He *was* his work." And in *The*

9 *The Tragic Muse*, VII, 148.

Real Right Thing the man who has been asked to undertake a biography of Ashton Doyne is doubtful of the value of the project because "the artist was what he *did*—he was nothing else" (XVII, 415). In *The Birthplace* Morris Gedge discovers that the only way to be true to Shakespeare is to stop making speeches about him as a "person" and start romancing on his own hook; the only way to be faithful to the meaning of Shakespeare is to try, no matter how inferior one's instrument, to celebrate life, instead of appropriating the past. James's sense of the world simply excludes this possibility for women, however. Women appear in his work in the guise of the Eve or selfhood (Kate Croy, Charlotte Stant), in that of the "church," the existing complex of institutions (Mrs. Newsome, Mrs. Lowder, Mrs. Assingham), or as the promise of life (the spontaneous American girl), but never as creators.

Isabel Archer is a changeling, both within the novel in which she figures and in the Jamesian canon at large. In one respect she is representative of a stage in the process of refinement which transformed Minny Temple into Milly Theale; in another, she is akin to the youthful narrator of *The Author of Beltraffio* or the young Henry James of *The Middle Years*, an artist who has not yet achieved his form and tries to borrow it from the world. These two lines of development intersect in Isabel, whose originals are Henry James *and* Minny Temple. In short, the reason that the ending of *The Portrait of a Lady* is unsatisfactory seems to be that it is impossible to make Isabel Archer over into a man and launch her on the career of an artist.

It is possible that in thinking about what might have happened had tuberculosis been his fate instead of Minny's, James hit upon the device of making an attenuated James (Ralph Touchett) the spectator of Minny's (Isabel's) descent upon Europe. Touchett, sexually impoverished though he is, grants the power which puts wind in Isabel's sails, gives her life to pursue an imaginary career. This may

help explain James's success in making Isabel seem a creature wonderfully formed for the highest demands of life.
It may also help to explain why her descent into the valley
of the middle years seems to belie that capacity for life.
Like Howells—who is forever leading his enchanted lovers
on a wedding journey into Canada, down through New
England, and then tumbling them into the drab and un-
relieved domesticity of Cambridge—James simply cannot
conceive of a third act for a woman. He tacks to the
career of his transmogrified Minny a promise of artistic
fulfillment; he gives her the pledge that he has given himself: that he will come through the period of conflict successfully and be able finally to make an assured and selfless
use of his powers. For this reason Isabel suggests spontaneity and intellectual grace in the first volume, and a
dogged, manly husbanding of creative energy toward the
end of the novel.[10]

Isabel is plainly enough saddled with the burdens of the
young writer who is trying to create a form or portrait out
of what the European world offers, and discovering the
error of such an attempt. The character of Isabel's spontaneity is questioned as well. She is not really ready to take
life in what Gabriel Nash calls the "free, brave, personal
way." In her declaration of principle ("Her life should
always be in harmony with the most pleasing impression
she should produce; she would be what she appeared, and
she would appear what she was.") James indicates Isabel's
worst error. She puts herself at the mercy of "the most
pleasing impression" she has made on others; she proposes
to live up to the portrait instead of the demands of the
inner life. What she must learn to do if she is to become

---

[10] A less hopeful possibility may be imagined. The doleful pre-
Raphaelite sister in *The Author of Beltraffio* opposes "form" to
"goodness" in a somewhat mechanical fashion. The first of these is
her brother's forte; the second is his wife's (XVI, 50–51). She enters
a nunnery and dies not long afterwards.

truly spontaneous is to invert the order. She must first of all learn to appear what she *is*. The elder James defines "Spiritual or essential freedom" as "being precisely what one wishes to be, and seeming precisely what one is." [11] Spontaneity of the unqualified sort is exemplified by Milly Theale and Maggie Verver, who possess Minny Temple's extraordinary generosity of spirit, together with a truly personal style which is not dependent on the world's image of them.[12]

Our most immediate sense of the virtues of *The Portrait of a Lady* as a novel depends in part on the way in which Isabel Archer engages the imagination. As a character, she has the authority of existence; her complications and contradictions suggest life. James's powers worked on her in a fashion which, happily, his "ideas" are unable to represent. She is perhaps a study of the Minny Temple one might have known, rather than the Minny Temple of the *Notes of a Son and Brother*. She is high and free and bold in her approach to life; yet James's development of what lies behind this manner leads us to feel that she is ignorant, self-centered, and afraid. In the world of James's later emblematic fictions this would be an anomaly, for in them the complications and contradictions of life are all fully known, fully explicated. But in the tradition of the novel with which F. R. Leavis connects *The Portrait of a Lady*—and in people as we know them!—there is nothing in the least incredible in a character whose innocence, ignorance, and self-absorption both charm and alarm us.

[11] *Substance*, pp. 431–432. "Spontaneity" is here said to be the "badge" of this freedom.

[12] The "gross male Adam" tries to impose his will on the world and the woman in order to make them reflect him. Insofar as Isabel does this, she is symbolically "masculine."

Leon Edel argues that James likened women to Diana or Artemis, and notes the connection of the name "Archer" with the divine huntress. This suggests a biographical basis for the novel, and accords with my emphasis on Isabel's masculine quality. (See "Venus and Diana," *The Untried Years*, pp. 252–260.)

James may very well have been intent on producing an American analogue to Emma Bovary, who likewise incorporates internal contradictions. To this end, he would logically make his European scene clear and relatively simple, almost posterish in its broad strokes: Warburton so quintessentially healthy and so proudly seated, the elder Touchett such a beautifully preserved Yankee banker, Osmond so black, Mme Merle so blandly and clearly designing, Henrietta Stackpole so merciless and so affectionate—they all seem adjuncts to Isabel's unseeing pursuit of her fantasy. The enchanted lawns of Gardencourt and the grim walls of the Palazzo Roccanera have a storybook quality. The clarity, the light and sure touch, of the prose playing about the figure of Isabel only to reveal an obscurity, a darkness within her lovely presence, has an effect which is among James's greatest achievements. In no other novel does so much of the world's strong light fall on a single person, nor is there any other character in James who could bear this much illumination without becoming emblematically transparent.

The emblematic incoherence of *The Portrait of a Lady*, which makes Isabel a cross between a young woman aspiring to be Milly Theale and a young man aspiring to become an artist, is a piece of good fortune for letters. It is evidence that the "ideas" which haunted James early and late could on occasion give way before "news of life" so haunting and compelling that his need for order had, temporarily, to take second place.

Whereas *The Portrait of a Lady* is so contrived that all our attention focuses on Isabel, *The Princess Casamassima* inverts our perspective; we are urged to see the whole world through the eyes of Hyacinth. He is the son of a woman of the people, whose maternal grandfather had fought at the barricades during the period of the Commune in Paris. His father, a dissolute nobleman, had been murdered by his mother. Hyacinth feels a strong bond with suffering humanity and at the same time an affinity with the dignity, power, and grace of established order. He has been led to believe (I borrow the elder James's terms) that the serpent or selfish self is identifiable with the order to which his father belonged, and that in sympathy for the people, the dove, or social self, finds its only proper expression. He is drawn to ask how beauty and manners may be reconciled with justice and equality; how, in a word, one may offer an "appearance" which represents all these things. James's scheme requires that Robinson have something of the authority of existence attributed above to Isabel Archer, but this is just what he lacks. Hyacinth escapes being a figure in an extended parable more than once, but never for long, and it is a condition of taking an interest in this book to admit that its pleasures are largely incidental to its main design. This is very splendid, but too exemplary, too emblematic. Hyacinth is stretched on the large gilt rack of his creator's scheme. We cannot see the world through his eyes, for he is too clearly the chief instance of the nature of the world we are asked to contemplate. He is not dramatically disposable; he is moved about like a camera rather than a man.

In this novel the house of life is really the subject. Hyacinth's question is the generic question: How may one take possession of the great house? By a kind of expansion of the implications of the Galerie d'Apollon passage we may arrive at a clear sense of James's end, which is to make Hyacinth confront the duality of the "beautiful horrible world" with a full awareness that he shares this duality. To put him squarely before this image of himself in the house of life, James dispatches him to Paris and Venice. The passages which have to do with this journey have a familiar ring: "He saw the immeasurable misery of the people, and yet he saw all that had been, as it were, rescued and redeemed from it: the treasures, the felicities, the splendors, the successes of the world. This quantity took the form sometimes, to his imagination, of a vast vague, dazzling presence, an irradiation of light from objects undefined, mixed with the atmosphere of Paris and Venice." The "diffused and reverberant" aspect of the Galerie d'Apollon here figures as a "dazzling presence" and is followed as we should expect by the "exaltation and dread" of Brooke on the Campagna. When Hyacinth is seated on Tortoni's terrace, watching the life of the Boulevard, he feels "a kind of pleasant terror of the place and hour" (VI, 140). From this dilemma the only escapes Henry James ever envisioned are those his father had described as the "social and aesthetic." One must either become an artist or wait until the divine society, which will finally reconcile the dove and the serpent, has been established. Hyacinth can do neither of these things, and his death is therefore the result of irreconcilable conflict. Hyacinth has no Milly or Maggie, no sweet Nan or Alice Staverton, to avert the fury of his outraged selfhood, no form or style in which to express his devotion to the sources. In order, at the ultimate instant, to establish his artist's vision, he must die, and make his death representative of the artist's triumph.

In order to see more clearly how the novel itself bears out the above analysis of its emblematic scheme, let us consider Hyacinth Robinson in the most overt terms the novel affords. He is a young man who feels an aching deprivation because he has been denied access to the beauty and power of the world in which his father had lived. He resents the injustice with which his mother had been treated, not because he feels that she as a person had particular claims on the world, but because she had suffered as a member of an excluded, disadvantaged class. His feeling of deprivation and his anger at those who maintain class privilege lead him to join an anarchist plot.

The feelings of the two Henry Jameses about violence directed against the existing order seem to have been much the same, and Hyacinth may serve as an example illustrative of the position of both father and son. Revolutionary violence (on the part of the individual) is a symptom of social disease.[13] It is hardly blamable, since it simply means that the institutional fetters man must wear in his imperfect state of consciousness have become unendurable to the persons involved. But no violence of this order occurs or is projected in *The Princess Casamassima.*

What James is studying is the principal instrument of revolutionary movements: the terrible aggressive power lodged in ideas which are used without reference to particular persons. Paul Muniment is after power; the Princess is trying to destroy the image (her status as "Princess") for which she has sold her soul—and ultimately to destroy herself; Eustache Poupin is working in a well-established convention of opposition to the powers that be. In other words, we have to do, as Lionel Trilling shows, with a variety of persons, not a revolutionary "movement" as such. Although James has Hyacinth perceive in the anarchists a "grudging attitude" and an "ulcer of envy" (VI, 142), he is most concerned with the fact that kindness can kill with a good conscience if it is kindness for the masses. This is the awful meaning of Paul Muniment's desire to "alter the conditions" (VI, 192) under which people live. The way in which James figures the moral extremes between which Hyacinth moves in this book may be understood by considering the attitudes of the characters toward the "personal" and the "impersonal." Lady Aurora is, as the elder James would say, a very good dove, but no longer a woman: she has identified herself with others and funked the job of identifying *herself.* The Princess does not have Paul Muniment's terrible self-righteousness, but she does have his desire to escape the personal, to make herself the engine of impersonal force. This will enable her to solve the problem she

[13] For the elder James's most explicit statement about social protest, see *Logic*, pp. 104–107

thinks Lady Aurora has solved, that of "getting out of herself" (VI, 224).[14]

The Bostonians is closely akin to *The Princess Casamassima* in asserting the horror of people who seek "impersonal" ends. Selah Tarrant in the former work tries to persuade Olive Chancellor's guests (before his daughter's exhibition of her rhetorical powers) that the success of his efforts and his daughter's were "thoroughly impersonal" (Macmillan, VIII, 65). And Olive herself notes that "a common end, unfortunately, however fine as regards a special result, does not make community impersonal" (Macmillan, VIII, 135).

What this comes to in *The Princess Casamassima* is that neither the Princess nor Paul can acknowledge the other self; they seek to create identities based on their denial of inner conflict. While Hyacinth sees himself as a mixture, they deny their greed only to assert their righteousness. When Hyacinth expresses a fear for the Princess's welfare, she asks, "Why am I so sacrosanct and precious?" He replies, "Simply because there's no one in the world and has never been anyone in the world like you." (VI, 406) This may serve as an instance of the complete fusion of moral and aesthetic meaning which James tries for. The Princess is sacred, as all individuals who have the promise of life to fulfill are sacred. She is discernibly unique because she *appears* so. Nonetheless she is lost, as the close of the passage shows: "And she turned from him as with a beat of great white wings that raised her straight out of the bad air of the personal." (VI, 406) Those who use ideas without reference to persons have not in the least escaped themselves. Hyacinth is made aware of this. He reflects that "her behavior, after all, was more addressed to relieving herself than to relieving others" (VI, 406).

To turn away from one's self is to meet one's self in

[14] See also XXIII, 219, for Charlotte Stant's desire for a motive outside of herself.

another form. The Princess Casamassima has an image of the revolution which flowers like an evil vine out of her own self-projection. With her, others collaborate; they share an image of destruction, yes, but the image is of their own destruction. This is the meaning of the Princess's wish to get out of herself. She hugs the very notion of the downfall of the world in which *she* is so deeply implicated; she asks of the revolutionary conspiracy, "Then it *is* real, it *is* solid?" (VI, 44) The most prized of her possessions would be the knowledge of an apocalyptic catastrophe. Her war on herself has become a war on society. She hates her love of possessions, of luxury, of beauty itself. She is rending herself. She will pull down the house of life to make sure that she will not meet herself there. Her righteousness struggles with her greed. In neither of these ways can one take possession of the house of life.

Hyacinth's case is almost diagrammatically simple. The point is that James shall have the luxury of putting before us an Adam awaking in the house of life—suddenly dowered with Medley, the Princess, Paris, Venice. To this end, the parable of the other self is placed at the very beginning of his career. He may enter, delighted and afraid, the "beautiful, horrible world" at one bound, like a second Adam, a redeemer, who perceives at the outset the whole extent of his temptation, and may thereafter be shown the world, the kingdoms of the earth.

James's comprehensive aim in this book is clearly Blakean. Society, the social world, is offered as a trap to engage our sensibilities and involve us in the contemplation of the primary problem—the problem out of which the whole "social question" springs: the problem of making a creative use of the relation between what Blake calls "innocence and experience" and what James symbolizes as the artist's impulse on the one hand and righteousness and greed on the other. Hyacinth knows himself as dove and serpent. How can he find an adequate representation of his knowledge, or, to repeat his own question, "How can one appear what one is when one is a mixture?" What is the fruitful use of the contraries? Once more, and inevitably, only as an artist can a single individual make this full acknowledgement of his dual nature.

We are forced to conclude that the task of making appearances reflect realities is in this book, as in *The Portrait of a Lady*, turned over to a protagonist who, in the terms of the action, cannot become an artist without giving the lie to the action itself.[15] Hyacinth wants to write; James allows him to glimpse the only possible opening, but the very mention of the possibility so distorts the values of the context that it is distressing, like a rent in the tapestry. To launch Isabel into the vale of the middle years, to contrive for Hyacinth a forced option of suicide—these are equally unsatisfactory resolutions, because the only one James really has to offer is not truly an option for the characters concerned, and he must conceal this fact.

James's three major ventures of the eighties were *The Bostonians*, *The Portrait of a Lady*, and *The Princess Casamassima*. *The Bostonians* is remarkably free of emblematic uses of father's ideas. This may also be said of *Washington Square* (1881) and *The Reverberator* (1888). The very titles of the two novels under discussion afford a sufficiently clear notation of the distinction. The relation of the "portrait" to the "lady" had been a symbolic device in James's work since 1870, and the house of life, the "great house" (Casamassima), is an emblem common to father and son. At the end of this decade James wrote a novel which carries the biographical suggestion that he was trying to come to terms with his father's ideas in a fresh way. *The Tragic Muse* (1890) is a kind of ritual farewell to the figure of his father, the "artist in life."

When James undertook to write plays, he was, it may be surmised, choosing a form which protected him against

[15] See VI, 155, where Hyacinth is called a "true artist."

an impulse in himself which frightened him, the impulse to become a "great explainer." *The Tragic Muse* is both a farewell to his father and a greeting to the future he imagined for himself. James tries to do something analogous to what William had done; to give himself an identity in the eyes of the world. But in January, 1895, when he was hooted from the stage on the opening night of *Guy Domville*, he found himself deprived of that public identity he had sought to create. The identification with the "great explainer" reasserted itself. The ground was prepared for the three novels which systematically represent his father's "spiritual cosmology": *The Ambassadors, The Wings of the Dove*, and *The Golden Bowl*.

VIII Manifest Providence : I

JAMES NOTES, IN THE PREFACE TO *The Golden Bowl,* THAT his works of the last dozen years had not required the revision, or "reseeing," that the earlier ones demanded. The world's wide scene has been translated into the terms of his ultimate vision; only the difficult and delightful question of form remains. The prefaces to the last three completed novels have little to say about subject matter and seem to justify the contention that the practice of art had become a wholly sufficient manner of life for the novelist. The *données* on which these last three novels are based are very simple, yet susceptible of great expansion. James intended them to flower within the work in a manner quite unconstrained by external circumstance. The three situations are in each instance painfully particular for the persons involved, yet they have the widest possible general significance. In *The Ambassadors,* Strether, who has an immediate moral responsibility for Chad, finds that he must come to a conclusion about a matter no less important than the meaning—the once possible meaning—of his whole life. Milly Theale, who is dying, must, though her strength ebbs, come to terms with the overwhelming revelation of the plot against her and play out the part of illimitable charity on the scene defined by Kate Croy's greed. The father and daughter of *The Golden Bowl* are deeply dependent on each other, and may almost be said to drive Charlotte and the Prince into each other's arms; yet their manner of resolving their difficulty has a universal significance which makes adultery the mere dramatic occasion of a final encounter between selfish and selfless love.

The Ambassadors, The Wings of the Dove, and *The Golden Bowl*[1] contain the clearest, simplest, and most carefully articulated representations of his father's ideas to be found in the whole range of James's work. This would seem to be compatible with the frequently expressed view that James was completely absorbed in his craft toward the end of his life. James's purest art—if one wishes to call it so—consorts logically with his unadulterated version of the bootstrap myth. This was inevitable on the very grounds which are sometimes employed to argue that these novels do *not* embrace a discernible system of values.

To create a novel which is very nearly sufficient unto itself—which demands a minimum of reference to familiar scenes and familiar manners—one must reduce and simplify one's principles to provide a basis for a unified view of the world. The complexity of a *Divine Comedy* must, if it is to be ordered, rest on something as fundamental and universally applicable as Dante's physics of love, which polarizes every created being in the field of God's providence. It is just as much their common reliance on a *mythos* as it is the texture of the prose which leads us to feel that these novels are related.

The purpose of this chapter and those which follow is to establish the nature of the emblematic relationships between these three works, and provide certain suggestive illustrations. Although the pattern is too intricate, the unexplored possibilities too numerous, to permit full explication at this stage of the inquiry, it can be established

[1] Named in the order of their composition (see XXI, vii).

that in these three novels we have to do with a trilogy. One may fairly represent James's intention by calling it a "divine novel."

James provides no external evidence to support this contention. Furthermore, without detailed support drawn from the elder James, one can hardly follow the pattern of the novelist's use of his emblems. There are, however, certain indirect clues to the conection between the last three novels. For example, all three involve an attempt on the part of an American or Americans to rescue someone in Europe from moral catastrophe. Was this choice of themes the result of James's final and exclusive commitment to his art? It is hard to see how such an argument could be supported. A progression in the kind and result of these attempts at rescue may be noted: Strether is unsuccessful; Milly is successful with Densher alone; Maggie and her father are triumphant.

What kinds of evidence are most useful in linking these three novels? In general, two sorts: a set of emblems representative of human nature and human destiny employed by both Henry Jameses; and the likenesses and differences between the functions of the characters in the three books. Take, as an instance of the first sort, the figures of Mrs. Newsome, Mrs. Lowder, and Mrs. Assingham. Each may be thought of as representative of the "church" of her time and place, of the governing principles of the mores and institutions, or, as William James might have put it, their "cash value" in conduct.

Mrs. Newsome, Mrs. Lowder, and Mrs. Assingham are close to representing ideal limits of human behavior. The first of the three is almost identifiable with New England's righteousness; the second with the acquisitive, the sentimental, the totally unimaginative British middle classes; and the third with an "international" worldly wisdom, a morality which equates a European care for social propriety, that is, appearances, with an American righteousness. All three may be identified with institutions or mores, "churches," in the elder James's terminology. Mrs. Newsome in *The Ambassadors* is, in essence, familiar to the reader of these pages. She is incarnate righteousness, "as intense as she can live," and quite incapable of understanding her spiritual likeness to her exquisitely acquisitive son, Chad Newsome. But her righteousness and Chad's exquisite greed will, as Mark Ambient so naïvely puts it in *The Author of Beltraffio*, "come to the same thing in the end," since greed and righteousness are both means of filling the bottomless cup of selfhood. That to which these two impulses are opposed, *caritas*, or the promise of life, has no voice, no representative, in *The Ambassadors*. The ideal limits in this novel are, at one extreme, righteousness; at the other, the ostensible, what shows, "the Vain Appearance" (XXI, 203).

Between these extremes, between Mrs. Newsome and Mme de Vionnet, Louis Lambert Strether is adrift. Mrs. Newsome, as James remarks, is a "reflection of his old self."[2] The novel has to do with Strether's attempt to find a new self, commensurate with his experience of Paris. He acts on the advice Little Bilham gives. "I commend you," says Little Bilham, "I commend you the Vain Appearance." As far as it goes, this is excellent advice. Strether finds himself in the house of life, confronted by "the vast bright Babylon, like some huge iridescent object, a jewel brilliant and hard, in which parts were not to be discriminated nor differences comfortably marked. It twinkled and trembled and melted together, and what seemed all surface one moment seemed all depth the next." (XXI, 89) This echo of the "diffused and reverberant" quality of what lies before us in Paris, an echo from the Galerie d'Apollon passage, *The Princess Casamassima*, and all the stories and novels in which we find a particular house of life, is an echo for Strether himself, who had experienced this

[2] *Notebooks*, p. 228.

"general sense of *glory*" as a youngster during his first trip abroad. The fact that "the temple of taste that he had dreamed of raising up" (XXI, 87) had not been completed "was surely proof enough of how his conscience had been encumbered." We have to do, then, with a Puritan whose conscience is about to be (as regards sensuous experience) disencumbered; who is capable of acknowledging what Woollett cannot acknowledge, the beauty and variety of appearance.

Woollett's version of the law will not serve in Paris, Strether discovers. He undertakes to make a new law, a higher law, based on the sublimity he finds in Mme de Vionnet. But Mme de Vionnet turns out to be a lovely lie. In the end she cannot help him to do what the artist does: use appearances to tell the truth. She is not a source but a contrived appearance concealing the ugly fact of adultery. Moreover, Strether is not even capable of learning from this (as the artist of *The Real Thing* learns what can be used to illustrate life and what cannot); Strether is a moralist, who has "lived only for Duty," [3] and he therefore conceives it to be his duty to discover a *law*, rather than a *style*, to justify his wonderful sensuous experience. This is of course generalization, in advance of the evidence, which will be presented later on the emblematic significance of the novel.

Before proceeding, I must say something of the meaning of James's use of his *donnée*, the remark attributed to William Dean Howells. James quotes his rendering of it in his preface: "Live all you can; it's a mistake not to. It doesn't so much matter what you do in particular so long as you have your life. If you haven't had that what *have* you had? I'm too old—too old at any rate for what I see. What one loses one loses; make no mistake about that. Still, we have the illusion of freedom; therefore don't, like me to-day, be without the memory of that illusion. I was either, at

[3] *Notebooks*, p. 226.

8

the right time, too stupid or too intelligent to have it, and now I'm a case of reaction against the mistake. Do what you like so long as you don't make it. For it *was* a mistake. Live, live!" (XXI, vvii) [4]

Howells's famous exhortation has a more equivocal meaning for James than his critics have suspected. Just how does it differ in intent from certain burlesque declarations in favor of experience in James's earlier work? Louis Leverett in *A Bundle of Letters* (XIV, 496-497) says, "The great thing is to *live*, you know . . . ," and Greville Fane, the tradesman of letters, urges her lazy son "to live, because that gave you material" (XVI, 128). James speaks in his preface of the danger that his theme might be mistaken because of its association with vulgar and trivial American adventures in Paris (XXI, xiii-xiv), but since these are matters of sensuous enjoyment, whereas Strether's adventures are actually of the mind, he concludes that the danger is illusory. Yet when Strether urges Little Bilham, "Live all you can," he offers no principle to guide his young friend, and we must inquire what, in the light of the values expressed in James's emblems, will happen to little Bilham if he carries out this advice. Will he not become, like the protagonist of *The Jolly Corner* or like William Wetmore Story, a submerged man, devoted to "the steady perception of the material present" and incapable of giving his experience that *form* which alone can rescue it from selfishness?

We have found, in earlier chapters, a good deal of evidence to support the remark in the preface that imagination is not Strether's "prime faculty" (XXI, viii). (Truly conscious persons do not try to arrive at a style by combining the forms the world offers.) Strether here makes his tentative formulation of a law opposed to the Law of Woollett, concluding that since righteousness has not served him, a younger man, little Bilham, who has the

[4] See also *Letters*, I, 375-377, 413-415.

adventure of life before him, may be better served by a mass of aesthetic impressions. This advice is not so very different, after all, from that which Louis Leverett gives his friend in Boston. Strether's prime faculty is the will; he conceives it to be his duty to work out a justification of the life of aesthetic acquisition, and he cannot easily be diverted from this task, once he has imposed it on himself. As little Bilham remarks, Strether is not a person to whom it is easy to tell things he doesn't want to know (XXI, 202). He has become the theorist of the sensuous, the defender of the ostensible; and he has done this because he feels that Chad has changed for the better. Chad has been schooled by Paris; he is a product of Paris, the product of a different law. What then is the law which governs his improvement?

Balzac's *Louis Lambert* perhaps had even more to do with the imaginative expansion of James's *donnée* than the figure of Howells. The name "Louis Lambert Strether" seems to announce an intention. We cannot be sure of this, but it is worth noting that Balzac's novel has to do with a figure who gets into a difficulty closely resembling Strether's. Louis Lambert is a theorist who writes a treatise on the will, which is also an attempt at a metaphysics, drawn in part from Swedenborg. His utter absorption in these all-embracing abstractions is interrupted by an overpowering rush of passion at the sight of a woman in a theater, during his stay in Paris. He returns to the provinces, where he falls in love with a Jewish heiress. Just before their wedding he goes mad, and the narrator conjectures that his madness may be the result of a sudden "transition from pure idealism to the most intense sensualism."[5] Balzac's tale is so incoherent, and so inconsequent in its attitude toward Louis Lambert, who is at one moment a transcendent genius, at the next, a pitiable object,

[5] *The Comédie Humaine*, ed. by George Saintsbury (Philadelphia: Avil Publishing Company, 1902), vol. entitled *Seraphita and Other Stories*, pp. 240–241.

that it is hard to say what impression James may have had of it. But Lambert has qualities and experiences in common with James's character: the violent revolution in feeling and conviction undergone by Lambert; his propensity to systematic inquiry; his obsession with the faculty of will, which had for the two Henry Jameses such an unpleasantly righteous connotation; and, finally, his loss of his position in the world through devotion to a woman of an alien faith.[6]

A more immediately useful way of indicating James's intention is to compare Strether's situation with those of Isabel Archer and Hyacinth Robinson. Isabel discovers her own doubleness, and she enters the period of the "middle years" with an awareness that she may, in the end, be able to come to terms with the fact that the world is both beautiful and ugly, loving and selfish, by coming to terms with her own inner duality. Hyacinth is aware from the beginning that one must find a form expressive of both the social and the selfish selves in order to give life meaning. Strether never attains to Isabel Archer's sense of the world, let alone Hyacinth's. He is ridden from beginning to end by the theory of the sheep and the goats: If Woollett is in error, Paris must, he feels, be right. Paris is, in the terms of the novel, an advance over Woollett, for Paris has a mode of acknowledging man's doubleness—Paris is Catholic. True, Catholicism is a frozen, a static, mode of representing our dual nature, but it is better than Woollett's righteousness.

Even this marginal moral advance is something Strether observes, rather than participates in. "He had the habit, in

[6] Since this novel is associated with Balzac's own childhood (Balzac is said to have written a treatise on the will as a schoolboy) and his passion for Swedenborgianism, it is tempting to ask whether James was covertly suggesting that Strether's marvelous capacity for perceiving the world of Paris and his inveterate tendency to impose his own private order on the data that world offered are representative of the imagination of the novelist of the order of Balzac.

these contemplations [in Notre Dame], of watching a
fellow-visitant, here and there, from a respectable distance,
remarking some note of behavior, of penitence, of prostra-
tion, of the absolved, relieved state; this was the manner
in which his vague tenderness took its course, the degree of
demonstration to which, naturally, it had to confine itself."
(XXI, 218) The "naturally" is a stroke of the sharpest
irony. There is to be no end to Strether's "middle years,"
since, when given a chance to see what Hyacinth sees at
the outset and what Isabel sees at the end—the great
simplicity that we are our own fate; that it is with ourselves
we do battle—Strether avoids the issue by trying to substitute his sense of Europe's ideal for New England's ideal.
He is far more reminiscent of Henry Adams than of
Howells; he finds in Mme de Vionnet something very like
Henry Adams's conception of the Virgin, a creature alien
yet fascinating, whom one might in the past have loved,
who had in the past ordered the world.

Strether resembles Henry Adams in a more important
respect. He is inclined to be a determinist; to believe that
we are made by conditions, rather than that we make ourselves. It is hard to imagine two men less likely to agree
about the human condition than Henry Adams and Henry
James. In a world in which, as the latter wrote Wells, "art
makes life," [7] the true recreants are those who declare that
life has us by the throat and that we can not affect its
course. Strether is of this company—as a part of his speech
in Gloriani's garden, the speech in which he urges little
Bilham to "live," will show: "The affair—I mean the affair
of life—couldn't no doubt have been different for me; for
it's, at the best, a tin mould, either fluted and embossed
with ornamental excrescences, or else smooth and dread-
fully plain, into which, a helpless jelly, one's consciousness
is poured—so that one 'takes' the form, as the great cook
says, and is more or less compactly held by it; one lives, in

[7] *Letters*, II, 490.

fine, as one can." (XXI, 218) The image is related to those which had first occurred to Strether in the presence of the mysteriously transformed Chad. "Chad was brown and thick and strong, and of old Chad had been rough. Was all the difference therefore that he was actually smooth? Possibly; for that he *was* smooth was as marked as in the taste of a sauce or in the rub of a hand. . . . It was as if in short he had really, copious perhaps but shapeless, been put into a firm mould and turned successfully out." (XXI, 152) Strether is not slow to make the connection: "He saw him in a flash as the young man marked out by women; and for a concentrated minute the dignity, the comparative austerity, as he funnily fancied it, of this character affected him almost with awe." (XXI, 153)

The reader will have recognized, both in the "mould" into which Strether's "consciousness" has been poured, and that which has formed Chad, one of the most familiar of the emblems shared by the Henry Jameses: that of the self-hood shaped by "nature and society," by the institutions, mores, manners, and so forth, which give us identity.[8] Strether of course has been quite as much molded by a woman as Chad, though he is less happy about the result. Maria says of him that he owes more to women than any

[8] The error Strether makes is precisely the error made by the right-eous man who conceives the bowl of selfhood to be unbreakable (that is, thinks of the law as an unbreakable form) and therefore feels that our experience must be put into a bowl given us by nature and society rather than a bowl (or style) worked out by the individual for himself. Louis Lambert, who is, like Strether, committed to an abstract way of handling experience, offers an interesting parallel: "Merely to live, was he not compelled to be perpetually casting nutriment into the gulf he had opened in himself? Like some beings who dwell in the grosser world, might he not die of inanition for want of feeding abnormal and disappointed cravings?" (*Seraphita and Other Stories*, p. 204.) Balzac's suggestion that the conflict between sensualism and idealism in Lambert led him to attempt self-castration, offers another parallel to the situation of Strether, who is caught between righteousness and sensuousness at the end of the novel.

man she has ever seen (XXII, 135). Of the alternative
mode of giving form to consciousness—that which involves
finding one's own note or style, involves, that is, being an
artist—no one in *The Ambassadors* seems to have any
knowledge. Gloriani himself, the great feral personage, is
simply the figure of an artist, the artist in society.[9]

James not infrequently used these tropes from cookery
when discussing artists whose form he found lacking in
firmness, or perhaps lacking altogether. Frank Saltram,
the figure of the artist without form *or* morality, who
appears in *The Coxon Fund*, is said to be "like a jelly
minus its mould" (XV, 350). But in order to define
Strether's situation we need the help of the elder James.
The following quotation suggests that Strether's moral
development is all to come: "My moral experience tells me
that justice is good and injustice is evil, that he who injures
his neighbour is an evil man, and he who refrains from
injuring him a good man. Now these moral judgements
serve simply as a mould or body to our spiritual perceptions, and being as such mould or body the exact inversion
of what is moulded or embodied in them, they have
obviously no more right to control our spiritual perceptions than an egg has to control the chicken, than the
foundation of a house has to control the superstructure,
than the kitchen has to control the drawing-room, than
the stream has to control the fountain." [10]

There is an embarrassment of emblematic reference
here: to the house with its savory and unsavory quarters
(the reader may recall that in the great gallery the infant
James "inhaled" his sense of glory); to the fountain, stream,
and, by implication, the sensuous sea in which we may

[9] See *Roderick Hudson*, I, 106–108; and *"The Velvet Glove,"* in *The Finer Grain*, p. 5.
[10] *Logic*, pp. 221–222. For another reference to the "fountain of life,"
see p. 222n. See also pp. 197–198 for a reference to the divinity who
is shut up in the "familiar mould of our passions and appetites."

drown; to the moral form which society imposes; and, again by implication, the individual form which the artist may create to hold his spiritual perceptions. These forms may be equated on the one hand with the bowl which is smashed in *The Golden Bowl,* and on the other with the "bowl as it was to have been, the bowl with all our happiness in it," to which Maggie Verver refers.

What Strether denies is his responsibility for the creation of a form fit to hold the sources. Here again is the epigraph from the title page of *Society: The Redeemed Form of Man:* "Man during his earthly life induces a form in the purest substances of his interiors, so that he may be said to form his own soul; or give it quality; and according to the form or quality of soul he thus gives himself will be his subsequent receptivity to the Lord's infinite life: which is *a life of love to the whole human race.*" In the following quotation from a letter the novelist wrote Hugh Walpole in 1912, we begin to see how his moral and aesthetic standards coalesce in the conception of form: "Don't let any one persuade you—there are plenty of ignorant and fatuous duffers to try to do it—that strenuous selections and comparison are not the very essence of art, and that Form *is* [not] substance to that degree that there is absolutely no substance without it. Form alone *takes,* and holds and preserves, substance—saves it from the welter of helpless verbiage that we swim in as in a sea of tasteless tepid pudding, and that makes one ashamed of an art capable of such degradations." [11] Strether has been molded by his wife, and by Mrs. Newsome; he attempts to adapt himself to Mme de Vionnet's mold, believing it fitter to contain his perceptions. He feels that it is his duty, that it is morally imperative, to subordinate the judgements of Mrs. Newsome to those of Mme de Vionnet. He is now in Mme de Vionnet's boat: "If Madame de Vionnet, under Sarah's eyes, had pulled him into her boat, there was by

[11] *Letters,* II, 237.

this time no doubt whatever that he had remained in it and that what he had really most been conscious of for many hours together was the movement of the vessel itself." (XXII, 111) Strether has become the righteous defender of the exquisitely ordered appearances of Paris. His view of Paris is the consequence of his indomitable will, operating on fresh materials. The elder James makes a parallel emphasis: "If we persuade ourselves that heaven consists in going to Paris and draining the cup of pleasure to the dregs, we find there a Paris perfectly accommodated to our will. . . ."[12] But he who trusts to the Vain Appearance is destined to a rude awakening—Strether is confronted by Mme de Vionnet and Chad on the river.

Before this climax Strether has figuratively emphasized what James calls his "false position" (preface, XXI, xiii). The "pilgrim from Woollett" (XXII, 185), James's "belated man of the world" (XXI, xiii), tries to marry off Mamie Pocock to little Bilham. " 'I want,' Strether went on, 'to have been at least to that extent constructive—even expiatory. I've been sacrificing so to strange gods that I feel I want to put on record, somehow, my fidelity—fundamentally unchanged after all—to our own. I feel as if my hands were embrued with the blood of monstrous alien altars—of another faith altogether.' " (XXII, 167-168) He wants his "conditions unmitigated" (XXII, 168), so that Chad's choice will be a choice between Paris and Woollett, quite unaffected by concern over Mamie's defeated expectation of marriage.

James's climax is almost obtrusively emblematic: Strether has been delighted to discover in the blue-green countryside a scene reminiscent of the landscape in Boston, a Lambinet with figures. Chad and Mme de Vionnet seem highly appropriate figures for the remembered landscape —until he recognizes them, and his whole elaborate structure of supposition about the change in Chad, the benefi-

[12] *Substance*, p. 522.

cent influence of Paris, and the "unmitigated conditions"
he had hoped to create for Chad falls into ruins. "He
recognized at last that he had really all along been trying
to suppose nothing. Verily, verily, his labour had been
lost." (XXII, 266) No matter how hard we try to will
our Paris into being, it somehow betrays its doubleness.
Neither the mold of Woollett nor the mold of Paris is fit
to contain the "beautiful horrible world." Unable to
recognize his own duality, Strether is unprepared to recognize it in others. He is a Pharisee, righteous to the last. The
elder James, in a letter on the harm that "churches" do by
encouraging us to believe that God prefers some men to
others, quotes the passage of Scripture which is echoed in
Strether's speech: *"Verily, verily, I say unto you that unless
your righteousness* EXCEED *that of the scribes and Pharisees,
ye shall in no wise enter into the kingdom of heaven."* [13]
Strether is sunk in moralism. Since Chad and Marie are not
innocent, they are guilty. If they are guilty, he is guilty. He
has been reveling in the ostensible, in people who are de-
lightfully conscious of the value of the thing he has been
starved for, the Vain Appearance. His joy in the magnificent human beasts in Gloriani's garden stems from his
sense that they wear masks with ease; that he *does not know*
the source of these appearances. His first encounter with
Mme de Vionnet leads him to reflect: "It wasn't as if she
tried; nothing he could see after they had been a few
minutes together was as if she tried; but her speech, charming, correct, and odd, was like a precaution against her
passing for a Pole. There were precautions, he seemed
indeed to see, only when there were really dangers."
(XXI, 210) Strether has sought to conceal his sense of
these dangers from himself. The wonderful manner of
Mme de Vionnet does indeed conceal (as he realizes after
seeing the couple on the river) a "typical tale" (XXII, 271)
of Paris. He has been "trying to suppose nothing," but this

[13] *Society*, p. 385.

act of will is fruitless. Mme de Vionnet had not appeared to
try at all, yet all the while she had been fighting to keep
Chad *and* to appear a lady; Strether had simply been trying to make a new law satisfactory to himself. When this
cherished ignorance is gone, Strether's new law goes with
it; he is forced, like the narrator of *The Sacred Fount*, "to
give up . . . the attempt to be a providence." [14]

It is perfectly plain to him that a repatriated Chad would
be a greater sinner than Mme de Vionnet's lover; for Chad
to leave her would be a betrayal of the person who has
given him a form superior to that of Woollett. Yet the way
in which Chad became the man he is cannot be justified by
either law. Both laws have failed Strether. He is no longer
an ambassador either from or to Woollett. He vanishes
into the limbo of a lonely righteousness. His only principle
is, "Not, out of the whole affair, to have got anything for
myself." (XXII, 326) He is firmly held in his tin mold.
Righteousness and a taste for the pictorial, for the Vain
Appearance, are not enough, singly or together. Chad's
wonderful façade on the Boulevard Malesherbes, Gloriani's
garden, the Lambinet with the figures of the lovers in the
foreground, Mme de Vionnet in Notre Dame—all these
have been seen as pictures, appropriated as impressions of
the house of life. Strether has not felt the fear which makes
our bones shake: the fear of the other self. He falls back on
the formula of righteousness; he has taken nothing for himself. This is an exorbitant demand—Strether has taken all
the moral credit available. He is self-righteous; he has
denied life, not affirmed it. [15] To use the terms of the portrait theme, Strether may be said to find that Mrs. Newsome is not simply a "reflection of his old self"; [16] she

[14] *Sacred Fount*, p. 176. For a use of the term "law" in the sense in
which I employ it to characterize Strether's activity, see p. 23.
[15] See *Notes of a Son and Brother*, p. 110. James writes: ". . . righteousness, as I mostly understood, was in our parents' view, I think,
the cruellest thing in the world."
[16] As James calls her in the *Notebooks*, p. 228.

remains his dominant image of himself. This is an unprecedented assertion about Strether, but I think it is forced upon us by a close reading of *The Ambassadors*, and reinforced by considerations drawn from the succeeding two novels.[17]

James's pleasure in *The Ambassadors* was very great because he had pulled off the extraordinary feat of projecting the vision of the world enjoyed by the disencumbered (though not finally disencumbered) Puritan. Strether, who moves between the poles of righteousness and worldliness, is only *comparatively* imaginative, because he is incapable of the great love of the artist who draws on the sources. The novelist has exquisitely articulated the insatiable hunger of the righteous man with the pictorial impressions which feed it. Strether's "constant tribute to the ideal" (XXII, 135) has been fully rendered *through* the reader's experience of Strether's Paris. Strether has indeed awakened in a world conformed to his ideal.[18] His moral quality is exhibited in what he sees and fails to see. What he sees

[17] In this discussion I have not associated James with Strether as have many readers of *The Ambassadors*. I can make nothing of this imputed connection. Strether, bereft of wife and child, is not akin to Henry James; Strether, seeing and discriminating for the first time after a lifetime of weighing and choosing among the alternatives of New England, is no more like the Henry James whose "visiting mind" took command in infancy than the man in the moon. It seems a rather vulgar error to connect the two at all, since the basis for comparing the "comparatively" imaginative Strether with the fully imaginative James seems to be the unspoken premise that they have both missed their Mme de Vionnet. James gives no sign that this is a matter of concern to him. James has entered into Strether's situation—has perhaps tried to feel what it would be like to play with people's lives as the novelist plays with his fictions—but this, as always, takes him out of himself, confirms his artist's passion. The error is very much the error of those who conceive that James is treating himself in *The Sacred Fount*, which is really an image of the artist manqué, who plays at being an artist in life, and for this reason denies life its rights.

[18] See Chapter III, note 47, and *Substance*, p. 522, for the elder James's discussion of Americans who go to Paris when they die.

and fails to see gives us the visual consequence of his
moral quality. We are led to conclude that righteousness
and sensuousness,[19] the demands of social conformity and
the demands of nature, are allied. Together they compose
the tin mold which Strether mistakenly assumes to be unbreakable in every case.

It is Strether's conscience which has given form to the
novel, and this is the meaning of James's assertion in the
preface that his use of Strether avoids "the terrible *fluidity*
of self-revelation" (XXI, xix). Or, rather, it is the moral
meaning of the aesthetic observation, and a good instance
of the teasing way in which, throughout the prefaces,
James refers to his emblems without ever announcing or
classifying them.

This view of the general significance of *The Ambassadors* in relation to the two novels which follow it is
supported by the fact that the emblematic significance of
the titles of the four novels James published between 1901
and 1904 is derived from his father's work and from the
Bible. The significance of these associated titles is paralleled
in the texts, which have an emblematic scheme in common.
The Sacred Fount, which begins this series, has a title
which is best explained in the fourth chapter of Zechariah.
Here we find the primary account of the golden bowl. This
bowl is filled by golden pipes which are fed by the branches
of two olive trees, one on either side. The bowl surmounts
a seven-branched "candlestick" (it is therefore a lamp fed
by oil). From the bowl there run seven pipes bearing oil
to the seven lamps. According to the symbolism of this
book, Christ is "the Branch" which feeds the oil through
the golden pipe. The commentators associate these symbols
with Ecclesiastes, 6:12; "Or ever the silver cord be loosed
or the golden bowl be broken, or the pitcher be broken at

[19] R. P. Blackmur seems, in general, to agree that the discovery
which characterizes Strether is a discovery of the life of the senses.
(See his Introduction to *The Golden Bowl*, p. x.)

the fountain, or the wheel broken at the cistern." These last are images of death. The silver cord, which some commentators take to be that by which the lamp is suspended, is by others associated with the tongue, or the power of speech. The "pitcher broken at the fountain" is of course a reference to the fountain of life, the waters of which the broken vessel can no longer contain. The golden bowl is usually held to be the head, the vessel of consciousness, and was so employed by Blake, whose motto for *The Book of Thel* runs:

> Does the Eagle know what is in the pit?
> Or wilt thou go ask the Mole?
> Can Wisdom be put in a silver rod?
> Or love in a golden bowl?

The rod, associated with the phallus, is here the form of human self-assertion, opposed to God's wisdom; and the vessel is Swedenborg's *proprium*, which man fills with the fruits of his greed, which must be emptied or symbolically broken to become a fit container of the divine love. (The commentators have been troubled by the fact that a golden bowl is not breakable. Charles H. H. Wright supposes that "the writer may have thought of some merely gilded lamp," [20] a description applicable to the bowl of *The Golden Bowl*, which is gilded and breakable.)

The sin of the narrator of *The Sacred Fount* is, symbolically, his attempt to "remount the stream." (This phrase is taken, out of context, from *The Coxon Fund* (XV, 324) to indicate James's familiarity with the figure.) The elder James was fond of this figure. It is his emblem for the attempt to impose our moral judgments on God, to constrain him to love us for being good, and hate our fellows for being evil: "How is it conceivable . . . that a relation should ever obtain between this affluent fountain

[20] *The Book of Koheleth, Commonly Called Ecclesiastes*, pp. 266–267.

and this strictly dependent stream, which should qualify the latter to become a judge of the former?" [21] *The Sacred Fount* is full of references to the vessels or bowls of consciousness, but a pair of instances relating to the source which fills them will suffice here. The first has to do with the "fount": "That we had suddenly caught Long in the act of presenting his receptacle at the sacred fount seemed announced by the tone in which Mrs. Brissenden named the other party. . . ." The second has to do with the "life" which Mrs. Brissenden is presumed to have drawn from her husband: "What was actually before me was the positive pride of life and expansion, the amplitude of conscious action and design; not the arid channel forsaken by the stream, but the full-fed river sweeping to the sea, the volume of water, the stately current, the flooded banks into which the source had swelled." The concluding sentence of the novel expresses the superiority of Mrs. Brissenden's style (form, vessel) to the defeated narrator's: "What I too fatally lacked was her tone." [22] The narrator's attempt to find the sources in other lives condemns him; it is an attempt to "remount the stream," to define the divinity, and an evasion of the task of forming his own soul that it may be fit to receive life. [23]

Numerous examples have been cited of the use of the "dove," in the elder James, as the principle of brotherly love, which is also called "conscience" and "God-in-us." We have just considered the origin of the golden bowl as an emblem. How may "ambassadors" be associated with

[21] *Nature of Evil*, p. 45. Also see note 10, above; and *Secret*, p. 162.
[22] Quotations from *The Sacred Fount* are on pp. 38, 245, 319.
[23] Taken alone, the relation between these figures in *The Sacred Fount* and the symbols of the Bible and the elder James does not compel us to any conclusion about the novelist's intention. But when it is juxtaposed with my evidence in earlier chapters and with what is said below about the other three novels of the period 1901–1904, the reader will, I believe, find that this relation is conclusive evidence as to James's most general moral intention in *The Sacred Fount*.

these religious symbols? There is a sense in which preachers have long been in the habit of using "ambassadors" which is completely in accord with my reading of *The Ambassadors*. Increase Mather, denouncing Baptists, writes, "Are they not generally of a bad Spirit? Bitter enemies to the Lord's most eminent Servants? yea, to the fruitful Ambassadors, spitting the cruel venoms of Asps against them." [24]

A convenient instance from the eighteenth century is to be found in the edition of *Letters on Theron and Aspasio* by Robert Sandeman, to which the elder James contributed a preface. Here we encounter unworthy vessels once more. "If the communication of the divine love be spoken of, the preachers are the earthen vessels into which it is poured, in order to be conveyed to the people. In short they are commissioned to bring Christ near to sinners, and sinners near to Christ. So that if they are so modest as to decline the title, they effectually assume the character and work of mediators betwixt God and the people. The title of ambassadors is that which they use the greatest freedom with, and they no doubt reckon that they put considerable honour upon Christ, while they call him *God's Ambassador Extraordinary*." The elder James's sympathy with Sandeman was largely due to a like scorn for those who arrogated to themselves the position of mediators between God and man. The novelist's father felt that no man had any spiritual claim to ascendancy over any other man. I am persuaded that the novelist himself chose the title for his novel with a view to suggesting the impropriety of the attempt on the part of his "ambassadors" from America to judge the conduct of Chad Newsome and Mme de Vionnet.

This case is strengthened by the following sentence from *The Heart of Midlothian* (Chapter IX): "It's evident that this puir callant of yours will never be able to do an usefu' day's wark, unless it be as an ambassador from our

[24] Kenneth B. Murdock, *Increase Mather*, pp. 138–139.

Master; and I will make it my business to procure a
license when he is fit for the same, trusting he will be a
shaft cleanly polished and meet to be used in the body of
the Kirk; and that he shall not turn again like the sow, to
wallow in the mire of heretical extremes and defections, but
shall have the wings of a dove, though he hath lain
among the pots." We know that the elder James was fond
of this work of Scott's, from which, as a boy, he read aloud
to a company of friends;[25] we also know that the novelist
was acquainted with this fact, since he had read his father's
"Autobiographic Fragment." [26] The sentence is part of
one of David Deans's frequent homilies on the theme of his
own true Presbyterianism, and the lapses of everyone else.
The "puir callant," Reuben Butler, had had a father who
was an Independent; hence he is said to have "lain among
the pots," that is, vessels unworthy of grace, persons prone
"to wallow in the mire of heretical extremes." Here, then,
are two of James's titles, *The Ambassadors* and *The Wings
of the Dove*, employed with a reference to vessels, which
may be emblematically associated with *The Golden Bowl*.
The elder James's taste for racy rhetoric, and his horror of
such sectarianism as that evinced by David Deans, may
well have made *The Heart of Midlothian* the common coin
of family discourse. To understand how the religious
significance of these three titles is related in each case to the
texts of the novels themselves, it is necessary to recall the
elder James's position on the three churches, the Jewish,
the Christian, and the new church, that is, the church of
the new Jerusalem.

The general function of the church is the removal of
spiritual wastes from the house of life; it is the cloaca of
the spirit through which our greed and moral pretensions
are discharged into hell. The church functions like the

---

[25] *Remains*, p. 191. For a characteristic use of the "dove" in the elder
James, see *Nature of Evil*, p. 226.
[26] *Notes of a Son and Brother*, pp. 164–165.

heart; it attracts "our personal ambition and avarice, the most selfish, the most despotic, the most worldly tempers among men." He goes on: "And as the heart, having gathered the corrupt or debilitated blood of the body to its embrace, makes haste to hand it over to the lungs to be defecated, washed, and renewed for use by contact with the atmosphere, so in like manner the church, in spiritually or inwardly reacting against the ungodly influences which as a carnal economy it attracts, becomes itself renovated or washed clean of defilement. . . ." Swedenborg's "spiritual physiology" cannot be understood unless one keeps it in mind "that heaven and hell are only the sharply contrasted processes of nutrition and waste, which go to the formation of the *maximus homo*, the lord, or divine NATURAL man, and hence bear a strict proportion to the varying states of the church on earth." This will serve to introduce a further description of the cloacal function of the church, of which the novelist made emblematic use.

As long as men believe in the unconditioned nature of morality, and therefore attribute to themselves a selfhood or freedom no less absolute in truth or unreality than it is in fact or appearance, so long, of course, they will be unable to recognize the truth of the divine natural humanity; and while this truth remains unrecognized, men must continue to eat of the tree of finite knowledge, or hold good and evil to be essentially irreconcilable. That hell (or self-love) in this state of things should be allowed freely to precipitate itself from heaven therefore, and come under the permanent though unconscious subjection of the latter, is as much a provision of cosmical order or spiritual hygiene, as the separation of the waste matters of the body from our houses, and their incarceration in appropriate receptacles, is a provision of civic order or domestic hygiene.[27]

This passage refers to the second in the series of three churches I have named: the Christian church. James

[27] Quotations in this paragraph are in *Secret*, pp. 197, 97, 98.

follows Swedenborg in believing that the immediately pre-
cedent Jewish church had presented a real threat to God's
sway over our consciousness—a state of dangerous spiritual
constipation. He quotes Swedenborg's *True Christian Religion* to this effect: "Again he [Swedenborg] describes the
'particular' faith of the new heavens and the new earth in
human nature thus: 'God is essential goodness and truth,
and he manifested himself in Christ for the purpose of
reducing all things in heaven, in hell, and in the church (or
representative earth) to order, because at that period the
power of hell or evil had got a greater purchase upon
the human mind than that of heaven or good, and hence
menaced a total destruction. This menace was averted by
the lord's HUMANITY. . . .' " [28]

Christ made the spiritual nutriment of heaven available
to us, and provided for the discharge of our self-love. The
ecclesiasticisms of the present day may appear to threaten
the invisible church as did the Jewish church, but the
threat is illusory:

To be sure, we have certain portentous Jewish phantoms of
our own to contend with—certain very orthodox Christian
enemies of the Divine Spirit—in the persons of our Popish
and Protestant ritualists, or high churchmen. But no one is
in any danger of mistaking these worthless pretenders for
authentic Divine persons, nor of gravely combatting their
ecclesiastical fopperies and gross covert disloyalty to the
human ideal. They are not natural Jews but only spiritual or
spurious ones: only simulated or imitative ones. They are not
the pure gold of the sanctuary, once famous but now vanished
from earth forever: they are a mere counterfeit and pinchbeck
image of it, with a view to impose upon simple and credulous
imaginations.

But the apostles had to deal with a much less effeminate
and contemptible class of zealots, whose superstitious regard
for their own law threatened, indeed, to stop the world's

[28] *Secret*, p. 99n.

progress, so hearty and malignant was their opposition to that
gospel which the apostles proclaimed, and whose sole burden
was that Jesus of Nazareth was the Christ. They esteemed
their own law a living Divine one already as to the minutest
jot or tittle of its letter, and this purported to bless them
exclusively as children of Abraham. . . .

This, I repeat, was a very important truth to those to
whom it was addressed, a typical "outside" people, subjects
of an external Divine law, who were directed to an external
Divine Saviour as the veritable end of their law for
righteousness. In short, the Jew was notoriously a frivolous
subject—as near to worthless as a people could well be that
still wore the human form—and cultivating only such base
ideas of the Divine righteousness as stood in a mere "outward
cleansing of the cup and platter, while inwardly they were
full of extortion and excess." [29]

The new church, the invisible church of the divine-
natural-humanity, has perhaps been described sufficiently
often to make the contrast clear. To be made social out
of moral, we must create a new sanctuary, a new vessel
of the spirit, fit to hold the divine love and wisdom, and in
doing so, we will create a community in which both
church and state will be superseded.

The emblematic themes of the three novels may now
be summarized. *The Ambassadors* has for its subject the
failure of the law, and its correspondent "church" is New
England's, here standing for the elder James's "Jewish"
church. *The Wings of the Dove* treats the redemption of
an individual by an exemplary savior, Milly Theale; the
correspondent church is "Christian." *The Golden Bowl's*
subject is the regeneration of mankind, and its correspondent church is that of the new Jerusalem announced by
Swedenborg.

Strether is a false prophet: He tries to do under the
aegis of the law what Milly Theale does through grace.

[29] *Society*, pp. 81–82 and 83–85.

These terms are in one sense inappropriate, since James sought to give us these significances through his form; yet in another sense they are indispensable, since James clearly teases, and makes game of our blindness—he wanted to be found out. Had he wanted to keep his secret forever, he would not have provided certain clues we shall presently come to. We may say of these first two novels that what James gives us is the naturalistic analogue of the operation of providence—two situations, in the first of which it is assumed that the law is really a sufficient moral guide for man, and the assumption fails; in the second of which love and wisdom incarnate in persons effectuate the redemption of an individual. *The Golden Bowl* is not, either dramatically or poetically, on quite the same plane, for in this instance James wishes to suggest, again through the device of naturalism, how an "achieved social fusion," a "sublime consensus," might be realized. Whereas it is the point of *The Ambassadors* that a moral law alone does not suffice in human affairs, and the point of *The Wings of the Dove* that the natural alliance of love and intelligence can save a man from wickedness, these possibly contemporaneous events have no counterpart in *The Golden Bowl*, which is naturalistic only by its adherence to a literary convention. This aspect of *The Golden Bowl* is therefore a poetic device, while the naturalism of *The Ambassadors* and *The Wings of the Dove* is necessitated by their themes. *The Golden Bowl's* theme is that of Revelation; it is an apocalyptic vision.

IX Manifest Providence : II

JAMES'S READERS HAVE OFTEN DESCRIBED THE LITTLE
American girl of *The Wings of the Dove* as in some way
carrying out the suggestion of the title and descending on
London as a visible image of the Holy Spirit. The perfect
congruence of the conditions and consequences of her
descent with the elder James's account of Christ's mission
gives this general impression a precise meaning.

Milly Theale's case is that of the domesticated, the
naturalized, the explicable redeemer. As love's agent in the
world she is confronted, like Christ, with the presumption
of her own arrogance and greed. She is asked to accept the
world's inverted image of her in her climactic scene before
the Bronzino portrait. The elder James defines the Redeemer's position as perilous simply because it offered such
a chance for "self-aggrandizement."

Yet He, adorable man of men, bore unflinchingly on, nor
ever ceased to eat the bitter bread of humiliation, until he had
made of his despised and suffering form the adequate and
ample temple of God, and so for ever wedded the infinite
Divine perfection to the most familiar motions and appetites of
our ordinary human nature. Jesus vindicated his prophetic
designation as above all men *"a man of sorrows,"* because
in the historic position to which he found himself born, he

was exposed on the one side to the unmeasured influx of the Divine Love, and on the other to the equally unmeasured influx of every loathsome and hellish lust of personal aggrandizement. The literal form of Christ's pretension was profoundly diabolic. View his personal pretension as literally true and just, as having an absolute basis, and you can imagine no more flagrant dishonour to the Divine name. To suppose that the universal Father of mankind cares for the Jew one jot more than for the Gentile, and that He cared for one Jew also more than for another . . . was manifestly to blacken the Divine character, and pervert it to the inflammation of every diabolic envy.[1]

Christ's achievement was an archetypal one. He set us an example and implanted within us the awareness that we have the power to open ourselves to heavenly influence and to discharge our merely selfish pretensions.

We must match the following passage, which recapitulates in part the preceding quotation, with Mildred Theale's descent upon London in order to understand *The Wings of the Dove* as an account of Densher's redemption.

This Jewish legalism and carnality, therefore, were the appropriate matrix and starting-point of Christ's redemption. Unless he had found himself from his very infancy in antagonism with human folly and conceit, some portion of his Divine labor must have been slurred over, and forever invited medication. In that case indeed He must have acquiesced in his family or national pretensions, and still further inflamed the existing Divine distance from man. But as it was he was born an object of the intensest fanaticism, and of the most selfish idolatry. He was looked upon from the hour of his birth as a Jew of Jews, born to be their Deliverer and King indeed, and to carry the national name to unprecedented summits of renown. From the very beginning of consciousness accordingly He was a stranger in his own home, a self-driven outcast from the sympathies

[1] *Logic*, pp. 213–214.

and hopes of His people. From the very beginning of his career the personal ambitions and aspirations, which you and I, by virtue of our finite derivation find so soothing and flattering awakened in him only the intensest sorrow and revulsion. The thoughts and lusts of personal aggrandizement which flowed into his soul, and fed themselves even by the holy texts which were assiduously cited to sustain his peculiar pretensions, encountered there the infinite Divine Love; and the amazement and the conflict and the anguish which this encounter generated on the infirm or human side of the illustrious sufferer, are only dimly shadowed by his wilderness states, by his hunger and thirst, by his flesh sweating blood, and the transcendent passion of the cross. Now all this conflict and anguish were patiently borne—to what end? Only that the human selfhood in the person of Christ might be perfectly united with the Divine Love, and the purification of human life go on, therefore, no longer by an outward pressure merely, or the force of circumstances, but by the inward and spontaneous law of its new and Divine source.[2]

In *The Wings of the Dove* Milly lives in and for Densher, and she encounters the "lusts" and "personal pretensions" in him as if they were her own.

For the character of Mildred Theale, James drew on his memories of the wonderful Albany cousins, who had so mysteriously and gracefully lived and died, as if their separation from business and all other grubby human concerns had literally made them ephemeral, or as if they had existed only through their style, and not as assertive greedy selves. In the terms of the novel, Milly may be said to be divine simply on the ground that she isn't anything else but mortal. She is divine by exclusion, by character. There is not enough of her in certain respects to make a wife or a mistress, and there is more than enough of *caritas* to make an effectual redeemer. She offers a perfect case of the function of individuals as the bootstrap myth projects

[2] *Nature of Evil*, pp. 339–340. See also p. 184.

it; in her, an individual recapitulates a function which in the days of the novelist's grandfather had been performed for all Christians by a designated and presumably historical character, Jesus.

If we put Chad Newsome, Merton Densher, and Prince Amerigo to one side and consider the rest of the characters in the last three novels, we find that each of them (with the exception of certain minor figures) has two aspects. Each appears as an individual in the world of the novel; yet each functions as one of the impulses determining human behavior, or as one of the ideal limits of moral motion. Newsome, Densher, and Amerigo are the figures on whom or within whom these impulses operate—who approach or recede from the ideal limits. These relationships are easier to illustrate than to describe. This is the logical consequence of James's devout application of his principle: The reality, or the "ideal thing," must be wholly incarnate in the appearance or the "real thing," if the common principle of morality and art—expression in truly individual form—is to be satisfied. By this time James's imagination had been so completely disciplined by attention to his principles that the presented appearance is almost without a seam.

In *The Wings of the Dove* we encounter love, wisdom, the finally disencumbered Puritan who has subordinated righteousness to love, the selfhood attended by figures representative of greed and of death, and two minor figures representative of the literal church and incarnate worldliness. The persons in whom these powers may be discerned are, in corresponding order, Milly Theale, Sir Luke Strett, Susan Shepherd Stringham, Kate Croy, Maud Lowder, Lord Mark, and two lesser persons, Mrs. Condrip and Lionel Croy. Merton Densher, mankind in the house of life, is the "field" in which all these persons move. Milly's palace is of course the house of life, but we also encounter an emblematic opposition not mentioned heretofore; that between the house of life and the "other" house, the otherness of which consists in its housing greed or selfishness in the forms appropriate to them. In this novel Mrs. Lowder's house at Lancaster Gate is one such; Densher's flat in Venice is another. These last two are houses of the serpent, as opposed to the palace of the dove. Mrs. Lowder's greed and Densher's lust are "honest natural evils," [3] but there is yet another house which may be called the house of death, Matcham, where Lord Mark tries to appropriate the divinity in the form of an image.

In emblematic terms once more, the action of the novel consists in the movement of the redeeming love to the point at which Milly is exposed to the "lusts of personal aggrandizement." Endowed with money as Christ had been endowed with the title to rule over the kingdom, she rejects every lure that the world can offer and determines that the best mode of expressing her love for mankind and her forgiveness for its selfishness and greed is to die for it. [4] Mankind meanwhile is exposed to the temptation to appropriate God. His attempt to do so brings on the vision of the other self, which he casts out. Redeeming love takes its place, and man becomes capable of a delighted dependence on the divine love and wisdom. Just as Alice Staverton in *The Jolly Corner* had seen and "accepted" Brydon's other self, so Milly with complete selflessness undertakes to give both Kate and Densher what they want. The effect is the same as in *The Jolly Corner*. Once Densher has seen his other self he gets rid of it, and Milly takes its place in his consciousness. Kate Croy functions emblematically as Densher's selfhood; that is, she is the form which governs the way he takes experience, just as Mrs. Newsome had shaped the "tin mould" into which Strether's perceptions had been poured. But when Densher perceives the possibility in himself of the ultimate sin,

[3] See *Society*, pp. 202–203, quoted in Chapter III, above.
[4] The elder James saw Christ's death as His own choice (*Logic*, p. 198).

spiritual greed, or the appropriation of the godhead, it corresponds not to Kate but to Lord Mark.[5]

How much of all this does James expect to be apparent to the reader of *The Wings of the Dove?* Did James expect him to see that he was dealing with a metaphysically inclusive psychology? I think we must grant that he did, partly on the ground that he had an extraordinarily provincial mind. He seems to have been almost totally unable to conceive of any morality other than that derived from the bootstrap myth. He had not that vision of life which makes for tragedy: the perception of unbridgeable gulfs, not simply between the totality of things and his understanding, but between his fellows and himself. He had no term for fate. He was alone with his intelligence. Most men meet a kind of primitive otherness in their wives; their world is at least dual. But James did not. His intelligence met no check and could have brooked none. He did, quite literally, expect that we would find in *The Wings of the Dove* an altogether sufficient account of the sources of appearance.[6] He was of course shrewd enough to know that what was so carefully concealed would be perceived only by an able reader, but he was clearly unaware that his sense of humanity was emotionally so private and historically so special that this scheme would not be apprehensible unless the reader used his father as a guide.

The young man who in the seventies had written so clearly and crisply about the dangers of provincialism finally succumbed to them. He wrote his last three novels out of a completely unified and consistent sense of the

[5] For the relation between Densher and Kate, see *The Sacred Fount* (p. 294) for a description of Mrs. Brissenden and Long as mutually mirroring one another.

[6] My prime instance of such a "source" in earlier chapters is the spontaneous American girl. But the term is equally applicable to the other impulses in human nature as the Henry Jameses saw it, provided we keep it in mind that love and wisdom are primary, while righteousness and greed are secondary, and will ultimately disappear.

meaning of human action. This is the very thing he had accused Hawthorne of doing in a passage on *The Scarlet Letter:* "The people strike me not as characters, but as representatives, very picturesquely arranged, of a single state of mind; and the interest of the story lies, not in them, but in the situation. . . ." [7]

What this comes down to is that James, though he went to Europe and stayed there just because he needed the density, the embodied complexity and the variety of surfaces offered by an old society, did not long profit by it in this respect. He never came to believe in society, to feel its actual variety, its abysses of difference. He put no limits on the power of consciousness. Specifically, *The Wings of the Dove* treats "representatives" of a *single* complex abstraction—human nature as James conceived it. Lionel Trilling has made the same point about a number of other American authors to whom it is somewhat easier to apply it. In discussing Dreiser, Mr. Trilling says, "It is not persons that interest him but more or less differentiated instances of the operation of abstract forces." [8] As an isolated statement, this would be quite inapplicable to James, but if we qualify it to read "operation of the components of human nature as James conceived it," the application is direct. And it suggests an important likeness. In the practice of both men society is neither loved nor understood. What is prized is a mode of relating isolated figures to one another which depends on some abstract thesis about the nature of their common humanity.

The reason that this fact about James, that is, his remoteness from society as the ground of judgments about the differences and complexities in the world, has not been emphasized in these terms is obvious. It was at first believed that James was exclusively occupied with one segment of society. The belief that succeeded this was that James was

[7] *Hawthorne,* pp. 110–111
[8] *The Reporter,* V, November 13, 1951, p. 40.

exclusively occupied with an imagined situation in terms of technique. Neither of these views is wholly at fault; the trouble with them is that, pushed to extremes, they negate the most important point about the social world in James's novels—that it is the world of his father's version of the bootstrap myth. This account of the world was neither arbitrary nor false; it was, culturally speaking, an instrument of considerable power and nobility. But it did not offer enough modes of recognizing difference; it was asexual, ahistorical, and inhospitable to a genuine play of ideas; in a word, it was provincial.

When we consider *The Wings of the Dove* with this in mind, it appears that its defect is not its involution or obscurity, but the transparency which a psychology enfolding a metaphysics involves. The sources of appearance are too few. The strong light of simplified motivation glows too brightly through each of these marvelously colored and animated figures. What shines through Kate Croy is simply selfhood, justified, explained, endued with an animal grace, pathetic in its inordinate hunger, but *in action* nothing but selfhood. Mrs. Lowder, on whom Kate depends, is the "church" of this novel, a figure representative of a greedy nation swathed in bourgeois respectability and utterly without imagination, or, as James describes her, "Britannia of the Market-Place" (XIX, 30). No doubt both Queen Victoria and the wonderful Podsnap of Dickens's *Our Mutual Friend* entered into her composition.[9] But just as in Kate Croy's case, Mrs. Lowder's *actions* are those of an impulse or force. James is explicit about her; she is "a grand natural force" (XIX, 216), "a car of Juggernaut" (XIX, 90), a "loaded projectile" (XIX, 169), a "vulture" or "eagle" with "wonderful gilded claws," or a "balloon" with a "car" into which she snatches the things of her choice (XIX, 73). The leading figurative impression

[9] See XX, 27, 188. Podsnap of *Our Mutual Friend* waves away, or simply denies reality to, all the things that displease him.

is of a great, moving, all-engrossing container. Simply as a container, she is "a capacious receptacle" or a "great slumbering fortress" (XIX, 168–169), or an enfolding "Eastern carpet" (XIX, 216). In *The Golden Bowl* this "church" has adapted itself to the problem of creating an equipoise between the power of America and the British Empire; "Britannia of the Market-Place" has become a "helmeted trident-shaking *pax Britannica*" (XXIV, 209), who, functionally speaking, supplants the "matron at a market-stall" (XX, 110) of *The Wings of the Dove*.

Conclusions can be drawn about the nature of Mrs. Lowder, Kate Croy, Milly Theale, Sir Luke Strett, and Lord Mark by observing their actions, and thereafter noting how their emblematic designations correspond to these. This is less true of Lionel Croy and Mrs. Condrip, who are easier to place emblematically. Lionel Croy is one of James's teasing jokes. One might put the riddle the novelist poses in this way: What well-known figure never tells the truth, is known as a "gentleman," has the worst possible name, and the best possible appearance, has committed every imaginable wickedness, and is no longer believed in? [10] He is of course the devil, whom we may call "father of the lies of appearance": Kate Croy the selfhood, and her sister Mrs. Condrip the literal church. He is permitted just two significant actions: He "wriggles away" (XIX, 70), abandoning Eve after he has forced her to eat of the tree and thus put her in the power of Mrs. Lowder; and he retreats defeated within the literal church when Milly's ascension on Christmas redeems mankind.

James frequently employed names for his characters which had the form of runic sentences, sentences whose meanings are often shocking and repellent. A few of these have already been pointed out, and now that the relation of the emblematic elements is clear, let us see how some of

[10] See XIX, 3–24, 66–70; XX, 382–383. For the elder James's description of the devil, see *Substance*, pp. 252–254.

the names were derived. We learn from the notes for *The Ivory Tower* that James chose names for both sound and significance (XXV, 271-273), but he nowhere gives any intimation of the intricacy of the patterns he sometimes employed. As a name, "Mrs. Condrip" has the suggestion of something indeterminately unpleasant; it also contains a clue to its emblematic force. With our knowledge of the figure of man as a conduit, the following sentence about "Mr. Condrip's widow" takes on its full significance: "She was little more than a ragged relic, a plain prosaic result of him—as if she had somehow been pulled through him as through an obstinate funnel, only to be left crumpled and useless and with nothing in her but what he accounted for." (XIX, 37) Mrs. Condrip *is* the filth of moral pretension and greed, functioning as a character, and her husband had been the church, now "dead" in England, and surviving only as a "relic." The name therefore refers both to the cloacal character of the church and to that which is discharged through it. The only survival of anything even faintly religious in Mrs. Condrip is her tendency to harp on Kate's duty. James even permits himself to remark on the smell that pervades her dwelling. The association of this name with Mrs. Condrip's function in *The Wings of the Dove* is not just an accident. There is another such cloacal figure in *The Awkward Age*: Nanda asks, "Doesn't one become a sort of a little drainpipe with everything flowing through?" and Mitchy, after demurring, assents, "What you take, you mean, you keep?" And Nanda says, "Well, it sticks to us." (IX, 358)

James's practice in making names is much like Blake's. Blake sometimes used anagrams such as "Orc" for Latin *cor*, "heart"; he occasionally used phonetic echoes as in "Urizen" (your reason). James uses both these devices, singly or in combination, along with directly suggestive names such as "Lionel" in Lionel Croy, which indicates that Croy goes up and down seeking whom he may devour.

Certain anagrammatic inversions dependent on sound values, such as "yorc" (Croy inverted), which is meant to point up the opposition between love (Milly Theale of New York) and selfhood (Kate Croy of London) contending for Densher's soul, may seem trivial or childish, but one is constrained, after studying the patterns James creates, to admit that he indulged in the kind of embellishment associated with Joyce. Milly is from New York, the region of blessedness; New York is also opposed to Lancaster Gate, by association with the Wars of the Roses.

One of the most important emblematic names in this novel is dependent on both sound and verbal meaning: "Matcham," the house in which Death (Lord Mark) seeks to appropriate life is "match-um" (match them), the place where the portrait is equated with its opposite. James seems to have felt that the sounds denoted in English by *uh* or *um* were the ugliest possible; consider, for example, the Miss "Lutches" of *The Golden Bowl*. These are instances of the "slack" or "passive" sounds which he denounces in *The Question of Our Speech*. Other sounds of the open or glottal sort, such as "Gaw" in *The Ivory Tower*, and "Maud," Mrs. Lowder's first name in the *The Wings of the Dove*, are indications of the character's emblematic function.

"Mildred Theale" is an instance of the elaborate suggestiveness of certain names. The Anglo-Saxon first name carries the meanings "mild" or "clement" together with "power" or "strength." We may also imagine that "gentle counsellor" (Anglo-Saxon "rede," or counsel) is also involved. "Theale," like Blake's "Enarithmon," [11] is an anagram from the Greek name "Alethea," from *aletheia*, "truth." James's emphasis on Milly's displacement, her wandering (XIX, 114–115), leads us to suspect that he had somehow come across Plato's playful etymology in the *Cratylus* (421B): "For the divine motion of the universe

[11] S. Foster Damon, *William Blake*, p. 69.

('being' or 'reality') is evidently called by this name, 'truth,' (aletheia) because it is a 'divine' (theia) 'wandering' (ale). The combined meaning of Milly's name and her identification with the dove of the spirit may be summed up: 'She who brings love, which is the truth of God, into the world.' " [12]

The effect of putting down too many of these details before the emblematic meaning of the action has been at least sketched is likely to be misleading. What we are given in the novel is not, after all, a statement of the opposed character of the impulses or forces James uses, but a representation of the result of their struggle, of the commerce between them. The names we affix to Lord Mark and Milly are less important than our perception of how these two function in the novel. We must first see the moral dynamics at work. The scene is one on which human drives or impulses create, through their relations with one another, a highly complex pattern. Its verbal complexity is the direct consequence of the simplicity of the elements employed.

In most novels of consequence every character is a sort of sacred mystery, which we cannot fully plumb. In *The Wings of the Dove* the complexity lies simply in the notation of the shifting relations between things which are as definable as musical notes; and the scholar who devoted his life to the job might reasonably expect to know this novel inside out. It is James's intention to make his persons hover on the very edge of worldly identity, identifiability; to make us feel that Kate Croy is knowable and lovable, Mrs. Lowder a Dickensian or Hogarthian genre figure, Densher an impecunious journalist. These are the faces that forces present, the masks thrown up to the surface of the cauldron of human love and greed which creates these appearances. James does not give us the

[12] I owe the reference to Plato's *Cratylus* to Fred Householder of Indiana University.

"character," in the sense in which we say that someone *has* character; he gives us the pictorial and dramatic consequences of the impulse as it is affected by its congeners.

It remains, then, for us to relate the naturalistic surface of the action to its emblematic significance, chiefly with reference to Milly and Densher.

Emblematically, Densher is a fallen man, Strether's successor, who is the son of greed and righteousness. Kate's conclusion is barely figurative. "If her last word for him in the connexion was that the way he saw himself was just a precious proof the more of his having tasted of the tree and being thereby prepared to assist her to eat, this gives the happy tone of their whole talk, the measure of the flight of time in the near presence of his settled departure." (XIX, 94) Our clue to Densher's relation to Strether, and fallen man in general, is his lineage. Kate is given this "bird's-eye view" of his life: "His father had been, in strange countries, in twenty settlements of the English, British chaplain, resident or occasional, and had had for years the unusual luck of never wanting a billet. His career abroad had therefore been unbroken, and as his stipend had never been great he had educated his children, at the smallest cost, in the schools nearest; which was also a saving of railway-fares. Densher's mother, it further appeared, had practised on her side a distinguished industry, to the success of which—so far as success ever crowned it—this period of exile had much contributed: she copied, patient lady, famous pictures in great museums, having begun with a happy natural gift and taking in betimes the scale of her opportunity." (XIX, 92–93)

He has the ancestry of the trapped. His father was a preacher, ostensibly concerned with spiritual things. His mother was a copyist, a reproducer. As parents, they sound as bad as Mark and Beatrice Ambient, although the roles in this case are reversed. Densher's mother exhibited Ambient's greed for the pictorial; his father was the purveyor of an empty righteousness like Mrs. Ambient's.[13] James adds a burlesque touch about Densher's mother: "Her son, who had lost her, held her image sacred, and the effect of his telling Kate all about her, as well as about other matters until then mixed and dim, was to render his history rich, his sources full, his outline anything but common." (XIX, 93)

The world of Kate's and Densher's London is vulpine, feral. Its prime verb is "to have." Milly remarks that all the people she and Susan encounter seem "to think tremendously of money" (XIX, 195), but this is not the worst aspect of the scene which is the fact that London is a place in which people "have" one another. Mrs. Lowder seeks to know Densher, "to see best where to 'have' him" (XIX, 57). Kate's mother had enjoined her to remember "that it was of the essence of situations to be, under Providence, worked" (XIX, 58). Kate means to make Densher's "long looks" her "possession," to "cherish them and yet, as regards the rigour of it, pay no price" (XIX, 61). Lord Mark and Milly are Mrs. Lowder's social possessions (XIX, 156). But Kate is her prize.

"Kate's presence is, in short, as fine as you know, and I've been keeping it for the comfort of my declining years. I've watched it long; I've been saving it up and letting it, as you say of investments, appreciate; and you may judge whether, now it has begun to pay so, I'm likely to consent to treat for it with any but a high bidder. I can do the best with her, and I've my idea of the best."

"Oh I quite conceive," said Densher, "that your idea of the best isn't me." (XIX, 82)

Later on, Kate explains to Milly the economy of London's social life. Lord Mark is a value that her aunt is betting on to appreciate, while Mark is himself getting

---

[13] Cf. Blake's "Tiriel," whom S. Foster Damon identifies as degenerate religion, one of whose daughters is "Heva," degenerate painting (*William Blake*, p. 71)

something in return: "And he [Mark] wasn't meanwhile himself indifferent—indifferent to himself—for he was working Lancaster Gate for all it was worth: just as it was, no doubt, working *him*, and just as the working and the worked were in London, as one might explain, the parties to every relation." (XIX, 178) Still later, Kate explains to Milly that the commerce between Lord Mark and her aunt is a matter of very close bargaining indeed. If Mrs. Lowder reckons an invitation to Matcham as worth much, she is mistaken: "He weighed it out in ounces, and indeed each of the pair was really waiting for what the other would put down." (XIX, 278) This suggestion of Matcham as a place where one *matches* things recalls Marian Condrip's lecture to her sister Kate on the necessity of doing what her aunt wanted her to with regard to marriage: "The exact identity of her candidate [Mrs. Lowder's] was a detail; what was of the essence was her conception of the kind of match it was open to her niece to make with her aid. Marian always spoke of marriages as 'matches,' but that was again a detail." (XIX, 44)

Some of the figures that have to do with being eaten, or those that link persons to devouring animals, will appear later in the discussion of Densher and Milly. One instance, the horror of which is reminiscent of *Gulliver's Travels*, is connected with Milly's London "success," the novelist's equivalent for his father's belief that the Redeemer's mission was misinterpreted as a search for worldly power. Susan Shepherd has taken part in the discussion of Milly's supposititious conquest of London, "and it was at that comparatively gross circumstance, now so fully placed before them, that Milly's anxious companion sat and looked—looked very much as some spectator in an old-time circus might have watched the oddity of a Christian maiden, in the arena, mildly, caressingly, martyred. It was the nosing and fumbling not of lions and tigers but of domestic animals let loose as for the joke." (XX, 42)

Our measure of Densher's moral awareness, and its possible complexity, comes from his early scenes with Milly. He had met her three times in America, during his journalistic tour. But he had not recognized her, except as one of the many little Miss Theales (XX, 10), a type of which America offered abundant examples. His first encounter with her in England takes place in the National Gallery. The scene on which she is to encounter Densher is carefully set by James. Milly has been watching the "lady-copyists." Sir Luke Strett, the great physician, had told her that she "could live if she would," and Milly is considering here, as she had in the park, after her interview with the doctor, those who "would live if they could" (XIX, 250). The "lady-copyists" have accepted the latter alternative. "She should have been a lady-copyist—it met so the case. The case was the case of escape, of living under water, of being at once impersonal and firm. There it was before one—one had only to stick and stick." (XIX, 288) These submerged creatures (who remind the reader of the business carried on by Densher's mother) are easier for the girl threatened with death to contemplate than the Turners and Titians: "They joined hands about her in a circle too vast, though a circle that a year before she would only have desired to trace. They were truly for the larger, not for the smaller life, the life of which the actual pitch, for example, was an interest, the interest of compassion, in misguided efforts." (XIX, 288–289)

James tries here to underline the fact that it is Milly's mortal disease which gives her "the interest of compassion." The redeemer is precisely the "life" shrouded in the body of this death. But it is not simply mortality which engages Milly in behalf of those who, "living under water," [14] like

[14] This is a prime emblematic theme. James chose London localities with names which emphasized the submerged lives of his characters. For this and other uses of the general emblematic theme involving the fountain, the river, and the sea, see XIX, 52, 174, 187, 199, 201;

Densher, are directed either by righteousness or greed. It is love for Densher, for mankind in Densher, who has no perception of a standard beyond poor Strether's "Live while you can. . . ."

Milly's encounter with the acquisitive reproducers is but a prelude to her meeting with Densher and Kate in the same gallery. James has already characterized these lovers as acquisitive with respect to each other: "Any deep harmony that might eventually govern them would not be the result of their having much in common—having anything in fact but their affection; and would really find its explanation in some sense, on the part of each, of being poor where the other was rich." (XIX, 50) Milly's response to the stimulation of Densher's presence and her doubt as to Kate's feelings about him is to become "as spontaneous as possible and as American as it might conveniently appeal to Mr. Densher, after his travels, to find her" (XIX, 296). Milly had been conscious before this meeting of the look Kate had when she was, so to speak, filled with Densher. Milly's love for him must always reckon with his selfhood.

We may figure Densher's movement through the rest of the novel as bounded on either side by his dove and serpent natures. He has entered on a path in which two kinds of love, the engrossing and acquisitive, and the spontaneous, which multiplies communications and contacts, are both open to him. We become aware, a good while before he does, that he will have to choose. The rest of the novel is a long sustained rush toward that choice. Will death come in before life, or life before death? These terms have, of course, a double meaning. Milly's physical decay and her rising moral ascendancy are movements which wear one meaning for London and another for the redeemed Densher. London thinks physical death is abso-

XX, 72, 80, 88, 295. See also *A New England Winter* (Macmillan XXV, 73).

lute; Densher learns that what is really absolute is spiritual death, the appropriation of the godhead. Just as in the elder James, death has three meanings, the physical, the moral, and the spiritual. To be redeemed Densher must die *to* selfhood, or, what is the same thing, confront his other self. We may think of him as moving down a corridor, impelled by Kate, his selfhood. At the end the corridor branches. To the left he will find Lord Mark, the final state of those under the domination of selfhood or that which he would become if he acted Lord Mark's part; to the right he will find Milly. But in order that he may be possessed of Milly he must first displace Kate. Thereafter he will no longer be impelled by greed, but drawn by spontaneity.

Densher is urged by Kate and her aunt to make up to Milly. He is not fully aware of their plot. He is surprised to discover "the positive extent of the old basis," that of the friendship he and Milly had established in New York. Recalling, in Venice, the drive they had taken together on the occasion of his second visit in London, he realizes that Kate's scheme has not really governed his relation with Milly: "He had more than once recalled how he had said to himself even at that moment, at some point in the drive, that he was not *there*, not just as he was in so doing it, through Kate and Kate's idea, but through Milly and Milly's own, and through himself and *his* own, unmistakeably—as well as through the little facts, whatever they had amounted to, of his time ·in New York." (XX, 186) His relation with Milly is a separate strand, not interwined with Kate's "silken web" (XX, 64). James has been at pains to make plain Densher's inability to make money and his capacity to "handle" any subject his newspaper might ask him to treat. This "pair of smudges from the thumb of fortune, the brand on the passive fleece, dated from the primal hour and kept each other company" (XIX, 73–

64).[15] Densher has the sensitive man's susceptibility to the shape and form, the simple quiddity of other existences, all of which appear so pleasant, mean so much to be themselves, whereas he feels chiefly the need to recognize the intent of others, and try to satisfy it, rather than to push ends of his own. (XX, 31–32)

What this comes to, as James puts it, is that Densher is still "in fusion and fermentation" (XIX, 49). He is consequently "handled" by Kate: "He would do as *she* liked —his own liking might come off as it would." [16] But he is no less open to Milly's influence: "Densher liked too much everyone concerned willingly to show himself merely impracticable." (XX, 71) This extreme sensibility of Densher's is illumined by the opposed instance of Tony Bream in *The Other House,* of whom it is said that he doesn't have "two grains of observation," and, "People like him too much." [17] Densher's extreme openness to experience is a rent in James's naturalistic surface. We accept Tony Bream, who has no observation, and about whom opposing forces may gather, without his noticing or assessing them, until, like a bourgeois marble faun, he is shocked into the widest consciousness by the loss of his child. Our difficulty with Densher is that he is made so aesthetically receptive, is so little jealous—like a god—of the wondrous multiplicity of existence, that he begins too plainly to appear an intersection, a human crossroad, responding gratefully to the pressure of conflicting impulses. James did not want him to appear as Everyman, but to function as Everyman; the novelist does not quite succeed in this.

During his second visit to Milly, which culminates in their drive together, Densher has realized that he is "at a

---

[15] See also XIX, 93.
[16] See XIX, 75; XX, 13, 63–64, 226.
[17] *The Other House,* pp. 94, 386.

corner" (XX, 86). This is his opportunity to tell Milly
that Kate does love him, despite the impression that Mrs.
Lowder and Kate have tried to convey. He does not tell
her; he goes for a drive instead, and he does so in his mixed
character, first as a person who likes, and likes to be liked
by, Milly, and second as a person who has fallen in with
Kate's views, Mrs. Lowder's views—a man in a "silken
web." Moreover, he does so as the man who has glimpsed
the possibility that Kate might find him boring. This leads
to his fall, or a dramatic recapitulation of *the* fall, in his
particular case. Having abandoned his power to arrive at a
form or style of his own, and having accepted Kate's
attempt to create an identity for them both out of things
appropriated, he comes to feel that he does not exist as an
agent. He is threatened with the loss of identity. He determines to "have" Kate. "His question, as we have called it,
was the interesting question of whether he had really no
will left." (XX, 177) He had "done absolutely everything
that Kate had wanted . . ." (XX, 177). She, meanwhile,
has done nothing that he wanted. He arrives at the plan of
getting Kate to become his mistress in the set of rooms he
has taken in Venice. He is so dominated by this scheme that
it seems horrible to let Milly visit these rooms. He is keeping the strands of his own fate apart by main force. His
anticipations would be spoiled by Milly's visit, and he has
the feeling as well that Milly should not be exposed to
what is to take place in his rooms.

Out of this conflict, and this conflict alone, what we may
now begin to call his character emerges. The phases of his
moral growth are very carefully indicated. His taste, and
his commitment to using his mind instead of flogging his
wits to some practical end; his perception that Mrs.
Lowder's drawing room is, in virtue of its ugliness,
"operatively, ominously . . . cruel"; his further perception that these ugly objects made for "the general attesta-
tion of morality and money, a good conscience and a

big balance," and were "a portentous negation of his own world of thought" (XIX, 78–79)—these are the things by which we first know him. He is like the infant Henry James in this first stage; he seems to feel that everything has more right to exist than he. The second stage is indicated by the reader's awareness of the conflict in him between his feeling for Milly and his feeling for Kate. This conflict is not yet (in this second phase) Densher's active concern, but the reader is apprised that Densher must sooner or later recognize the fact that he is a riven man. This recognition takes place in Venice.

We must now follow in some detail the redeemer's preparation for her meeting with Densher in Venice. She must first subject herself to Mrs. Lowder's London, and Lord Mark's London. The scenes in which she does so are those of Mrs. Lowder's dinner party and the gathering at Matcham at which she confronts the Bronzino.

When Densher returns to London and meets Milly once more, we are prepared with the knowledge that Milly offers an alternative to the situation in which Kate and Mrs. Lowder have placed him. The groundwork is laid in the talk between Lord Mark and Milly at Mrs. Lowder's (XIX, 150–166). Milly has been reflecting that the relations she now enters into are likely to be the sum of what she is to know. "It was queerly a question of the short run and the consciousness proportionately crowded." (XIX, 159) Her dinner companion, Lord Mark, has advanced the question of her value to Mrs. Lowder as a social resource. "Milly had practically just learned from him . . . that he gave her the highest place among their friend's actual properties. She was a success, that was what it came to, he presently assured her, and this was what it was to be a success; it always happened before one could know it." (XIX, 157) Mrs. Lowder, Mark assures her, will not lose by her: "Nobody here, you know, does anything for nothing." (XIX, 160) Milly is finally moved to a direct attack:

". . . you all here know each other—I see that—so far as you
know anything. You know what you're used to, and it's
your being used to it—that, and that only—that makes you.
But there are things you don't know." "Things that *I* don't—
with all the pains I take and the way I've run about the
world to leave nothing unlearned?"
  Milly thought, and it was perhaps the very truth of his
claim—its not being negligible—that sharpened her impatience
and thereby her wit. "You're *blasé*, but you're not
enlightened. You're familiar with everything, but conscious
really of nothing. What I mean is that you've no
imagination." (XIX, 161–162)

London is in this respect, though for a different reason,
very much like Woollett, Massachusetts. Strether, in describing Mrs. Newsome to Maria Gostrey, employs a
phrasing which is reminiscent of Densher's sense of Mrs.
Lowder's drawing room as representative of her (XIX,
78–79), and he is just as emphatic as Milly is here, about
the lack of moral or intellectual elbow room: ". . . she's
all, as I've called it, fine cold thought. She had, to her own
mind, worked the whole thing out in advance, and worked
it out for me as well as for herself. Whenever she has
done that, you see, there's no room left; no margin, as it
were, for any alteration. She's filled as full, packed as tight,
as she'll hold. . . ." (XXII, 222) Righteousness and greed,
singly or in combination, cover the ground of their own
preoccupations so thoroughly and are so tightly enclosed
that the imagination has no room to function. The very
shapes of things can tell us this, and this is what Mrs.
Lowder's furniture tells Densher: "He had never dreamed
of anything so fringed and scalloped, so buttoned and
corded, drawn everywhere so tight and curled everywhere
so thick." (XIX, 78–79) Milly's attack on Mark is the
response of spontaneity to a world which is both aesthetically and morally static, a world in which the exchange

of stamped images, the acquisition of prestige, and spiritual greed are the rule.

In this talk with Mark, Milly takes the privilege of her mortality and speaks out. She has chosen this world because it is the world of Densher, whom she loves. But the gulf across which she speaks to those who live in it is extraordinarily wide. This is perhaps clearest in the many references to her London "success," which is the particular cruelty to which this redeemer is subjected. All assume her to be as greedy as they themselves are, and only Susan Shepherd and Densher know how horrible an imposition this is. But Milly has engaged herself in this world, and she suffers its pains with a bravery which (although it appears to have moved James more than most of his readers) the novel presents as deeply touching.[18] Densher binds Milly to a world in which people can not imagine her possible difference; a world in which they can but "jump" at her or snatch her, because this is the thing they know how to do (XIX, 154–155).

The first and second chapters of James's Fifth Book (XIX, 207–229) which deal with the party at Matcham and Milly's confrontation with the Bronzino, have an extraordinary emblematic complexity. James is playing a double game to a somewhat bewildering effect. In these chapters Milly's life in the world culminates, although it may be more nearly accurate to say that it is comprised within them.

James gives us in the scenes at Matcham a symbolic account of Milly's entry into, and exit from, the world of "*appointed* felicity," [19] which is on the surface the world of

[18] Milly's social success is heavily stressed (XIX, 157–158, 160, 164, 168, 210, 228–229, 281, 290; XX, 37–39, 42–44, 51, 79, 83, 87).

[19] James's emphasis here may be compared to his father's description of "addled conservatism": "Law consequently as the symbol of order and the enemy of our unrestrained freedom is the pole-star of the conservative imagination, and respect for it as *established* the sum of all human duty" (*Remains*, p. 204).

the English nobility, but is emblematically representative of the domain of those who live through their identities alone. Their "style" is simply the manner common to all who have their status; and they are all dead, frozen by their claim to status. Later when Milly walks through the throng with Mark, these people flock about the pair, like the shades in the *Odyssey* and *Aeneid*, and their "kind eyes" reflect the desire to gain some increase of status from acquaintance with Milly, the "success" who is Mark's social capital at the moment.

The chief emblematic clue in these two chapters comes from James's use of pictures or portraits. The following is the opening of the passage which deals with Milly's response to the scene of "*appointed* felicity."

The great historic house had, for Milly, beyond terrace and garden, as the centre of an almost extravagantly grand Watteau-composition, a tone as of old gold kept "down" by the quality of the air, summer full-flushed but attuned to the general perfect taste. Much, by her measure, for the previous hour, appeared, in connexion with this revelation of it, to have happened to her—a quantity expressed in introductions of charming new people, in walks through halls of armour, of pictures, of cabinets, of tapestry, of tea tables, in an assault of reminders that this largeness of style was the sign of *appointed* felicity. The largeness of style was the great containing vessel, while everything else, the pleasant personal affluence, the easy murmurous welcome, the honoured age of illustrious host and hostess, all at once so distinguished and so plain, so public and so shy, became but this or that element of the infusion. (XIX, 208–209)

"The largeness of style was the great containing vessel . . ." holding an "infusion" into which many elements entered. This figure will serve to suggest the parallelism between James's figures relating to containers and bowls, and those having to do with the house of life, which, as we have often noted, offers us an experience of "diffused and reverberant" quality.

Since the portrait theme is dominant in these two chapters, they may be studied as an instance of James's combined use of his three great emblems, the portrait, the house of life, and the bowl. It is perhaps unnecessary to remind the reader of the basic moral principle exemplified by the relation of these members of the British nobility, who hold "appointed" stations in Britain and the Empire, to the house of life which they occupy. Since their style is a *public* one, they have no spiritual individuality whatever, and their tenure of the house of life is based on appropriation. They are identities, who have stolen the world's beautiful forms to reflect themselves. Godfrey Sholto of *The Princess Casamassima*, in whom Lord Mark is foreshadowed, is described by the Princess in terms applicable to the creatures of Matcham: "He was a cumberer of the earth—purely selfish for all his devoted disinterested airs. He was nothing whatever in himself and had no character or merit save tradition, reflexion, imitation, superstition." [20] (VI, 82) Character gained through reflection—through getting the world to mirror oneself—is just the sort that Lambert Strether tries to acquire in Paris, Or, to shift from the portrait theme to the theme of the bowl, this is the sort of thing with which Strether tries to fill the "tin mould" of his consciousness. The reader must recall that the appropriation of the promise of life, God's love as represented by the spontaneous American girl, is an ultimate evil, whereas Strether's attempt to get the world to

[20] Cf. this sentence describing the persons whom Mark and Milly encounter as they pass through the gardens at Matcham: "They might have been moving a good deal by a momentum that had begun far back, but they were still brave and personable, still warranted for continuance as long again, and they gave her, in especial collectively, a sense of pleasant voices, pleasanter than those of actors, of friendly empty words and kind lingering eyes that took somehow pardonable liberties" (XIX, 218).

reflect him, or to use the forms of the world to create an identity for him, is an "honest natural evil" which may be overcome. This warning is necessary here, because we shall presently have to deal with an instance of this ultimate sin in Lord Mark.

Milly is seated with Mrs. Lowder during the garden party at Matcham. It dawns on her that in this lady's plans she figures, or her money figures, as a great value with which much may be done, especially in association with Kate's wonderful appearance. "It couldn't be less than a climax for a poor shaky maiden to find it put to her of a sudden that she herself was the matter—for that was positively what, on Mrs. Lowder's part, it came to." The atmosphere of bargain and exchange is figuratively reinforced by James's use of the colors pink and blue, which play through this and the following scene, and stand for girls and boys. Mrs. Lowder is weaving together pink and blue: She is projecting *matches,* matches of the sort that the elder James would call, not marriages, but states of concubinage. These involve, in the terms of this figure, the *imposition* of blue on pink. "It came back to Lord Mark again, as he seemed slowly to pass and repass and conveniently to linger before them; he was personally the note of the blue—like a suspended skein of silk within reach of the broiderer's hand. Aunt Maud's free-moving shuttle took a length of him at rhythmic intervals. . . ." The reader of the novel is aware at this point that Aunt Maud's use of Milly as a "value" is very much the same thing as taking the portrait for the lady.

Milly, however, is a source. She is not something to be bartered, nor can she consent to a marriage which would impose an identity on her. Such things mean death to her. The immediate cause of her death will be the knowledge that she has been made part of a bargain, a Judas bargain, a betrayal. She tells Lord Mark what her true function is when he asks her to marry him in Venice. The speech is one of a number in which she makes it plain that she can only *give*. " 'No, I mustn't listen to you—that's just what I mustn't do. The reason is, please, that it simply kills me. I must be as attached to you as you will, since you give that lovely account of yourselves. I give you in return the fullest possible belief of what it would be—' And she pulled up a little. 'I give and give and give—there you are; stick to me as close as you like and see if I don't. Only I can't listen or receive or accept—I can't agree. I can't make a bargain.' " (XX, 160–161)

The scene of the garden party provides a wonderful setting for Kate Croy, about whom Milly's imagination plays as she sits sipping her iced coffee. The occasion has the strangeness, the exotic character of a "durbar," attended by "a contingent of native princes." But Kate is at home on this scene. Milly praises her opposite, the portrait itself, which is walking about out of its frame: "She knew people, and people knew her, and she was the handsomest thing there—this last a declaration made by Milly, in a sort of soft midsummer madness, a straight skylark-flight of charity, to Aunt Maud." Milly had earlier thought of the scene as representative of "great pictures," and of the Matcham occasion as the close of her period of involvement with London society: "The parenthesis would close with his admirable picture. . . ."

To follow the rest of this chapter and the succeeding one, in which Mark takes Milly to view the Bronzino, which is said to resemble her, it must be kept in mind that the Kate Croy whom Milly is contemplating is "other," in virtue of being Densher's Kate Croy.

Kate had for her new friend's eyes the extraordinary and attaching property of appearing at a given moment to show as a beautiful stranger, to cut her connexions and lose her identity, letting the imagination for the time make what it would of them—make her merely a person striking from afar, more and more pleasing as one watched, but who was

above all a subject for curiosity. Nothing could have given
her, as a party to a relation, a greater freshness than this
sense, which sprang up at its own hours, of one's being as
curious about her as if one hadn't known her. It had sprung
up, as we have gathered, as soon as Milly had seen her after
hearing from Mrs. Stringham of her knowledge of Merton
Densher; she had *looked* then other and, as Milly knew the
real critical mind would call it, more objective; and our
young woman had foreseen it of her on the spot that she
would often look so again. It was exactly what she was doing
this afternoon; and Milly, who had amusements of thought
that were like the secrecies of a little girl playing with dolls
when conventionally "too big," could almost settle to the
game of what one would suppose her, how one would place
her, if one didn't know her. She became thus, intermittently,
a figure conditioned only by the great facts of aspect, a figure
to be waited for, named and fitted. This was doubtless but a
way of feeling that it was of her essence to be peculiarly
what the occasion demanded when its demand was highest.
There were probably ways enough, on these lines, for such a
consciousness; another of them would be for instance to say
that she was made for great social uses. (XIX, 211–212)

London is the place where people "have" one another;
where individual persons are themselves "containing vessels." Mrs. Lowder, like her furniture, is stuffed with
"morality and money"; Kate Croy, when she is aware of
Densher, looks "more objective"! The consciousness of
such persons is often intermitted, since it is an awareness
simply of things they *have*—and when they are not jerked
by desire, or stuffed by such an awareness of their possessions, they are like dolls, splendid dolls perhaps, like Kate;
they are fit for "great social uses," occasions when it is
simply the ostensible, the vain appearance, that counts.
Milly really is in a sort of nursery of the human spirit, and
the figurative use of pink and blue chimes in with her
musing about Kate as if she were a doll. When Mrs.
Lowder speaks of Milly and Susie as having come to her

"out of a fairy-tale," the impression is confirmed that we are in a magnificent nursery full of wonderfully behaved children who are at the same time as greedy as hogs and as vain as peacocks.

The occasion turns serious when Milly and Mark stand before the Bronzino. Mark had earlier (at Mrs. Lowder's dinner party) made a tacit offer of himself, which Milly had phrased for herself as, "*I'm* the way" (XIX, 159). Since Milly herself is the truth and the life—and consequently the way—Mark's unspoken offer has already announced itself as a kind of monstrous inversion, as if he were willing to kill her in order to have her. This is precisely what he proceeds to try to do. What is crucial for Milly is the sight of the portrait itself. To be taken for the portrait, to be taken *as* the portrait, is to be taken for dead, is to be denied. She has touched, like Christ himself, in the elder James's account, the "lowest point conceivable of human degradation."[21] It is not Mark's offer which, a moment later, makes her give way; it is being taken for this picture of "a very great personage." Here is the passage which deals with her contemplation of the picture.

It was all the while for Milly as if Lord Mark had really had something other than this spoken pretext in view; as if there were something he wanted to say to her and were only —consciously yet not awkwardly, just delicately—hanging fire. At the same time it was as if the thing had practically been said by the moment they came in sight of the picture; since what it appeared to amount to was "Do let a fellow who isn't a fool take care of you a little." The thing somehow, with the aid of the Bronzino, was done; it hadn't seemed to matter to her before if he were a fool or no; but now, just where they were, she liked his not being; and it was all moreover none the worse for coming back to something of the same sound as Mrs. Lowder's so recent reminder. She too wished to take care of her—and wasn't it, *à peu prés*, what

21 *Social Significance of Our Institutions*, p. 46.

all the people with the kind eyes were wishing? Once more
things melted together—the beauty and the history and the
facility and the splendid midsummer glow: it was a sort of
magnificent maximum, the pink dawn of an apotheosis coming
so curiously soon. What in fact befell was that, as she
afterwards made out, it was Lord Mark who said nothing in
particular—it was she herself who said all. She couldn't help
that—it came; and the reason it came was that she found
herself, for the first moment, looking at the mysterious
portrait through tears. Perhaps it was her tears that made it
just then so strange and fair—as wonderful as he had said: a
face almost livid in hue, yet handsome in sadness and crowned
with a mass of hair, rolled back and high, that must, before
fading with time, have had a family resemblance to her own.
The lady in question, at all events, with her slightly
Michaelangelesque squareness, her eyes of other days, her
full lips, her long neck, her recorded jewels, her brocaded
and wasted reds, was a very great personage—only
unaccompanied by a joy. And she was dead, dead, dead.
Milly recognized her exactly in words that had nothing to do
with her. "I shall never be better than this." (XIX, 220–221)

"Once more things melted together" recalls Maggie's
sense of the "infusion" within "the great containing vessel"
and the reverberant life of all James's great houses. But
why should Milly at this moment have an "apotheosis";
that is, be elevated from a mortal state into the state of a
goddess? The elder James may assist us here. He regards
the terrible query Jesus addressed to his mother as peculiarly significant. When Jesus asks Mary, "Woman what
have I to do with thee?" He is thinking of her as the mold
or matrix into which the divine love had been poured, and
recognizing that Christ's mission had involved touching the
"lowest point of human degradation." The elder James
infers that Mary was probably "one of the basest of her
kind." [22] Milly might well have repeated the words of
Jesus to his mother at this moment. She is no longer to be

22 *Nature of Evil*, p. 184.

numbered among the daughters of Eve or selfhood; she is conscience incarnate. The spiritual analogue of this woman of appointed station is Kate Croy, not Milly. Christ's agony is, in the eyes of the elder James, the consequence of being mistaken for the most worldly and selfish creature the world had ever known. The Bronzino with its "wasted reds" is a picture of "a very great personage." With every naturalistic and emblematic resource at James's command, he has presented Milly Theale as a person incapable of assuming an identity, of being a "somebody." The resemblance that Kate and Lord Mark have found is precisely parallel in meaning with the resemblance that Brooke had asserted between his painted Madonna and Miss Evans in *Travelling Companions*—the great lady is an inversion of Milly, and she is "dead, dead, dead." Lord Mark is re-enacting the temptation of Christ, offering the kingdoms of this world which Milly had contemplated from the height of the Brünig pass (XIX, 124–125) before her descent upon London.[23] To accept his offer would be to accept an earthly kingdom from Satan. We may now see the doubleness of Milly's words. When she says, "I shall never be better than this," she is saying what is literally true, both physically and morally. She will never, on earth, have a better moment, in the sense that she will never again encounter such a test of her capability for her mission. It is also asserted that divinity is visited upon her, imposed on her, at this moment. The "pink dawn of an apotheosis" is the moment when her love, divine love, triumphs over its prime enemy, spiritual greed, or Lord Mark, who may be called Satan.[24]

Milly's physical illness recurs a moment later, as if her

[23] See *Society*, 374–377, and notes 1 and 2, above.

[24] Although the elder James distinguishes between the Devil and Satan, his use of these designations is not quite consistent. I have used the term "Satan" to refer to a creature emblematic of the idea, recurrent in the elder James, of spiritual death. (See *Substance*, pp. 252–254.)

body were unable to bear this ultimate denial of her spirit. She will never again feel as well as she did in the garden with Maud Lowder. Her increasing spiritual ascendancy is inversely proportional to her growing illness. Never, however, will she appear any more ill than she does at this moment. Even at the end Densher sees nothing but "her beauty and her strength." James apparently wants us to feel that her body has finally been so disciplined by her style that it is like the body of the risen Christ, a "glorified" natural body, as the elder James might have described it.

There is a final emblematic involution of this scene, in the passage in which Milly is overcome by an awareness from which her illness is a kind of escape. "Thus it was that, aloft there in the great gilded historic chamber and the presence of the pale personage on the wall, whose eyes all the while seemed engaged with her own, she found herself suddenly sunk in something quite intimate and humble and to which these grandeurs were strange enough witnesses. It had come up, in the form in which she had had to accept it, all suddenly, and nothing about it, at the same time, was more marked than that she had in a manner plunged into it to escape from something else." (XIX, 225) The "something else" which Milly tries to escape is something in Kate, "something that was perversely *there*, she was more and more uncomfortably finding, at least for the first moments and by some spring of its own, with every renewal of their meeting. 'Is it the way she looks to him?' she asked herself—the perversity being how she kept in remembrance that Kate was known to him."

James here presents two emblematic oppositions which are hard to interpret without close reference to the elder James's works. These are, first, Lord Mark's attempt to take Milly in the form of the Bronzino; second, Densher's use of Kate Croy to reflect him. This statement of the second opposition sounds like a distortion, since what Milly had asked herself was, "Is it the way she looks to him?" It may be recalled that Milly felt Densher's *presence* in Kate and that Kate seems "more objective" (XIX, 212) when she is full of Densher. We have to do with two emblems, both of which are being used to report the same thing about Densher: Kate is the form or (using Strether as an instance) the "tin mould" by which Densher's consciousness is constrained.

When we shift, as James does, from the form or bowl theme to the portrait theme, Kate is the portrait Densher has chosen to give him identity. The phrasing of this quotation from the dinner party scene will help to make this clear. Milly has been reflecting on the kind of relation it will be open to her to establish with Lord Mark. "She saw already . . . that there would be a good deal more of him to come for her, and that the special sign of their intercourse would be to keep herself out of the question. Everything else might come in—only never that; and with such an arrangement they would perhaps even go far." (XIX, 163) This passage makes it plain that Milly had known from the outset that she could not serve as anything but an *appearance* for Lord Mark, who "took her, kindly enough, but imperturbably, irreclaimably, for granted . . ." (XIX, 152–153). Now Kate is precisely the sort of woman a man may choose to mirror him; Milly is precisely the opposed sort, the woman to whom a man must subordinate himself if he is not to commit the ultimate sin of appropriating the godhead. This disposes of the meaning of the first emblematic opposition: We know that Lord Mark's attempt to appropriate Milly is an ultimate sin, and that Densher reflected in Kate, or using Kate as a mold, will not be a hopeless sinner.

What then, is the explanation of Milly's distress over Kate's "Densher look"? The question which causes her distress may be put this way: What can I give, how can I help Densher, if he is using Kate as Lord Mark wants to use me, as a reflection of himself? Yet a moment later she is trying, as she does throughout, to make up to Kate for having in thought blamed her. "It wasn't a fault in Kate— nor in him assuredly; and she had a horror, being generous and tender, of treating either of them as if it had been." (XIX, 225) The extent of this generosity is perhaps greater than we at first realize. Milly's highest praise for Kate, her "skylark-flight of charity," had been to assert that Kate "knew people, and people knew her, and she was the handsomest thing there . . ." (XIX, 211). To *know* people in this world is to *have* people, for one use or another, and what Milly has had to face is that Densher and Kate are related in this way.

The Bronzino scene is a kind of emblematic set piece. It contributes something, though not a great deal, to the story about which James is so insistent in his preface, the story of the little girl who is attending her first and last garden party. This surface story, though, is so encrusted with emblematic reference that if one takes it seriously, the general effect may be compared to what one might expect if Richardson's Pamela were sent to a garden party at which the décor had been contrived by Cecil Beaton.

At the beginning of the eighth part of the novel, James brings Milly and Densher together in her palace in Venice. Densher is still unaware of the strength of his feeling for her. Milly tells him that she has determined not to leave the palace: "She wouldn't let him call it keeping quiet, for she insisted that her palace—with all its romance and art and history—had set up round her a whirlwind of suggestion that never dropped for an hour. It wasn't, therefore, within such walls, confinement, it was the freedom of all the centuries: in respect to which Densher granted good-humouredly that they were then blown together, she and he, as much as she liked, through space." (XX, 174) The experience of the "diffused and reverberant" wealth of life which echoes through the great house is not of spatial movement, although Densher so characterizes it. The turn he gives Milly's figure is reminiscent of the Paolo and Francesca episode in the *Inferno*, in that it suggests lovers buffeted by desire, driven by lust. He speaks as the man who is shortly to sleep with Kate would speak.

The other strand in his consciousness, however, has grown stronger, more intricately inwoven with memories, and he begins to show a love of the very spectacle of Milly, as distinguished from his desire for Kate, and his admiration for Kate's high capacity and "the greatness of knowing so well what one wanted" (XX, 226). This is the passage in which his fresh sense of the "dove" begins to take form.

This spectacle had for him an eloquence, an authority, a felicity—he scarce knew by what name to call it—for which he said to himself that he had not consciously bargained. Her welcome, her frankness, sweetness, sadness, brightness, her disconcerting poetry, as he made shift at moments to call it, helped as it was by the beauty of her whole setting and by the perception, at the same time, on the observer's part, that this element gained from her, in a manner, for effect and harmony, as much as it gave—her whole attitude had, to his imagination, meanings that hung about it, waiting upon her, hovering, dropping and quavering forth again, like vague, faint snatches, mere ghosts of sound, of old-fashioned melancholy music. It was positively well for him, he had his times of reflecting, that he couldn't put it off on Kate and Mrs. Lowder, as a gentleman so conspicuously wouldn't, that —well, that he had been rather taken in by not having known in advance! There had been now five days of it all without his risking even to Kate alone any hint of what he ought to have known and of what in particular therefore had taken him in. The truth was doubtless that really, when it came to any free handling and naming of things, they were living together, the five of them, in an air in which an ugly effect of "blurting out" might easily be produced. He came back with his friend on each occasion to the blessed miracle of renewed propinquity, which had a double virtue in that favouring air. He breathed on it as if he could scarcely believe it, yet the time had passed in spite of this privilege, without his quite committing himself, for her ear, to any such comment on Milly's high style and state as would have corresponded with the amount of recognition it had produced in him. Behind everything, for him, was his renewed remembrance, which had fairly become a habit, that he had been the first to know her. (XX, 184-185)

I have so far spoken as if the split in Densher's awareness were simply his own, but it is in fact correspondent to the actual division between the parties, between Kate and Mrs. Lowder on the one hand, and Susan Shepherd and Luke Strett on the other. The first are the plotters, who conspire with Milly to carry on her gallant masquerade in the face of death, and also plot (with death in mind) to secure the money. There are two sources of appearance here: the motives of these plotters, which lead them to fall in with Milly's desire to appear wholly unaffected by illness; and the motives of Susan Shepherd and Sir Luke, which lead them to take what appears in Milly's behavior as a finality —as ground for love and respect. In Densher, who has drifted into Kate's plot, the first set of motives is combined with the second, a belief that in Milly as she appears to the world, there is something ineffable and adorable. This means that these two sources of appearance converge in Densher. The book moves toward a climax which may be stated in the form of the questions: What shall be the meaning of this death? Will love or greed prevail among those who survive?

The fact that Milly is dying casts a lurid light on one of the premises of James's fiction, a premise which tends to a most unfictional generality. Is life to be loved for the wondrous appearances which love can create, or is it to be loved as a snatching game, an awful, cannibalistic, gothic, nursery tale? We may of course anticipate the conclusion: Salvation lies in style, and style is the consequence of making love the source of appearance.

Two emblematic figures help Milly to help Densher as the book draws toward its end. Susan Shepherd Stringham, the first of these, is Strether's successor, "the Puritan finally disencumbered . . ." (XIX, 256). Strether had discovered the world of appearance; Susan Shepherd discovers the world as it appears if you turn and follow one whose illimitable charity makes blind faith appropriate. Susan's stories for New England periodicals had centered about heroines who had "an appetite for motive" (XIX, 201); she is still in the habit of "giving an account of herself" (XX, 107).[25] But "all categories failed her—they ceased at least to signify—when she found herself in presence of the real thing, the romantic life itself" (XIX, 107). "She had had it seemed to her, a revelation. . . ." She had already concluded that "Boston was not in the least seeing" Milly (XIX, 106), while she was: "*She* was seeing her, and she had quite the finest moment of her life in now obeying the instinct to conceal the vision. She couldn't explain it—no one would understand. They would say clever Boston things—Mrs. Stringham was from Burlington Vermont, which she boldly upheld as the real heart of New England, Boston being 'too far South'—but they would only darken counsel." (XIX, 106) (Job's friends, the obstinate defenders of God's literally righteous dispensation, are those who "darken counsel," while Job himself proclaims an unwavering faith.) The passage continues: "There could be no better proof (than this quick intellectual split) of the impression made on our friend. . . ." (XIX, 106)

Susan's role in James's emblematic scheme is that which his father assigned to the rational, or the scientific mind; it prepares us for the realization of the nullity of mere science or mere moralism, and it is finally schooled by love to devote itself wholly to God. Susan knows that she is giving up everything for Milly. Her reflections on the fact

[25] See also XIX, 169.

are reminiscent of the elder James's definition of love: "Love consists in willing what is our own to be another's, and *feeling that other's private delight as our own*." [26]

When Susan Shepherd is invited to accompany Milly to Europe, she is aware of the finality of her acceptance: "She had wanted, very consciously, from the first, to give something up for her new acquaintance, but she had now no doubt that she was practically giving up all." (XIX, 112) Her only fear is that she may "act on her companion clumsily and coarsely" (XIX, 111). "To attach herself for an indefinite time seemed a roundabout way of holding her hands off. . . . This in fact she fully recognised, and with it the degree to which she desired that the girl should lead her life, a life certain to be so much finer than that of anybody else. The difficulty, however, by good fortune, cleared away as soon as she had further recognised, as she was speedily able to do, that she Susan Shepherd— the name with which Milly for the most part amused herself—was *not* anybody else. She had renounced that character; she had now no life to lead; and she honestly believed that she was thus supremely equipped for leading Milly's own." (XIX, 113)

This earnest responsible little person had been schooled in Switzerland with Maud Manningham, now Mrs. Lowder, and thinks of herself as a "woman of the world" (XIX, 119), but of course it is only the world of righteousness she has known with any comprehension. This is comically apparent in her description of Mrs. Lowder as "the world" (XIX, 170) and her acknowledgment that she is clearly so ponderous that nothing like her has ever been shipped to Boston. In the emblematic scheme we may figure these schoolfellows as the poles of Strether's preoccupation with the world: Susan is New England's righteousness; Mrs. Lowder is England's worldliness or sensuality. At the

[26] *Society*, p. 213.

time we encounter Susan she has become a disciple of the Princess, who is the Lord's vicegerent.[27]

Sir Luke Strett, as Milly realizes, also sees her as "romantic" (XIX, 236). He has a name which recalls that of Sir Matthew Hope, the great physician of *The Portrait of a Lady* and *The Tragic Muse*. In his case the name is more apparently related to his office in the novel, since it suggests the physician who was the companion of St. Paul (Colossians, 4:14). Another Gospel reference comes to mind when we consider what Sir Luke does. In Matthew (9:12) Christ proclaims himself the physician of the sick, not of the well,[28] and Sir Luke's behavior toward Densher gives us ground for the conclusion that Sir Luke is treating Densher's moral illness. The divine wisdom cannot be felt in us until the divine love has made a place for it. Sir Luke is the representative of that wisdom in *The Wings of the Dove*, and Densher's curious feeling that he and Luke have the relation of doctor and patient is its emblematic expression (XX, 305). The most explicit account of Sir Luke's ministrations relates to Densher. They amount, oddly enough, to keeping quiet about Milly, to accompanying Densher on rambles in Venice, and silently sustaining him, forgiving him. "Nothing in his predicament was so odd as that incontestably afraid of himself, he was not afraid of Sir Luke. He had an impression, which he clung to, based on a previous taste of the visitor's company, that *he* would somehow let him off. The truth about Milly perched on his shoulders and sounded in his tread, became by the fact of his presence the name and the form, for the time, of everything in the place; but it didn't, for the difference, sit in

---

[27] For other expressions indicative of Susan Shepherd's discipleship, see XIX, 200, 219. See also Luke (8:33) for Susanna, who was among those "which ministered unto him [Christ] of their substance."
[28] See *Moralism and Christianity* (p. 130) for the elder James's application of this text.

his face, the face so squarely and easily turned to Densher at the earlier season." (XX, 300–301)

We are of course chary of accepting the notion that the "truth about Milly" which alights on Sir Luke's shoulders is a reference to the dove of the spirit which is seen to descend in the Gospels. But James meant nothing less. The "truth about Milly" is that she is mortally ill, and in this, there is a burden of guilt for Densher. The "truth about Milly" is also that she *is* Milly; she offers the possibility of a wholly new way of life that Densher is just coming to realize. It is in the interest of this positive result that Densher is "*being* let off" by Sir Luke (XX, 304). Densher's sense of Sir Luke is a foretaste of what he will finally feel about his last interview with Milly: "He had been, to his recovered sense forgiven, dedicated, blessed . . ." (XX, 343). Densher's passages with Sir Luke may be glossed by saying that one cannot be afraid of the truth when one knows it for the truth, though one may feel, as Densher does about Sir Luke, "not much less affected by his mercy than one might have been by his rigour" (XX, 305). Sir Luke's importance in the novel is considerable, but James's mode of establishing it is largely emblematic, and the unschooled reader must be content with his impression of Luke's great authority,[29] and the depth of his relation to Milly established in "their brown old temple of truth" (XIX, 241), that is, the great doctor's office.

Sir Luke is of course only one of the looming figures

[29] The coming of the storm is associated with Lord Mark's fatal mission—"the weather had changed . . . *because* of Lord Mark" (XX, 263). The weather becomes fair with the arrival of Sir Luke. Luke "the beloved physician" (Colossians, 4:14), patron of physicians and painters, is associated with the sporadic occurrence of good weather in the Fall. His day is October eighteenth. (See also the storm on the Lake Gennesaret [Luke, 8:22–24], which is stilled by Jesus.)

Through Sir Luke, Milly makes her only institutional tie with the world of appearance. He is "half like a general and half like a bishop" (XIX, 231).

which confront Densher in the course of his Venetian stay. The reader has occasion to feel that the great doctor, Mrs. Stringham, Lord Mark, Milly herself, and the Venetian scene are functioning both within and without Densher's consciousness, or that that consciousness itself consists in an awareness of relations among these persons and this place—and nothing more. One of James's means of noting the successive stages of his awareness of these persons is to shift his vocabulary as he enters a new phase. When Kate's plot and his conquest of Kate are still in the forefront of his mind, he talks or muses in commercial or acquisitive figures; when he has become a Strether, abandoning greed for righteousness, he uses the terms of moralism; and the last phase is signalized by his attempt to get Kate to see that the wonderful spectacle of Milly enacting her sacrifice had been *in itself* a consummation. The last vocabulary, that is, is beyond words: It is vision. Yet Kate sees only a series of appearances which may or may not indicate that they are to get the money.

Densher, while ministering to Milly's magnificence, as if to admire it were a part of the plot, comes to admire it for itself and to believe that the source of this wonderful spectacle is love, and love alone. Maud and Kate grow remote, ancillary, like the crooked labor bosses one might bribe to get a splendid building finished. What they had taken for mere (though sentimentally touching) appearance becomes his reality. He and Kate drift far apart before they have found any means to acknowledge the fact. When they meet in London, Kate says that Densher has fallen in love with Milly, but this is not the fact, since it implies that he has fallen out of love with Kate. Rather, he has found another kind of love. And when Kate presses him to describe his last meeting with Milly, Densher says:

"She showed nothing but her beauty and her strength."

"Then," his companion asked, "what's the use of her strength?"

He seemed to look about for a use he could name; but he had soon given it up. "She must die, my dear, in her own extraordinary way." (XX, 329)

This juxtaposition tells us more. The "use" of Milly's strength is not bargain and exchange; it is in being Milly —in giving—but this has no force for Kate in whose eyes Milly is a means. Once more, Densher tries to explain what Sir Luke had done for Milly and for him. He had treated Densher as he had *before* Milly "turned her face to the wall" (XX, 323). He had, Densher says, "understood." Kate asks: "But understood what?" Densher replies: "That I had meant awfully well."

"Ah, and made *her* understand? I see," she went on as he said nothing. "But how did he convince her?"

Densher put down his cup and turned away. "You must ask Sir Luke."

He stood looking at the fire and there was a time without sound. "The great thing," Kate then resumed, "is that she's satisfied. Which," she continued, looking across at him, "is what I've worked for."

"Satisfied to die in the flower of her youth?"

"Well, at peace with you." (XX, 332)

The gulf between Densher's having "meant awfully well" and the thing Kate has "worked for" is impassable. Sir Luke has not of course persuaded Milly of Densher's good faith. He has simply allowed Densher to perceive that he regards him as aware of "the truth about Milly," of her extraordinary value as a person, her peril, and her love for Densher. Densher has realized all the values of the created scene in Venice and taken them for the actuality. Kate has seen only what will serve her—seen it with great clarity, true, but never as a good in itself.

The Wings of the Dove has at its center the contrast between those who apprehend the lives of others as aesthetic finalities, art in life, and those who analyze the lives of others simply with a view to self-aggrandizement. Milly's moral goodness seems to entail the perfection of her manners, and even of her furnishings. This is one more way of enforcing the contrast between the two loves. It is only under the aegis of love that one can "live." Milly alone has lived because she has lived in and for Densher, as Maggie Verver comes to live in and for the Prince. Densher himself will be rescued from the world of the dead appropriators when he recognizes this.

As is always the case, the most direct clues to comprehension of the Jamesian crossroad of impulse such as Densher are afforded by his references to his fear of himself,[30] and the particular appearances that inspire his fear. Densher first feels this fear during Mrs. Stringham's visit. He notes it once more when he is about to go to the station to meet Sir Luke, and he thinks of his fear as a fear of self-betrayal—as if he might give himself and the *plot* away. A moment later he is thinking that perhaps the best reason for meeting Sir Luke is that he has a chance to feel as Susan had described his feeling earlier—to feel that he and Sir Luke shared their concern for Milly without in the least articulating it. The next occasion on which he feels this fear has been dealt with above. He is now afraid of himself, but *not* of Sir Luke, and it is now plain that what he had thought a fear of giving away the plot is a fear of his own impulses. These impulses had been completely represented in all their ugliness and greed by the figure of Mark sitting in Florian's Café (XX, 262). "The weather had changed, the rain was ugly, the wind wicked, the sea impossible, *because* of Lord Mark. It was because of him *a fortiori*, that the palace was closed." (XX, 263) His first recognition of the figure seated within is of a naked purposiveness: "This wider view showed him *all* Lord Mark—Lord Mark as encountered, several weeks before, the day of the first visit of each to Palazzo Leporelli. For

[30] See XX, 295.

it had been all Lord Mark that was going out, on that occasion, as he came in—he had felt it, in the hall, at the time. . . ." (XX, 262) He is at first comforted by the difference in their conduct which he guesses. "It was for all the world—and he drew a long breath on it—as if a special danger for him had passed." (XX, 265) For three days thereafter he keeps quiet, reassured by the contrast between Lord Mark and himself.

Densher's "middle years" are extraordinarily compressed, as they no doubt must be when love *constrains* one to accept it. *The Wings of the Dove* treats a case of redemption, and redemption is, so to speak, a far rougher and more peremptory process than being "made social out of moral," that is, being regenerated. The Prince and Charlotte in *The Golden Bowl* become regenerate; Densher, however, simply learns what such a state may come to mean in the future; he is himself left alone, with only Milly's spirit to comfort him. The three days he passes after seeing Lord Mark in the Café comprise his "middle years," the period in which, like Strether, he believes in the theory of the sheep and the goats. If Lord Mark is to blame, he is not. "It was *he*, the brute who had stumbled into just the wrong inspiration and who had therefore produced, for the very person he had wished to hurt, an impunity that was comparative innocence, that was almost like purification." (XX, 265)

The vocabulary of righteousness replaces, as I have noted, the vocabulary of bargain and exchange. He has said of Kate, for example, that she is "good for" what he wants; and he is continuously aware of the "treasure" of memory which fills his rooms, where he and Kate had consummated their bargain. He keeps still, and rejoices in the contrast between Mark and himself: "The day or two passed—stretched to three days; and with the effect, extraordinarily, that Densher felt himself in the course of them washed but the more clean." (XX, 265–266) But when Susan Shepherd comes to see him, his fear of himself, his *fear of himself as Lord Mark*, begins to mount: "He knew soon enough that it was of himself that he was afraid, and that even, if he didn't take care, he should infallibly be more so." (XX, 282) To be afraid of oneself is to recognize death in oneself; while to overcome that fear is to die to selfhood. Densher recognizes this in saying to Susan Shepherd: "I *am* dead." (XX, 272) This sequence of feelings in Densher contributes to the momentousness of his declaration to Kate after his return to London. Kate has just said that if Susan has seen through their plot he need not be afraid, because Susan too is fond of him. To this he replies: "I'm not afraid." (XX, 330) The reply covers far more ground than Kate knows, can ever know in fact. What he is saying is that he is not afraid of himself. Riven man though he is, at once drawn to Kate and possessed by his sense of Milly, he need no longer entertain the fear of his own impulses. He will, in the end, become as dependent on the "Life" as the elder Henry James.

Toward the end of the novel its figures arrange themselves somewhat statically, as if for a final exemplification of the meaning of the interrelation of human impulses in the story. Milly's death falls, for an apparent emblematic reason, on Christmas. Densher is reborn on this night, and he is thereafter animated by Milly's spirit. Meanwhile the other characters, who have escaped from the hells, fall back into them. Lord Mark, Satan (whom the elder James distinguishes from the Devil), falls back on Mrs. Lowder; Lionel Croy, the Devil, retreats to the home of his daughter, the "church" of anti-Christ. Densher asks Kate whether it was "want" which had driven Croy home.

"No, not of food, of necessary things—not even, so far as his appearance went, of money. He looked as wonderful as ever. But he was—well, in terror."

"In terror of what?"

"I don't know. Of somebody—of something. He wants, he says, to be quiet. But his quietness is awful."

She suffered, but he couldn't not question. "What does he do?"

It made Kate herself hesitate. "He cries." (XX, 383)

The reader gets no further explanation. But in the terms of the elder James this is all we need. The death of Christ produces an "instant equilibrium" [31] in the heavens and hells; the possibility of redemption for all restrains those creatures who had heretofore been able to go to and fro in the earth, and to walk up and down in it (Job, 1:7).

Some time after writing this account of Lionel Croy I read a letter of the elder James's to the New York *Daily Tribune* (January 16, 1855), which is headed "London, Christmas-day, 1855." In it he writes: "European countries are full of traditional customs at Christmas, which indicate a sort of instinctive popular apprehension of the great mystery of Redemption. At Dewsbury in this country, they toll the bell at midnight to celebrate *the death of the devil*, and in many other localities similar customs exist with similar intensity of meaning."

Densher, who has sat all night through on Christmas Eve with Milly's unopened letter before him, is reborn in Milly's persuasion. Milly's last act as Densher's redeemer is to complete her subjection to the world of appearance by convincing Mark that Densher loves her, rather than Kate (XX, 381). This lie becomes the truth; Densher does in the end love her. He sets out to find and save Kate, to consummate a marriage between wisdom and love and the world—to reconcile appearance with reality. Densher fails, but his failure foreshadows the successful consummation of a similar marriage in *The Golden Bowl*, brought about by what would be unimaginable in this novel; a marriage between Luke Strett and Kate, which would have the ef-

[31] See Chapter X, note 39.

fect of forcing her to see what in the world is worth having and what is not. The ground the novel offers for Densher's failure is, most simply, Kate's perception that he is Milly's man; that her attempt to get everything (XIX, 72–73) has failed. She says of Milly: "She died for you that you might understand her. From that hour you *did*." (XX, 403) Kate goes further: "And I do now. She did it *for* us." The "dove," as Kate again calls her, "covers" them. As it is said in Luke (1:35), "the power of the Highest shall overshadow thee. . . ." But Kate cannot live under Milly's dominion. She is still of the other party. She is as "proud as the deuce" (XX, 389), her father, and must have all or nothing. The hells have not yet been abolished.

The Ambassadors and *The Wings of the Dove* deal with two modes of redemption: first, the false mode, the Old Testament mode, obedience to the Law, which turns out to mean through righteousness; second, the true, though incomplete, because personal rather than social, redemption through love. A third mode is that of love and creative law or wisdom, and it is communal redemption, or regeneration for all.

What is the standing of these first two novels in relation to the others in which James pushed the attempt to make moral principle and aesthetic practice coincide? To my sense these novels cannot be reckoned a part of a "major phase." In them the writer's gifts were not happily distributed. Something was sacrificed, though much was gained. The inward complexity of Isabel Archer was sacrificed; the outward complexity of *The Princess Casamassima* was sacrificed. Principle and practice work, as it were, too harmoniously. The difficulty of the material has vanished, and only the difficulty of the internal structure remains. That this was for James a wonderful challenge and that he rose to it magnificently we must acknowledge. But the acknowledgment need not take the form of saying that a genius discernibly feeding on its own roots is in a state of ripeness. There are many moments, especially in *The Wings of the Dove*, about which it is meaningful to say that James knew too much about too little. At these moments his very virtuosity suffices to show that he is asking too much of his somewhat attenuated ethos. The bootstrap myth lets him down.

X The Golden Bowl

PRINCE AMERIGO, IN WHOM MAGGIE VERVER DELIGHTS BE-
cause he is descended from the ostensible discoverer of
America who gave his name to the world from which she
comes, first appears in *The Golden Bowl* as the walking
sum of history.[1] His name figures inclusiveness, since it
begins with Alpha and ends with Omega.[2] He recalls that
Maggie had asked, "What was it else . . . that made me
originally think of you? It wasn't—as I should suppose you
must have seen—what you call your unknown quantity,
your particular self. It was the generations behind you,

[1] For Maggie's expression of pleasure in the Prince's ancestry, see
XXIII, 79–80. The figurative use of boats and voyages reinforces
the emphasis on the Prince as a descendant of Amerigo Vespucci,
the ostensible discoverer of America—who, in the end, discovers
America itself (XXIII, 14, 22, 27).

[2] See Revelation, 1:8, 11, and *Logic*, p. 37: "And when we shall see
Nature's order and harmony, we shall assuredly see her reflecting in
every glorified lineament and feature, the LORD, or that Divine
NATURAL man who is the Alpha and Omega, the Beginning and the
Ending of creation, who is, and who was, and who is to come, the
All-powerful." The novelist's clear intention in naming Christopher
Newman of *The American* was to refer to a discoverer of the Old
World who hailed from the New World; here he uses a name figur-
ing inclusiveness in order to suggest that the Prince is at once the
sum of history and its emblematic consummation, a union of Europe
(appearance) with America (reality).

the follies and the crimes, the plunder and the waste. . . .
Where, therefore . . . without your archives, annals, in-
famies, would you have been?" (XXIII. 9–10) To com-
press all nature and all history within the compass of the
human form is the goal of providence.[3] Prince Amerigo
is an analogue of the house of life. He has what Maggie
calls an "unknown quantity," his "particular self." [4] His
selfhood is nothing more nor less than his relation to Charlotte Stant, the "twentieth woman" (XXIII, 50). This implies that Prince Amerigo has been formed in the image
of the lordly male, whose sense of himself depends on his
ability to subordinate women to himself, and that he is
therefore obliged to use them as mirrors or molds to give
him identity. The women who appear subordinate are
themselves emblematic of the selfhood or greed.

The representative character of the figures with which
this novel deals is much more directly and openly conveyed than it is in *The Wings of the Dove*. One of the
reasons for this is simply that the domestic situation of *The
Golden Bowl* lends itself much more readily to indefinite
emblematic expansion than does the situation of the dying
American heiress betrayed by European adventurers. The
first few chapters are very much like a prologue in which
each of the characters is exhibited in the round.

Prince Amerigo epitomizes history. He has no capacity
for self-realization, no irritable consciousness; he has simply the generic quality of the aristocrat, the ability to take
for granted his position and the whole train of the past
which informs his manner.[5] He is not aware that he has

[3] See *Substance*, pp. 250–251: ". . . our hitherto neglected body shall
become the only visible and acknowledged temple of God. . . ."
[4] Maggie's perception of the nature of this self in the Prince is reserved for the second volume; Milly Theale sees Densher *in* Kate
Croy rather early in *The Wings of the Dove*. (See XIX, 189–190,
and XIX, 207–229 *passim*.)
[5] See "*The Velvet Glove*," in *The Finer Grain*, for a rather explicit
account of the meaning of aristocracy.

done anything unprecedented in taking an American heiress for a wife: "What was it but history, and of *their* kind very much, to have the assurance of the enjoyment of more money than the palace-builder himself could have dreamed of?" (XXIII, 10)

There is, however, a qualification. The "element that bore him up" was money, yes, but into it, he reflects, "Maggie scattered, on occasion, her exquisite coloring drops. They were of the colour—of what on earth? of what but the extraordinary American good faith? They were of the colour of her innocence, and yet at the same time of her imagination, with which their relation, his and these people's, was all suffused." (XXIII, 10) These two, the Prince and Maggie, have been brought into relation by the ostensible, the "Vain Appearance"—to use the phrase employed in *The Ambassadors*—that is, by the Prince's wonderful heritage and Maggie's money. It is this additional thing, Maggie's innocence, or "the extraordinary American good faith," which seems to make their relation personal. But it does not in fact do so. The good faith is no more capable of discrimination than is the money. The good faith is extended to all. Maggie seems at the outset to believe that money and good faith can do anything for anyone.

We are dealing once again, as in *The Wings of the Dove*, with a group of related impulses. We have already encountered Adam Verver's power, Maggie's innocence, which is, so to speak, its impassioned expression, and the Prince as a kind of quintessential commodity, the sum of history. We are aware that these impulses do not at first comprehend one another. Maggie, for instance, has no sense of the Prince's need to get identity from women, which shows in him as an assurance "that he had after all gained more from women than he had ever lost by them" and that his "books" show "a balance in his favour that he could pretty well as a rule take for granted" (XXIII, 350–351).

Our sense of the ignorance of each of these impulses or natures of the others is matched by a sense of their power. Innocence backed by unlimited money is a very great power, but it appears that it cannot find expression save in buying things up; it has no meaning without Europe and the things Europe contains. Even in these first few pages the reader may feel that the problem of the novel has been established: What is the middle term between the Ververs and the world which they are buying up, buying up, that is, in the measure in which it has found form, in art, in manners, or in whatever may be said to *represent* the meaning of human history? (The Prince, for example, is not what Santayana calls the "sensuous pulp" of history. He is rather its consequence; through him the past works, or is represented.)

Some of the things which James asks us to accept at the outset are hard to swallow. What, for instance, is the quality of Adam Verver's wonderful taste? Does the novelist ask us to take it as a datum that this millionaire is unerring in his selection of objects of art? The conversation the Prince is recollecting while he walks toward Mrs. Assingham's, at the beginning of the novel, raises a second question. He had said to Maggie:

"You Americans are almost incredibly romantic."
"Of course we are. That's just what makes everything so nice for us."
"Everything?" He had wondered.
"Well, everything that's nice at all. The world, the beautiful world—or everything in it that *is* beautiful." (XXIII, 11)

We have already gathered that it is within the purview of the father and daughter that crimes and follies and wastes may somehow produce valuable things—this is true of the Prince himself. Still, it is a puzzle how such an inclusive "good faith" can absorb objects with this sort of history and be untouched by their "mixed" origins. Can we in the least believe that the project Maggie describes as having grown like "the programme of a charity performance"—the collection of objects of art to be housed in the museum in an American city—has in the mind of its projector a meaning commensurate with the extraordinary human achievements it involves? Maggie's phrase suggests an emblematic rather than a directly fictional answer. The Swedenborgian trinity of love, wisdom, and use appears to be involved. A parallel phrase employed by the elder James in *The Logic of Creation* runs, "programme of the operations of the Divine Spirit," and we shall later have reason to identify Maggie with love or charity, Adam with wisdom, and their joint activity with "use" or "operations."

We learn something more explicit from the Prince in these opening pages. He has described Adam as more "natural" than himself, as a "galantuomo." He discusses his own title to the latter designation in this passage: "Say, however, I *am* a galantuomo—which I devoutly hope: I'm like a chicken, at best, chopped up and smothered in sauce, cooked down as a *crème de volaille*, with half the parts left out. Your father's the natural fowl running about the *bassecour*. His feathers, his movements, his sounds—those are the parts that, with me, are left out." (XXIII, 8)

In *The Ambassadors* James had described Chad both as a sauce and a comestible turned out of a mold, and it appeared that Mme de Vionnet was responsible for his taste and his shape. When we relate the Prince's description of himself to this earlier figure, it becomes clear that the Prince is likewise contained, or given form, by a woman, and that Adam enjoys a distinctive sort of life which does not involve being formed by a woman. We must be alert, then, for evidence as to the difference between Adam's relation to Maggie and the Prince's to Charlotte Stant.

But we cannot at this point say that we know much

more of Adam Verver as a "natural fowl" than that he is prepared to gobble up the Prince, whom Maggie affectionately refers to as a *"morceau de musée"* (XXIII, 12). We are carried much closer to our sense of the "natural" when it occurs to the Prince as he muses that he would like "to do something or other, before it was too late, for himself" (XXIII, 20). His "too late" does not imply that there is nothing to be gained by marrying Maggie, but that action really on his own account is likely to be far less frequent in the future. It seems unlikely that he ever has acted for himself; he has simply followed conventions. A passage from an earlier part of his reflections is apropos here. "If there was one thing in the world the young man at this juncture clearly intended it was to be much more decent as a son-in-law than lots of fellows he could think of had shown themselves in that character. He thought of these fellows, from whom he was so to differ, in English; he used, mentally, the English term to describe his difference, for, familiar with the tongue from his earliest years, so that no note of strangeness remained with him either for lip or ear, he found it convenient, in life, for the greatest number of relations. He found it convenient, oddly, even for his relation with himself. . . ." (XXIII, 5) Action appropriate to one's position, action appropriate to certain standards which other "fellows" visibly violate— this, for the Prince, is clearly customary. He sets off to visit Mrs. Assingham, who has done much for him, and the determination to acknowledge this is in a sense his only *act*, save prowling for the gift with Charlotte, up to the moment at which he perceives the shattered fragments of the bowl on the polished floor.

What cannot be acknowledged to Maggie or to his prospective father-in-law is that he is indebted to Mrs. Assingham for the opportunity to court Maggie. She has "made" his marriage (XXIII, 20–21). To my first tentative posing of the question of the book the reader has a tentative answer: The link between the associated power and innocence of the Ververs and the Prince is the intelligence of Mrs. Assingham. She it is who has seen how the two worlds may be united; who has created a situation in which the Prince may live up to his name by making a specious discovery of America and in which the Ververs may crown their quest for representations by acquiring this consummately finished product of European civilization.

The curious quality I have attributed to the Prince's musings, that they introduce us to a world of "natures" or of impulses figured in persons, persists in the scene with Mrs. Assingham.[6] Of course the names we have so far given these natures are not quite commensurate with one another. The Prince is history, manners, tradition. Maggie is innocence, her father the pure power of money; together they represent American "good faith." And we may even now ask whether the collocation does not involve the assertion that this "good faith" depends equally on money and innocence.

Mrs. Assingham may be called the "church" of the novel. She has put her wits to the problem of ending the "adventures" (XXIII, 27) of the Prince, Colonel Bob, and herself; she will shortly begin to devote herself to the task of finding a place for Charlotte; and thereafter she will busy herself with the fundamental job of keeping up appearances. In her desire to keep her moral books balanced we find something reminiscent of Mrs. Newsome of *The Ambassadors*; in her eye for the main chance and her interest

[6] Maggie, while reflecting, after she has become aware of the relations between Charlotte and the Prince, on Charlotte's ability to keep up appearances, uses "virtue" in a sense close to the Latin *virtus:* "Charlotte had done that . . . during the numerous months of their [Charlotte's and Adam's] hymeneal absence from England, the period prior to that wonderful reunion of the couples, in the interest of the larger play of all the virtues of each, which was now bearing, for Mrs. Verver's stepdaughter at least, such remarkable fruit." (XXIV, 137)

in keeping up appearances we find something reminiscent of Mrs. Lowder. It appears that this final "church" is somehow a cross between those of the preceding novels. Her origins accord with this impression, for although she looks like "a daughter of the South, or still more of the East," James assures us that she is "neither a pampered Jewess nor a lazy Creole; New York had been recordedly her birthplace and 'Europe' punctually her discipline." She has a "flagrant appearance," with which she contends by making her clothes so startling that her person seems less so. On this account she wears yellow, purple, crimson, and gold. "Her character was attested by the second movement of her face, which convinced the beholder that her vision of the humours of the world was not supine, not passive. She enjoyed, she needed the warm air of friendship, but the eyes of the American city looked out, somehow, for the opportunity of it, from under the lids of Jerusalem." (XXIII, 34–35)

This description is rather a riddle in the text, and the details I have extracted are not immediately helpful. James makes it clear that her marriage to an English colonel is an earlier, or even the earliest, form of the marital alliance between America and Europe. This permits the reader to suppose that Mrs. Assingham's worldly wisdom about America and Europe is to be put to a new test in the novel, and this is the fact. But the emblematic significance of this fact—that Mrs. Assingham represents the wrong way of uniting Europe with America and that the Ververs represent the right way—is still hidden from the reader. It may be surmised that James is once more teasing us, as he does with Lionel Croy. Fanny Assingham's original is no less a figure than the whore of Babylon, who is described in Revelation in a way that makes her highly appropriate to the role of the culminating "church" in the system of the elder James, and consequently in this apocalyptic novel. Before going further with the exploration of the emblematic definition of these impulses or natures in *The Golden Bowl*, let us see how they are complemented in *The Wings of the Dove*.

Innocence and the power of money, serving, as in Adam Verver's case, to the most gently beneficent ends, as a part of one's character rather than as a separable instrument—these are apparent in Milly Theale, who is also an instance of American good faith. Adam Verver's other dimension, that of the taste which is the wisdom of the "great and deep and high little man" (XXIV, 274), is less clearly paralleled in the connoisseurship of Luke Strett, exhibited in his rambles with Densher in Venice.

Mrs. Lowder's role as the focus of relationships in the world of the appropriators is closely paralleled in the activities of Fanny Assingham, whose name carries forward the unpleasant suggestiveness of "Condrip" and recalls the cloacal function of the "church." [7] In discussing Mrs. Condrip I spoke of her as the literal church, subordinate in function to Mrs. Lowder ("Britannia"). Mrs. Lowder suggests, in all her bourgeois ugliness and heavy moralism, the Victorian era. Mrs. Assingham, her successor, is less bumptious, far more concerned with diplomacy and questions of adjustment to a diminished British power—James calls her a "helmeted trident-shaking pax Britannica" (XXIV, 209). The Establishment seems to have no importance whatever in *The Golden Bowl;* however, Catholicism has come to the fore. Maggie, her father, and the Prince are all Catholics. Mrs. Assingham may therefore be thought

[7] Eric Partridge dates the use of "Fanny" for the female pudendum back to 1860; its American use to refer to the buttocks occurs in 1910, but it is surmised that the usage is somewhat older. "Ass" seems, in this instance, to be reinforced by "ham." For the whore, popularly identified with Catholicism, who is "arrayed in purple and scarlet" and gold and pearls, see Revelation, 17–20. James's curious emphasis on Mrs. Assingham's *not* being "passive" or "supine" seems to be a reference to the fact that the great whore is said to be *sitting* on the beast. James calls London "the great grey Babylon" (a phrase quoted by F. W. Dupee, *Henry James*, pp. 135–136).

of as succeeding to the functions of both Mrs. Newsome of *The Ambassadors* and Mrs. Condrip of *The Wings of the Dove.*

With respect to the question of marriage, so important in *The Golden Bowl,* there is a fundamental likeness to the events of *The Wings of the Dove.* Just as the Prince is parted from Charlotte and united to Maggie, so is Densher parted from Kate and united, after the fashion of Henry James and Minny Temple, to Milly. In both cases the lovers are separated by the realization on the part of the man that he is loved by another in a mode of which Kate and Charlotte are quite incapable.

James has led us to suspect either that he is too weary to invent or that he has an intention which ought to be looked into. Charlotte and Kate are too similar to go unquestioned. Does James mean to have these tall, slightly square girls, who coerce men in parks, dominate his fiction? Are they in some intended way related? And again, there is the functional likeness between Sir Luke Strett and Adam Verver—each provides sagacious assistance to an American girl bent on redeeming somebody; and the functional likeness between Mrs. Newsome, Mrs. Lowder, and Mrs. Assingham—each a representation of the view of the world that a particular society prizes, hence the proponents of its chief institutions; and, finally, the recurrence of the man who is somehow to be saved—Chad, Densher, and the Prince. All these likenesses pose a problem for those who assume that James's imagination was working to ends it had clearly seen.

We may now go back to the Prince's visit to thank Mrs. Assingham. When he reaches that lady's dwelling, he is full of polite appeals for more assistance. Mrs. Assingham may serve him further by helping him to see. "I'm sure, after all, that the more you're with me the more I shall understand. It's the only thing in the world I want. I'm excellent, I really think, all round—except that I'm stupid. I can do pretty

well anything I see. But I've got to see it first." (XXIII, 30)
Mrs. Assingham discovers that the Prince's conception of
his particular difficulty is that he lacks the "moral sense." "I
mean always as you others consider it. I've of course something that in our poor dear backward old Rome sufficiently
passes for it. But it's no more like yours than the tortuous
stone staircase—half-ruined into the bargain—in some castle
of our *quattrocento* is like the 'lightning elevator' in one of
Mr. Verver's fifteen-storey buildings. Your moral sense
works by steam—it sends you up like a rocket. Ours is
slow and steep and unlighted, with so many of the steps
missing that—well, that it's as short in almost any case to
turn round and come down again." (XXIII, 31) He thinks
that this "moral sense" will carry him to the region of
Maggie's innocence and Adam's power.

Of Mrs. Assingham, "for whom life was multitudinous
detail" (XXIII, 35), one may say what Maria Gostrey says
of herself, that there is nothing she doesn't know (XXI,
18). She is promptly prepared to discriminate on the question of Charlotte Stant's rather disconcerting arrival in
London. It doesn't "properly" concern the Prince. The
adverb amuses him; he thinks it a good instance of the
working of the "moral sense" (XXIII, 37).

Later on, at Fawns, he makes good his statement that
he will always want Fanny's eyes (XXIII, 30). She is "in
charge of his mere intelligence." "She was there to keep
him quiet—it was Amerigo's own description of her influence; and it would only have needed a more visible
disposition to unrest in him to make the account perfectly
fit. Fanny herself limited indeed, she minimised her office;
you didn't need a jailor, she contended, for a domesticated
lamb tied up with pink ribbon. This wasn't an animal to be
controlled—it was an animal to be, at the most, educated.
She admitted accordingly that she was educative—which
Maggie was so aware that she herself inevitably wasn't; so
it came round to being true that what she was most in

charge of was his mere intelligence. This left, goodness knew, plenty of different calls for Maggie to meet—in a case in which so much pink ribbon, as it might be symbolically named, was lavished on the creature." (XXIII, 161-162) Mrs. Assingham fills a real domestic need, "Amerigo always being, as the Princess was well aware, conveniently amenable to his friend's explanations, beguilements, reassurances, and perhaps in fact rather more than less dependent on them as his new life—since that was his own name for it—opened out" (XXIII, 160).

Let us examine some of these details. The Prince says of himself that he lacks the "moral sense," and this suggests his emblematic role. As William James puts it in his father's *Literary Remains*, "Mr. James, following Swedenborg, often calls the creature abstracted from moral consciousness the Adam, the moral consciousness being the Eve." [8] Prince Amerigo—history—is, taken by himself, a handsome abstract of the whole of the beautiful horrible world; he becomes history when he is stirred up to activity by one of the long line of Charlotte Stants he has known. And it follows that the form of his relation to society must always be given by some "church" or other. This is Mrs. Assingham, whose office consists in furnishing "explanations," or, to use the punning expression of which James is so fond, *keeping up appearances*. At the moment when Mrs. Assingham is represented as furnishing these explanations to the "lamb" swathed in "pink ribbon," who calls this new existence his "new life" (*vita nuova*), the principal characters of the novel are arranged as if for emblematic exemplification. Maggie and Adam, love and wisdom, are conferring apart under the tree of life; Amerigo, the deluded Adam, is being fed from the "tree of the knowledge of good and evil" by Mrs. Assingham.[9] His Eve or

---

[8] *Remains*, p. 40n.
[9] "Two trees grow in the garden of the created intelligence, which cannot be eaten of simultaneously: one called *the tree of the knowl-*

selfhood is still in the wings; she will presently enter and effect that liaison with him which makes the falsity of uniting man to God through the "church" and "state" (Colonel Assingham) obvious.

Using the emblematic clues that have been listed, we may now summarize the situation of the Prince. He is the first Adam, who is incapable of understanding invisible things; he must *see* to understand, as he tells Mrs. Assingham. Bound as he is to the world of appearance, he must be awakened to the moral life of righteousness by the self-hood, and the church which is its institutional expression. Only after he has enjoyed a liaison with his Eve will he be able to comprehend the nullity and vileness of the satis-factions his Eve urges him to seek; and only then will he understand the completely inverted character of the knowledge Mrs. Assingham has offered him. He will then see that what he calls his "new life" [10] amounts to an appropriation of the godhead. After this discovery he will be transformed into the "Lamb" of Revelation, swathed in

---

edge of good and evil, i.e. the knowledge of the finite, whose fruit is death; the other *the tree of life*, i.e. the knowledge of the infinite, whose fruit is immortal life. Or to drop figurative and confine our-selves to scientific speech, there are two sources of knowledge prac-ticable to the human bosom: 1. Experience, which gives us self-knowledge; 2. Revelation, which gives us divine knowledge. And by Adam's being told 'that he should die if he ate of the tree of the knowledge of good and evil,' is symbolized that law of human destiny which makes the seeming life but most lethal death we encounter in ourselves, or reap from our physical and moral experience, altogether subordinate and ministerial to the seeming death but most vital life we realize in God, or reap from our spiritual and historic culture—from our social and aesthetic regeneration." (*Secret*, p. 150.)

[10] Dante's *Vita Nuova* is in praise of "ladies who have intelligence of love," and might seem to satisfy the condition—that we are to live and write under the inspiration of a woman—which is laid down by the Henry Jameses. But the fact that Beatrice is "European," that she subordinates herself to a church which is, in the view of the two Jameses, idolatrous and full of both greed and righteousness, is deci-sive. See Chapter V, above, for the young man who seeks a portrait of his "blessed lady," and turns out to be the narrator's other self.

the pink ribbon emblematic of Maggie's good faith, or illimitable charity.

The novel is a fable almost as much out of time as the original story of Adam and Eve, and all its episodes imply the whole emblematic narrative. Turning back now to the Prince's reflections at the beginning of the novel, we find James employing the imagery appropriate to a descendant of Amerigo Vespucci. The Prince figures his adventure in marrying Maggie as a voyage reminiscent of *The Narrative of Arthur Gordon Pym*, "by Allan Poe, his prospective wife's countryman. . . ." Pym, drifting farther toward the Pole than any man had ever done, "found at a given moment before him a thickness of white air that was like a dazzling curtain of light, concealing as darkness conceals, yet of the colour of milk or of snow. There were moments when he felt his own boat move upon some such mystery. The state of mind of his new friends, including Mrs. Assingham herself, had resemblances to a great white curtain." (XXIII, 22) This figure inverts the "iridescence" or the "diffused and reverberant" quality of the house of life. It is an image of purity, an image of the awful moral pretensions of the righteous. It has nothing to do with Adam and Maggie, but at this stage the Prince must assume that it has, since Mrs. Assingham, who is the mediator between the world of sense and the world of the spirit, offers him the only connection he can *see*. That is, the visible church contains and represents the invisible church—Maggie's love and Adam's wisdom. Adam and Maggie, by subjecting themselves to Mrs. Assingham in order to save mankind, have allowed it *to appear* that they are righteous.

In the second volume Maggie, trying to protect herself against Charlotte, finds it expedient to use Mrs. Assingham just as the Prince does—to define the form of the experience that all these persons are sharing: "Our young woman's idea in particular was that her safety, her escape from being herself suspected of suspicion, would proceed from this friend's power to cover, to protect and, as might be, even showily to represent her—represent, that is, her relation to the form of the life they were all actually leading." (XXIV, 100) This is probably James's most explicit statement as to the function of his "church."

Mrs. Assingham affords what was earlier called a "middle term" between Maggie's *caritas*, the wisdom which is represented in Adam's infallible taste, and the awful power of their millions—and the beautiful and wicked world which the Prince and Charlotte consummate. The Prince finds Mrs. Assingham indispensable and somewhat puzzling as well. Her moralism, which he compares to a steam elevator, her righteousness, which is like an impenetrable curtain of whiteness, are unintelligible to the purely sensuous Latin mind. He does not know how Mrs. Assingham's dodge is worked. What has Mrs. Assingham to gain but a kind of hypocritical self-esteem? Yet, since he is laboring under the misapprehension that Mrs. Assingham offers the only way to deal with the Ververs, he feels that he must follow her lead. Indeed, Mrs. Assingham herself is not aware that her dodge will not work in this case. She has an unlimited belief in the efficacy of intelligence to arrange matters decently. As Maggie puts it to Adam later on, Mrs. Assingham's morality is chiefly a matter of the obligation to use one's wits: " 'She only thinks people are sometimes fools,' Maggie developed; 'she doesn't seem to think so much about their being wrong—wrong, that is, in the sense of being wicked. She doesn't,' the Princess further adventured, 'quite so much mind their being wicked.' " (XXIV, 261) Mrs. Assingham's esteem for the sort of intelligence that the elder James (a trifle quaintly) calls "scientific" is unlimited. Moral self-esteem of this order is a possession she will fight to keep, as we discover when she breaks the golden bowl. Most of her conversations with her husband, the Colonel, are a kind of stock-taking. Has she or has she not succeeded in serving both God and

Mammon? The Colonel's role is invariable. His cigar points only one question. How can anyone serve both? Mammon must come first.[11]

Charlotte's reappearance is disturbing to Fanny. It means that she must arrange her pieces anew and play the game differently. But she has a faith that by the use of her wits and the preservation of the "forms," anything can be done, no matter how difficult it seems. Addressing the Colonel, she observes: "But stupidity pushed to a certain point *is*, you know, immorality. Just so what is morality but high intelligence?" (XXIII, 88) And again, to the same patient auditor, in what is a part of the remarkably concise and accurate summary of the worldly view of the situation of the two couples which she makes at the end of the first volume, she speaks of the adulterous Charlotte:

> "She observes the forms," said Fanny Assingham.
> "With the Prince?"
> "*For* the Prince. And with the others," she went on.
> "With Mr. Verver—wonderfully. But above all with Maggie. And the forms"—she had to do even *them* justice —"are two thirds of conduct. Say he had married a woman who would have made a hash of them." (XXIII, 390–391)

The high capacity of this "church" is exercised exclusively in bringing about and trying to perpetuate the book's two marriages—on *her* terms. She has no social position aside from this—she barely figures in the high society of Matcham—and she may therefore be said to function almost exclusively as the rational middle term

[11] For the Colonel's emblematic role, see XXIII, 66–68, 77. These passages indicate that we have to do with a devil of sorts. He is representative of both force (as a military man) and materialism, since he regards life as "for far the greater part, a matter of pecuniary arrangement." Since he is subordinate to a "church," he may be assumed to be a rather dim presentment of the "state," as well as the sheerly mechanical and materialistic element in human affairs,

between the world of the senses and the world of the spirit.[12] If we consider the emblematic significance of marriage for the Henry Jameses, it is evident that the antithesis between the true marriage and concubinage (or the liaison) is the chief emblematic theme of *The Golden Bowl*. The high society of Matcham is not prepared to recognize what the apostate American, Mrs. Assingham, has fully seen: America has come to Europe in its final form, a combination of financial omnipotence, finished taste, innocence, and unlimited capacity for love. Mrs. Assingham understands what the people of Matcham cannot—that it is not possible to handle the Ververs as Matcham had handled Milly Theale—with total incomprehension, simply as something to be snatched at, or appropriated. Mrs. Assingham realizes that her world hangs in the balance, that either America or Europe will prevail, and she proposes to assimilate and neutralize the Ververs before it is too late. She treats them as if they were crucial and final cases, but her method is an old one. She will bamboozle them into an acceptance of the mere *forms;* she will get them to take appearance for reality. Her failure is total.

The figure with which James dismisses the Assinghams at the end of the book is both playful and serious. They have seen Adam Verver's rented country place, Fawns, dismantled, and they have fled as if they had witnessed Samson's destruction of the temple. This is a clear indication that what Adam had all along planned, and Maggie's victory over Charlotte has now made possible, is about to take place: The false temple was necessary, but it is so no more, and the new temple at American City will offer the

[12] A gloss on Milly Theale's experience of "*appointed* felicity" is the fact that Matcham is the breeding ground of extramarital adventures for Lady Castledean, its occupant in *The Golden Bowl*, as well as for the Prince and Charlotte (XXIII, 361). For Milly's experiences at Matcham, see Chapter IX, above.

For one of the elder James's descriptions of the relation between these three divisions, see *Social Significance*, pp. 43–44.

Assinghams the barest subsistence, since it does not represent appearance but reality alone.

Let us return to the scene in which the Prince meets Charlotte. When he is left alone with her at Mrs. Assingham's, he has a series of perceptions so convenient for the purposes of exposition that they may be quoted at length.

Once more, as a man conscious of having known many women, he could assist, as he would have called it, at the recurrent, the predestined phenomenon, the thing always as certain as sunrise or the coming round of saint's days, the doing by the woman of the thing that gave her away. She did it, ever, inevitably, infallibly—she couldn't possibly not do it. It was her nature, it was her life, and the man could always expect it without lifting a finger. This was *his*, the man's, any man's position and strength—that he had necessarily the advantage, that he only had to wait with a decent patience to be placed, in spite of himself, it might really be said, in the right. Just so the punctuality of performance on the part of the other creature was her weakness and her deep misfortune —not less, no doubt, than her beauty. It produced for the man that extraordinary mixture of pity and profit in which his relation with her, when he was not a mere brute, mainly consisted; and gave him in fact his most pertinent ground of being always nice to her, nice about her, nice *for* her. She always dressed her act up, of course, she muffled and disguised and arranged it, showing in fact in these dissimulations a cleverness equal to but one thing in the world, equal to her abjection: she would let it be known for anything, for everything, but the truth of which it was made. That was what, exactly, Charlotte Stant would be doing now; that was the present motive and support, to a certainty, of each of her looks and motions. She was the twentieth woman, she was possessed by her doom, but her doom was also to arrange appearances, and what now concerned him was to learn how she proposed. He would help her, would arrange *with* her— to any point in reason; the only thing was to know what appearance could best be produced and best be preserved.
(XXIII, 49–50)

They had known and been very much drawn to one another in Rome, but when the Prince's great opportunity came, Charlotte, like a second Kate Croy, had effaced herself in order to let the Prince have his chance at the money. Alone in the world with Maggie and her father, the Prince might, though quite unable to comprehend the Americans, live a life of grateful boredom. But there is Charlotte—in fact there has always been a Charlotte. Just as Mrs. Assingham later remarks, "It *is* always the Prince, and it *is* always, thank heaven, marriage" (XXIII, 81), so Amerigo recognizes in Charlotte a persistent, a repeated event. "Once more, as a man conscious of having known many women, he could assist, as he would have called it at the recurrent, the predestined phenomenon, the thing always as certain as sunrise or the coming round of saint's days, the doing by the woman of the thing that gave her away." (XXIII, 49) The obvious and essential difference between James's spontaneous American girls and his "European" women, subject to "gross Adamic servitude," is that whereas the former seek opportunities to *give*, the latter are characterized by their *wants*. The Prince cannot understand Maggie by asking himself what she wants—she is quite cut off from the world of the appropriators, at least in their eyes, by the fact that she seems to have everything.

Charlotte is described in a variety of interesting, though not quite translucent, figures in this scene. She is like a "muse" (XXIII, 47), perhaps Melpomene, though Clio fits the Prince's sense of a historic connection with her kind, as does the extension of his voiceless recognition of the girl he had last met in Rome, whose "presence in the world" was "so closely, so irretrievably contemporaneous with his own . . ." (XXIII, 45). He reckons up her aspects as if they were "a cluster of possessions of his own," and, in a complicated figure, suggests their solidity for him: "He knew above all the extraordinary fineness of her flexible waist, the stem of an expanded flower, which gave her a likeness also to some long loose silk purse, well filled with gold-pieces, but having been passed empty through a finger-ring that held it together. It was as if, before she turned to him, he had weighed the whole thing in his open palm and even heard a little the chink of the metal." (XXIII, 47)

The figure of Charlotte as a purse full of coins reminds us that the Prince, in the course of his musings before he reached Mrs. Assingham's, had compared himself to a gold coin, so old and valuable as to defy estimation of its worth (XXIII, 23). Both the Prince and Charlotte are later imagined by Maggie in the form of the face and reverse of a "gold medallion" (XXIV, 35–36). Charlotte, like Kate, is full of things, and the Prince can measure her worth with assurance.

This extraordinarily various, commanding, and attractive woman has no home, no relatives who don't want something of her (XXIII, 180)—as Kate Croy's all do—no possessions except her two large, empty trunks, and no prospects of marriage, nothing in fact save the small "social capital" which consists in her detachability and mobility. James has cleared the scene of all possibilities for her, with the exception of those that reside in Mrs. Assingham and Maggie. The fact that she had fled Rome so that their liking for one another would not deprive the Prince of his great chance for a fortune, *but* that the strong current of feeling between the two is renewed at their first London meeting, makes the Prince a little afraid of her, and makes her, James indicates, a little afraid of herself (XXIII, 50–51). Has she come to get something out of someone? The Prince is sure of it. Some light on her intentions is apparent in her glancing account of her American journey. "No one would have" her; that is, no one offered to marry her. Referring to the wedding gift she wishes to offer Maggie, she says: "It was impossible to get in America what I wanted." (XXIII, 57–60) But when, having gotten the

Prince to give her an hour or two to help choose her gift, she meets him in the park, she tells him that she has come back "to have one hour alone" with him (XXIII, 89). Nonetheless, they set out on a "prowl" for a gift. This gift appears to the reader to be a reference to the larger gift, the gift of the Prince himself, and Charlotte is made to insist on it almost like a jealous woman. This is not what the reader concludes her to be. Rather, he is persuaded of the truth of Mrs. Assingham's observation to the Colonel, "She has done this great thing for him" (XXIII, 84); at the same time the reader is aware of Charlotte's eagerness to get some explicit recognition of what she has done from the Prince.

The pair know London well, though the Prince is somewhat irritated to observe that Charlotte knows it better than he. The fact is interesting: "It was a fresh light on Charlotte and on her curious world-quality, of which in Rome he had had his due sense, but which clearly would show larger on the big London stage." (XXIII, 90) This "world-quality" of Charlotte's is the consequence of her universal hunger, the hunger she later on expresses as a desire to sleep with the Prince: "I've wanted everything." (XXIII, 362) James has sent his Adam and Eve on a curious mission. They are to discover an object emblematic of the relation between them, and at the same time to initiate the train of events which leads to the apocalyptic conclusion of the novel. They come upon the golden bowl in a little curiosity shop run by a Jew. They do not, in the end, buy it, because Charlotte finds it too expensive and the Prince is all along aware that it has a crack. We must here follow the emblematic pattern in some detail (XXIII, 104–121).

Somewhat later, just before Charlotte reveals her plan for an afternoon alone with him in the inn at Gloucester, the Prince speaks of the opportunity the day affords as "like a great gold cup that we must somehow drain together." Charlotte is reminded of "the gilded crystal bowl in the little Bloomsbury shop" (XXIII, 359). What the cup of the Prince's figure contains is the anticipated pleasure of making love to Charlotte.

One of our emblematic clues here is the relation of Kate Croy to Densher. We are prepared to find that Charlotte is full of the Prince—or, to put it schematically, that the world of things is incorporated in the selfhood. If we now return to the comparison of Charlotte to a silk purse (XXIII, 47), we may understand somewhat more clearly what the golden bowl represents. The reader may visualize this silk purse in the likeness of those little money bags which statisticians employ in their charts to represent so many millions of dollars. The bottom of the bag is full of money, which here stands for the material aspect of the world, conceived as that which is most valuable.[13] The bag is *held together* by a ring, and above that it opens out some-what more widely than the bags commonly depicted in the symbols to which I have referred—so widely that it is like a flower. We have, then, a material base (money), a stem, and a flower. It occurs to us that James has hidden the scriptural proverb, "The love of money is the *root* of all evil," in his figure, for we are familiar with the thesis that the selfhood's devotion to the world conceived as a mélange of objects to be appropriated *is* the root of all evil. So it is not money in any literal sense but an attitude toward material things which the figure suggests.

Returning to the bowl which Charlotte and the Prince examine in the Bloomsbury shop, we first note that it too has three parts, a base, a stem, and a bowl. It is described as follows: "Simple but singularly elegant, it stood on a circular foot, a short pedestal with a slightly spreading base, and, though not of signal depth, justified its title by the

[13] See the passage (XX, 37) in which Densher concludes that only the precious metals can afford to be ugly in form—to appear as mere stuff, unqualified by style.

charm of its shape as well as by the tone of its surface. It might have been a large goblet diminished, to the enhancement of its happy curve, by half its original height." (XXIII, 112) The shallowness of the bowl itself increases its likeness to a flower. The question that follows is this: Can we identify the three parts of the bowl with those of the silk purse, and how are they to be designated? James's figure gives us license to associate flowers with containers, and we gain support for this view in *The Ambassadors* from the figure of Jeanne de Vionnet as a flower which will open only to the *illumination* provided by *money*. Little Bilham is acknowledging the attractions of Mlle de Vionnet and deploring the poverty which makes it impossible for him to court her: "She's certainly immense. I mean she's the real thing. I believe the pale pink petals are folded up there for some wondrous efflorescence in time; to open, that is, to some great golden sun. I'm unfortunately but a small farthing candle." (XXI, 277)

We may remember, too, that the novelist employed his father's contrast between the fruits of the "tree of the knowledge of good and evil" and that of the tree of life. Both trees may be described as having a root, a stem, and a flower.

Stated in more general terms, Swedenborg's doctrine practically amounts to this: that the creative operation in humanity is under a certain necessity imposed by its own perfection to put on a strictly historic guise; or to struggle up from a natural root, through a rational stem, into a consummate spiritual flower, His method of demonstration may be formulated in three propositions of surpassing philosophic breadth, to which accordingly I invite the reader's close attention, namely: 1. God's perfection is such that He cannot create life, but only communicate it; 2. It is of prime necessity therefore that a suitable form exist prepared to receive each communication; 3. This form, thus necessary to enracinate creation or separate between creator and creature, must be itself natural.[14]

In this passage the elder James, like the novelist, uses the root, stem, and flower image as an equivalent for man's natural form, that form which determines our "receptivity to the Lord's inflowing life. . . ."[15] The figure of the mold or vessel of selfhood, and the opposed figure, that of the truly individual form of the artist, the vessel of style, are both familiar. We now see that the first is equivalent to the tree of the knowledge of good and evil, and the second equivalent to the tree of life.

The comparison of Charlotte to a purse may therefore be put into schematic terms. Those who take experience under her aegis have a material root, a rational stem, and a cup full of "spiritual filth."[16] The Prince's figurative cup —"a great gold cup" that he and Charlotte "must somehow drain together" in Gloucester—thus joins the bowl of the Bloomsbury shop; both are full of the sinfulness of the appropriators. The stem of the bowl, like Densher's rooms in Venice, which hold a "treasure" of memory after he has slept with Kate, is comparable to the cloaca of the spirit, the church. For what had *held together* the loose silk bag of our earlier comparison save Mrs. Assingham's intelligence? She it is who provides the *form* used by the appropriators to grasp their world in its public dimension (in this case ostensible marriage), while Charlotte provides the form used for private enjoyment. If Charlotte is the bowl, Mrs. Assingham is the stem, the "rational" form which upholds the world of the appropriators; and her

[14] *Substance*, p. 397.
[15] See Chapter III, note 47, for the whole of the epigraph from *Society*.
[16] *Substance*, p. 397. Here the elder James, in a passage just preceding the one quoted above, speaks of "the spiritual filth of all sorts—the exuberant pride, inhumanity, and concupiscence—which lies concealed in every motion of our moral power."

husband, the completely materialistic Colonel Assingham, is the material foot or root.

The golden bowl—the one Mrs. Assingham smashes—is an emblem of Charlotte or the selfhood. It is offered for sale by a Jew, who is representative of a merely external law. He calls it "My Golden Bowl" (XXIII, 112), and we may conclude that he is willing to sell it to Charlotte because he perceives that she is its living form. This recalls a previous quotation from the elder James: ". . . the Jew was a notoriously frivolous subject . . . cultivating only such base ideas of the Divine righteousness as stood in a mere 'outside cleansing of the cup and platter, while inwardly they were full of extortion and excess.' " [17] The bowl is of crystal covered with gilt, and is therefore breakable. It was made in a "lost time" by a "lost art," and the Prince (who has the capacity to *see* with absolute clarity) knows that it has a flaw.

When (in the second volume) the shopkeeper sells Maggie the bowl, he is conscience-stricken, and seeks her out at her home to plead with her not to give it to her *father*. In other words, he fulfills both branches of the elder James's characterization of the Jew. He first sells the bowl for an extortionate price, but he is then troubled because it is to be presented to a father; it is an impiety to give an unclean thing to God's surrogate in the Jewish household (XXIV, 222–224). The high price Maggie pays for the bowl corresponds to the high price she pays for a Prince who is enclosed in the form bestowed by the selfhood (Charlotte). We therefore find references to this price at the beginning and end of the novel (XXIII, 13, and XXIV, 368).

We may obtain further light on the curious fact that Mrs. Assingham looks like a Jew, while at the same time resembling the great whore of Revelation, by considering the relation between the Jews and the Romans as the

[17] *Society*, p. 84.

elder James conceived it. As a "church," she is outwardly
righteous, while inwardly foul. The following quotation
explains her eagerness to serve the Roman prince—to "make"
a marriage which will constrain him to follow her law:

The jewish [*sic*] law was admirably contrived accordingly,
by its peculiar atoning ordinances and its perpetual implication
of personal uncleanness in its votary, to suggest to every one
of the least spiritual insight how futile this moral aspiration on
our part is, since it is invariably energized by a carnal spirit,
or is all the while pursuing really fleshly ends by apparently
ascetic methods. This being the exact inward condition of the
jewish church (and that church represents the distinctively
religious conscience of man everywhere)—namely, that its
zeal for sound morality was a mere cloak to its real
unconscious immersion in all manner of carnal cupidity and
uncleanness—it is not surprising that it outwardly at last
[least?], or correspondentially, fell under the roman [*sic*]
yoke, which symbolizes the unbridled worldliness or ambition
of the human bosom.[18]

Mrs. Assingham's feat is to unite Roman universality with
Jewish particularity—to put the Prince in the golden bowl.
This is a precise inversion of the situation at the end of the
novel. We shall find that the Prince becomes the bowl and
that he is filled by Maggie's love; and it is Adam Verver
who becomes the stem, or link, between Adam, or earth
(the regenerate Prince), and the divine love. The table on
page 307 may make these inversions less confusing.

What the reader who has the whole book in mind must
conclude about the hunt for the gift and the finding of the
bowl is that Charlotte has begun to realize that the situation
in which she and the Prince find themselves is literally
desperate. They will have to struggle to keep their identities because Adam Verver has taken possession of everything in the world which might serve to give them identity
—except Charlotte herself. The adultery will be necessi-

18 *Secret*, p. 110n.

		Bloomsbury Bowl	The Perfect Crystal
(Flower)	CUP	Charlotte filled with Prince Selfhood (inversion of the divine love)	Amerigo filled with Maggie Divine love
(Stem)	STEM	Mrs. Assingham Rationality (inversion of the divine wisdom) (church, cloaca)	Adam Verver Divine wisdom
(Root)	FOOT	Colonel Assingham Matter	Museum at American City [19] Earth completely correspondent to human meanings—works of art
		Despotic state	Spiritual democracy

tated by the hunger for identity: This final pair is alone on earth with God.[20] Like Adam and Eve, they must transgress to exist as selves. This of course is excellent elder Jamesian doctrine. How can man exercise his freedom save by appropriation? Again, how can man be redeemed, save by undergoing self-confrontation in the house of life?

Adam Verver, master of the great house in this work, is accorded a status which James's readers have been loath to grant him. Their reasons are often excellent, but they do not argue the case against James's own fable, because James has so carefully concealed it. To give Adam Verver his proper weight we must see his relation to the theme of the house of life and ask—as so many have asked, in dif-

[19] For a reference by the elder James to "God's great museum," see *Notes of a Son and Brother*, p. 182.
[20] Charlotte and the Prince are the only persons in the book who may be called human. The rest seem to be either angels or devils. And, since women of Charlotte's ilk are themselves representative of an impulse, we may say that the Prince is all humanity—the unique crossroad of impulse in the novel.

ferent terms—how *he* has been redeemed. As we first meet him in the billiard room at Fawns, he is conveniently meditating on the house of life and the steps which had led to his taking possession of it in the most thoroughgoing, imaginative, and yet literal sense.[21] He has entered the billiard room with the intent of escape. He is, James suggests, pretending for the moment that he has no conscience, and is not even aware that Mrs. Rance, who has marital designs on him (or would have if she could only dispose of a remote Mr. Rance), has stayed home from church in order to catch him. His pretense is transparent, even to himself. He is a man who never really escapes the claims that others make.

James moves from this trait to another of an apparently contradictory sort: Adam Verver's mind had served as "a strange workshop of fortune" (XXIII, 127). He is, we are to believe, incredibly rich. Single-minded acquisitiveness must then have been at work in him. Yet James is preparing us for acceptance of still another trait. "Variety of imagination—what is that but fatal in the world of affairs unless so disciplined as not to be distinguished from monotony?" (XXIII, 128)

We shall see in a moment in what measure James endows him with this quality so suspect in a financier, but first certain other aspects may be noted: "His greatest inconvenience, he would have admitted had he analysed, was in finding it so taken for granted that as he had money he had force." (XXIII, 130–131) He can hardly complain that people are wrong about his having power—yet he is not occupied in making them feel it.[22] He can hardly deny the fact of his position; the fact is plain to sight. "The latter [his eyes] showed him what he *had* done, showed him

[21] We get our view of Adam Verver through James's report of his reflections (XXIII, Book Second, Chapters I and II).
[22] See XIX, 120–121, on Milly's attitude toward her wealth, which is much like Adam Verver's.

where he had come out; quite at the top of his hill of difficulty, the tall sharp spiral round which he had begun to wind his ascent at the age of twenty, and the apex of which was a platform looking down, if one would, on the kingdoms of the earth and with standing-room for but half a dozen others." (XXIII, 131) [23]

We see from this that Adam is endowed to an awful extent with the power to make money. He is selfless in the sense that his pursuits are all dictated by his sense of the claims of others: Maggie, the residents of American City, and in fact all who approach him have a claim. He is not anxious to manifest power but to transmit it to fulfill larger aims. He has, moreover, the "variety of imagination" which may show as taste.

His "peak in Darien" was the sudden hour that had transformed his life, the hour of his perceiving with a mute inward gasp akin to the low moan of apprehensive passion that a world was left him to conquer [he is already wealthy] and that he might conquer it if he tried. It had been a turning of the page of the book of life—as if a leaf long inert had moved at a touch and, eagerly reversed, had made such a stir of the air as sent up into his face the very breath of the Golden Isles. To rifle the Golden Isles had become on the spot the business of his future, and with the sweetness of it —what was most wondrous of all—still more even in the thought than in the act. The thought was that of the affinity of Genius, or at least of Taste, with something in himself— with the dormant intelligence of which he had thus almost violently become aware and that affected him as changing by a mere revolution of the screw his whole intellectual plane. He was equal somehow with the great seers, the invokers and encouragers of beauty—and he didn't after all perhaps dangle so far below the great producers and creators. (XXIII, 141)

He is so uncharitable as to wonder whether his late wife's fondness for "depravities of decoration" might have

---

[23] See XXIV, 296, for James's reference to these seven persons, who are identifiable with the characters of the novel.

continued to lead him astray had she lived. "Would she have prevented him from ever scaling his vertiginous Peak . . .?" (XXIII, 143)

However this may be, he now perceives that his moment of illumination had marked, not the abandonment of his past, but its culmination:

What was at all events not permanently hidden from him was a truth much less invidious about his years of darkness. It was the strange scheme of things again: the years of darkness had been needed to render possible the years of light. A wiser hand than he at first knew had kept him hard at acquisition of one sort as a perfect preliminary to acquisition of another, and the preliminary would have been weak and wanting if the good faith of it had been less. His comparative blindness had made the good faith, which in its turn had made the soil propitious for the flower of the supreme idea. He had had to *like* forging and sweating, he had had to like polishing and piling up his arms. They were things at least he had had to believe he liked, just as he had believed he liked transcendent calculation and imaginative gambling all for themselves, the creation of "interests" that were the extinction of other interests, the livid vulgarity even of getting in, or getting out, first. That had of course been so far from really the case—with the supreme idea all the while growing and striking deep, under everything, in the warm rich earth. (XXIII, 144)

The reader will have been struck by the recurrence of "good faith." Like all the figures with whom we have been dealing, Adam is like a fresco in a public building. He is representative; he is meant to open out to widely illustrative use. Perhaps it has already become plain: The transition in the life of this second Adam,[24] this innocent in possession of Europe's garden, may stand quite generally for what is described in *The American Scene* as the intel-

[24] See *Substance*, p. 149.

ligible hope for America, that with our innocence unimpaired, and our power accumulated, our need for taste will one day be fulfilled. Adam has prepared a form fit to receive the divine; or, in terms of the correspondent emblems of growth, he has come into spiritual flower. His career exemplifies that of mankind. He has had to believe in and like being acquisitive, and this very belief had furnished the soil in which a wholly contrary set of beliefs and perceptions had grown.

Can we believe that what Adam Verver had performed during his "years of darkness" were works of darkness as well? Those who do so overlook James's manner of describing Verver and his explicit assertions that Verver is a person of high moral worth and real discrimination. That he is out of place in a novel may be argued, but James's intent to incorporate in him a pair of Blakean contraries is perfectly clear. His worldliness has been sanctified, and his case is put forward as broadly representative. To neglect this representative quality in him is to neglect the drama implicit in James's use of his character. The proof lies in Adam's relation to Maggie. This has also occasioned raised eyebrows because its plainest meaning is not novelistic. It is through Maggie somehow that Adam's acquisition of his fortune has been blessed; the reason he is not guilty is that he stands in a proper (rather than improper!) relation to Maggie. Our initial clue to this lies in the fact that Maggie too is representative. She is the final flowering of that "type" by which James has been haunted; she is the American redeemer endowed with a species of universal efficacy. Note first of all that nowhere in James has such a figure earlier met with understanding and a full measure of devoted appreciation. Adam Verver is the male complement of the wonderful American girl. As such, he may not satisfy us, but he does satisfy James. The relationship between Adam and Maggie is not directly sexual, but a kind of fusion of the paternal and the filial; paternal with respect to worldly matters, filial with respect to the life of the spirit. These are crude terms for a scheme to which James has given poetic precision.

"He had wrought by devious ways, but he had reached the place, and what would ever have been straighter in any man's life than his way henceforth of occupying it?" (XXIII, 145) With this reiteration of Adam's contrariety, and of the figure of the ascent of the "Peak," I put the question once more: How has Adam been redeemed, or how have his contraries been transcended? We remember the necessity of both dove and serpent natures described by the elder Henry James, and the significance of the great scenes of self-confrontation in the house of life, which in this case inspires the "low moan of apprehensive passion" (XXIII, 141). This is of course identical with the "exaltation and dread" encountered so often above. The crookedness had been a necessary preliminary to the straightness. The "middle time" (for which we may read "middle years") had been an unconscious struggle toward an end realized with the suddenness of vision: a discovery in himself of something akin to genius "that affected him as changing by a mere revolution of the screw his whole intellectual plane" (XXIII, 145).

Adam Verver is not an artist, but akin to one. It is for this reason that his relation to Maggie is his chief determinant as a nature. The artist bears within himself the love and wisdom required to represent the world, invoke life, live in the great house as if it were a representation of his own nature. Though not an artist, Adam may be—the final American may be—a godlike patron of art if he has properly subordinated himself to *caritas*, to Maggie. He may even be spoken of in this gayly apocalyptic work as the Christ founding a new temple. "It hadn't merely, his plan, all the sanctions of civilisation; it was positively civilisation condensed, concrete, consummate, set down by his hands as a house on a rock—a house from whose open doors and windows, open to grateful, to thirsty millions, the higher, the highest knowledge would shine out to bless the land." (XXIII, 145) [25] Subordinating himself to Maggie involves of course subordinating himself to mankind too, getting man to represent what is godlike, emerging from his winding pursuit as something very like a god, but putting his godhood at man's service.

It had only seemed logical (both to the American and the god) to marry Maggie off to the quintessential piece of all, the man who most fully represented what Europe had produced, whose manner was so finished, so exquisitely modulated by his sense of his whole past that he barely needed to think. Adam's effort to describe the Prince's quality is one of the delightful passages in the book. Quite as if he were addressing the globe itself, he praises the Prince for being composed of roundness rather than angularity:[26] "It all came then, the great clearance, from the one prime fact that the Prince, by good fortune, hadn't proved angular. He clung to that description of his daughter's husband as he often did to terms and phrases, in the human, the social connexion, that he had found for himself: it was his way to have times of using these constantly, as if they just then lighted the world, or his own path in it, for him—even when for some of his interlocutors they covered less ground." (XXIII, 136) To the Prince himself, Adam puts it thus: "You're round, my boy . . . you're *all*, you're variously and inexhaustibly round, when you might, by all the chances have been abominably square." (XXIII, 137–138) Noting that he is not sure that

[25] See *Notes of a Son and Brother*, p. 182. Cf. Revelation 3:12 (the prophecy of the new Jerusalem). For the symbolic meaning of Adam's acquisitions for the museum, see "Property as a Symbol," *Lectures*, esp. p. 64.

[26] Is James playing off the triangles of Plato's *Timaeus* creation story against Democritean atoms? For the aristocracy's freedom from "angularity," see *Notes of a Son and Brother*, p. 110; and *"The Velvet Glove"* in *The Finer Grain*, p. 10.

the Prince is not square in the mass, but that the point is his roundness "in the detail," he goes on:

"Say you had been formed all over in a lot of little pyramidal lozenges like that wonderful side of the Ducal Palace in Venice—so lovely in a building, but so damnable, for rubbing against, in a man, and especially in a near relation. I can see them all from here—each of them sticking out by itself—all the architectural cut diamonds that would have scratched one's softer sides. One would have been scratched by diamonds—doubtless the neatest way if one was to be scratched at all—but one would have been more or less reduced to a hash. As it is, for living with, you're a pure and perfect crystal. I give you my idea—I think you ought to have it—just as it has come to me." The Prince had taken the idea, in his way, for he was well accustomed by this time to taking; and nothing perhaps even could have more confirmed Mr. Verver's account of his surface than the manner in which these golden drops evenly flowed over it. They caught in no interstice, they gathered in no concavity; the uniform smoothness betrayed the dew but by showing for the moment a richer tone. (XXIII,138) [27]

After an account of the Prince's musings on the propensity of the Americans to give reasons for the things they said and did, James has him reply: "Oh if I'm a crystal I'm delighted that I'm a perfect one, for I believe they some-times have cracks and flaws—in which case they're to be had very cheap!" (XXIII, 139)

It had indeed seemed logical and delightful to incor-porate this young man in his family, but Adam Verver, as we meet him first, is discovering that in the process he has gotten himself into a difficulty. The process begun as a young man of twenty, the process of acquisition, of doing others that he might not be done by them, has been

[27] The Prince, we here discover, is a crystal without a flaw; in other words, he is the ultimate bowl. (This passage sounds like an echo of the Latin tag, *totus, teres atque rotundus*—complete, polished, and round.)

brought to a transcendent conclusion, a synthesis with that to which it appeared opposed, and by a "mere revolution of the screw" he has changed "his whole intellectual plane." Maggie too has been at the work of redemption, not, as he has, to make whole and complete the world's image of itself (or, as the elder James would say, to make of Adam or earth a reflection of the divine-natural-humanity),[28] but at the work of love, to make men fit beholders of the image of God in themselves.

In the terms here employed, Maggie has married the world, or the sum of it, the Prince; and Adam must somehow reckon with this cosmic disarray. He is, moreover, afraid, as Wisdom without Love must be. He is afraid, as the reader has guessed, of himself. Apropos of Mrs. Rance and the discomfited Miss Lutches who had introduced her, James writes: "He feared not only danger—he feared the idea of danger, or in other words feared, hauntedly, himself." (XXIII, 133) (It is worth noting how the adverb confirms my account of the fear of the self as of the *other* self.) He has quite come to terms with the Prince's presence, the Prince who has been set down like a Palladian church in the midst of a "pleasant public square" representative of his and Maggie's "decent little old-time union," for the prospect is still fine, or, as he muses, "the piazza took care of itself" (XXIII, 135).

Adam's reflections come to an end when Maggie, returning from church, divines Mrs. Rance's importunity, and he becomes aware of the depth of her anxiety. "When, in their common past, when till this moment, had she shown a fear, however dumbly, for his individual life? They had had fears together just as they had had joys, but all of hers at least had been for what equally concerned them. Here of a sudden was a question that concerned him

[28] *Substance*, p. 405: "Space and time are really mental substances having no other function than to compel all the objects of Nature and all the events of History into the compass of the human form."

alone, and the soundless explosion of it somehow marked a date. He was on her mind, he was even in a manner on her hands—as a distinct thing, that is, from being, where he had always been, merely deep in her heart and her life; too deep down, as it were, to be disengaged, contrasted or opposed, in short objectively presented." (XXIII, 154) [29]

Needing to be together to discuss their plight, this extraordinary father and daughter go for a stroll which takes them in a manner out of the world, or at least far from the terrace where Mrs. Assingham is ministering to the possible needs of a Prince who does not know quite what to expect of his destiny. Passing through a gate in the brick wall around the garden, a gate above which the date 1713 appears in Gothic lettering, they proceed to a white gate in a green field, beyond which there is an oak on a bit of rising ground. On a bench under this tree they have a colloquy which makes it appear that they are indeed creatures from another world. [30]

If we expect for the moment the supposition that this pair is godlike, that together they are God, we find it amusingly in accord with the difficulties of the regenerative and redemptive mission of the divinity in the elder James. God must somehow become man in order that man may become God. To do so he must get into a dramatic fix. The ensuing scene under the oak seems to confirm the supposition that these final Americans are in just such a fix. The marriage of love to the world or mankind must be complemented

[29] See XIX, 211–212, quoted in Chapter IX, above, for the look Kate Croy has when filled with Densher: She then becomes "objective." For the fashion in which divine love (particularity) contains divine wisdom (universality), and the inversion by which love becomes universal in the particular form of mankind, here the Prince, see *Substance*, p. 413; and for history as the *marriage* of the human and divine, see p. 429.

[30] For the scene under the great oak (identifiable as the tree of life), see XXIII, 158–190. See also XXIV, 91, 256. For James's assertion that the pair are, like the Prince and Charlotte, "contemporary," see XXIII, 206.

by the marriage of wisdom to the world. Their silver cord has been loosened, to a purpose they have not yet worked out—to the purpose that the self which has occupied the world's attention may be led off in a silken halter, that Adam may marry Charlotte. At this moment that scheme is but a gleam in Mrs. Assingham's eye. But Maggie, for different reasons, has begun to consider it. Maggie states their position in this way:

"We must think together—as we've always thought. What I mean," she went on after a moment, "is that it strikes me I ought at least to offer you some alternative. I ought to have worked one out for you."

"An alternative to what?"

"Well, to your simply missing what you've lost—without anything being done about it."

"But what *have* I lost?"

She thought a minute, as if it were difficult to say, yet as if she more and more saw it. "Well, whatever it was that *before* kept us from thinking, and kept *you*, really, as you might say, in the market. It was as if you couldn't be in the market when you were married to *me*. Or rather as if I kept people off, innocently, by being married to you. Now that I'm married to someone else you're, as in consequence, married to nobody. Therefore you may be married to anybody, to everybody. People don't see why you shouldn't be married to *them*." (XXIII, 172)

Adam is mildly doubtful of the notion that he "had better get married just in order to be as I was before," but Maggie explains that if he *should* wish to, she would understand: "But I only wish that if you ever should like anybody you may never doubt of my feeling how I've brought you to it. You'll always know that it's my fault."

"You mean," he went on in his contemplative way, "that it will be you who'll take the consequences?"

Maggie just considered. "I'll leave you all the good ones, but I'll take the bad." (XXIII, 173)

The redeemer here engages to fulfill her office. The marriage to "everybody" duly takes place. Adam marries Charlotte Stant—constrains universal selfishness within the form of the divine wisdom.

Before we consider the bad consequences of which Maggie speaks, let us pursue the situation of Adam Verver in the world. We return to the involved figure of the "Peak," or "hill of difficulty," with which the change of Adam's "whole intellectual plane" by a "mere revolution of the screw" is associated. The complicated doctrine in the elder James which his son seeks to represent through a symbolic screw is called by Frederic Harold Young the "involution" and "evolution" movement—the descent of God into man in order that man may ascend to God.[31] Here are two passages from *Substance and Shadow* which bear on this simultaneous ascent and descent.

The moral experience of the race necessarily involves this double or divided historic movement which we name Church and State; the former a descending or centrifugal movement by means of which the creature becomes self-convinced of his essential antagonism, as naturally constituted, to the Divine perfection: the latter an ascending or centripetal movement, by means of which the creature acknowledges himself as such recognized antagonist of the Divine perfection, to be rightfully under law to his fellow-man. . . . The play of these two forces fills the page of human history, until they succeed at last in generating a third or grandly unitary force which we call society, in which they both willingly coalesce and disappear, and which consequently thenceforth assumes the undivided responsibility of human destiny.

In a word according to Swedenborg God creates us or gives us being only by thoroughly incarnating Himself in our nature; but inasmuch as this descent of the creator to creaturely limitations incidentally involves of course, on the

[31] *The Philosophy of Henry James, Sr.* A useful diagram illustrating these movements is on p. 168 of this work.

part of the creature, the strictest inversion of the creative
perfection, or a spirit of the utmost pride, rapacity and
tyranny, so it must itself necessarily provoke a corresponding
ascending or redemptive movement on God's part, giving us
spiritual extrication from this infirmity. Otherwise creation
would remain utterly inoperative save in a downward
direction. If God should simply give me natural substance or
identity without at the same time insuring me spiritual form
or individuality, I should remain like the animal forever
unconjoined with Him spiritually, and immersed in sensual
delights. Let us clearly understand then that the Divine
operation in creation is made up of two movements: one
strictly objective or creative, which is a movement of
humiliation consisting in giving us natural being or identity;
the other strictly subjective and redemptive, which is a
movement of glorification consisting in giving us the amplest
individual or spiritual expansion out of that base root. The
prior movement—the descending, statical, and properly
creative one—gives us natural selfhood or consciousness, a
consciousness of separation from God, of a power inhering
in ourselves and independent therefore of Him. The posterior
movement—the ascending, dynamical, and properly
redemptive one—gives us spiritual consciousness, a
consciousness of union with God, and makes us abhor and
recoil from nothing so much as the spiritual filth of all sorts
—the exuberant pride, inhumanity, and concupiscence—
which lies concealed in every motion of our moral power.[32]

"The play of these two forces fills the page of human
history. . . ." Here is a figurative connection with the
passage (quoted on page 309) in which Adam Verver takes
possession, "with a low moan of apprehensive passion," of
his "peak in Darien." In this passage the novelist carries
forward his father's figure: "It had been a turning of the
page of the book of life—as if a leaf long inert had moved
at a touch and, eagerly reversed, had made such a stir of the
air as sent up into his face the very breath of the Golden

[32] The two passages above are in *Substance*, pp. 153–154 and 396–397.

Isles." And this account of history as suddenly and quietly culminating in some climactic inversion is reported by the novelist as his father's, in *Notes of a Son and Brother*. The novelist has noted that his father did not entertain the idea of revolution in "the vulgar or violent sense," and he describes the apocalyptic change in terms which parallel the "mere revolution of the screw" in Adam Verver's musings: "The case was really of his rather feeling so vast a rightness close at hand or lurking immediately behind actual arrangements that a single turn of the inward wheel, one real response to pressure of the spiritual spring, would bridge the chasms, straighten the distortions, rectify the relations and, in a word, redeem and vivify the whole mass —after a far sounder, yet, one seemed to see, also far subtler, fashion than any that our spasmodic annals had yet shown us." [33]

Adam is represented as thinking to himself that he had "wrought by devious ways, but he had reached the place, and what would ever have been straighter in any man's life than his way henceforth of occupying it?" (XXIII, 145) A further correspondence may be noted here. In both cases, making the crooked straight is associated with a single revolution—of a "screw" (in the novel) and of an "inward wheel" (in the reminiscences). The most complete parallel is afforded by a comparison of the passage (page 310) in which the novelist uses the root-stem-flower emblem to express motion in two contrary directions, just as his father does in the passages just quoted from *Substance and Shadow*.

A comparison of these two passages gives us the clue to the use of the root-stem-flower emblem. Its appropriateness depends on the fact that before a plant can grow *up* it must grow *down*. My explication of the figure of the screw which represents Adam's ascent and descent must satisfy the condition here indicated: The screw must

[33] *Notes of a Son and Brother*, p. 225.

somehow represent motion *both* down and up. Relevant here is a passage on this *double* or divided historic movement, as it affects God himself, and culminates in the "second Adam." [34] The elder James says of God: "Before the Incarnation he could truly claim to have been the source from which all things proceeded. It is only since that event that he can claim also to be the haven to which they all return." [35]

The complication of the figure of the screw is such as to serve precisely the need of describing the involvement of man in God and God in man. I find so much precision in the figure that I cannot doubt James's intention. Observe what the figure does: First, it represents the antithesis between Adam's "years of darkness" and his illumination, or discovery of his taste; second, it makes a connection between these apparently antithetical elements, for "the tall sharp spiral" around which Adam had at the age of twenty begun to wind his way must of necessity have precluded any view of the "kingdoms of the earth" in their totality, so that emergence at its point (or on the "platform") would, as by a single revolution of the screw, bring total vision. Since a screw is simply a continuous inclined plane, the association of planes with screws is patent.

Adam's motion upwards, then, is analogous to our blind struggle through the middle years to the point at which the house of life or the kingdoms of the earth lie open before us. For man in general this is the moment when we clearly see and fear the other self. In Adam's case the fear which comes belatedly, long after he has taken possession of the house of life—or, in the specific terms of the novel, has begun to collect in order to give the American millions a view of the wondrous character of human achievement—is a fear of the importunities of mankind. He

[34] *Substance*, p. 149.
[35] *Nature of Evil*, p. 332.

is afraid because the divine love is busy saving Europe, and he is alone.

Yet the figure of the screw attentively considered tells the reader that this fear is necessary but in the end unwarranted. If one takes a screw between finger and thumb with the point held upward and revolves it slowly with the other hand, the spirals will appear to rise while the head is actually sinking. The platform on which Adam and half a dozen others finally stand is reached by the divinity at the moment that it is reached by Adam. God involves himself in us in the precise degree in which we involve ourselves in him. On this account the platform appears to signify the point at which the apocalyptic union is realized, and the "half a dozen others" who are to stand on it are precisely the natures of man and God who figure in this book: Mrs. Assingham, the Colonel, Charlotte, the Prince, his son, and Maggie. I suggest that the date over the gate through which Maggie and Adam pass into the realm of their rarefied discourse, one of the very few dates in James, refers to a union of the one in seven, man, with the one in three, God.

A secular account of the meaning of Adam's figure would run in this way: When in America money-grubbing has served its purpose of piling up the goods of the earth, those American men who have completed this process will discover the world under the guidance of the daughters of America. Money, good faith, innocence, and taste in the arts will thereupon confront the institutionalized selfishness, worldliness, manners, and so forth, of Europe; in a word will come to terms with evil and with history—not for the purpose of destroying or erasing either, but in order to create a cultural order in which every human institution serves the human imagination, is at once spontaneous and controlled, selfish yet stylistically distinct, humanitarian yet capable of discriminating.[36]

[36] See "Property as a Symbol," *Lectures*, esp. pp. 63–64.

The energy which turns the screw, so that we appear to be mounting it, has all along been descending into us. Nor is God himself God nor man man until the process is complete.

Now that we have discerned Adam's function as a nature, we may go back to his difficulty as the book presents it. He has lost momentarily, but with no less strain on his sense of his world for that, his consort, his balance wheel. Maggie and Mrs. Assingham now propose to set him straight again, Mrs. Assingham for worldly reasons, Maggie for reasons of her own. They both hit on Charlotte as the solution. Charlotte, whose selfishness informs the world and has guided the destinies of Princes since the world began, is to be married to Adam's impersonal power and benignity, to be allied with a wisdom which is foolishness to Mrs. Assingham. Charlotte will be in for trouble, for to conduct herself successfully in such a marriage she must use her husband's sense of the world as her own; but to retain an identity she must think as Mrs. Assingham thinks, and the dramatic consequence is that she must cling to the Prince. (Selfishness cannot see itself reflected in the divine wisdom; nor contain it.) He is the only prospect in the book for her kind of experience. She is too much herself to enter into the communion of Maggie and Adam, just as the Prince is at the outset too much himself to love his wife. To do so he must invert all his feelings about women, must, for instance, concede them a priority in defining his relation to others, which is unthinkable. The marriages are made under Mrs. Assingham's aegis; love and wisdom become subject to worldliness and greed.

Quite as important as giving Adam Verver the place James provided for him is the job of establishing the compelling character of the situation in which Charlotte and the Prince find themselves. It has been freely and invidiously charged that father and daughter shut them out (XXIV, 82), but what has not been clearly seen is that shut out from the world of the Ververs, which can only be inhabited on the Ververs' terms, they are also excluded from everything else because the world of the novel is a world in which the Ververs, like newly landed conquerors, set the scene, engross the interest, command the property— have, in brief, all that is worth having.[37]

Charlotte's cry on the day of her peregrinations through the London fog—during which she looks in on her husband and her stepdaughter three times to see if they have missed her—is definitive: "What in the world else can we do?" (XXIII, 297,303) It is of course one thing to sympathize with Charlotte as a trapped nature, a final version of the selfhood, and another to scold James for creating a fully alive woman, marrying her to a man whom she believes to be sterile, and subjecting her to Maggie, a woman comparatively without salt or savor. But if we are to follow James's emblematic pattern, we must not become partisans of one character as against another.

Putting this question to one side, it is plain that in the sense of the book I seek to establish, the adultery must be both fated and wicked; it must exhibit the inadequacy

---

[37] I have omitted the long train of emblematic references which Adam's courtship of Charlotte involves. James seems to have had a great deal of fun in detailing emblematically the marriage of the second or universal Adam, the Grand Man or *Maximus Homo*, to the Eve, or *minimus homo* (also called *vir* by the elder James). He first named her Charlotte, the emblematic significance being "little man" or *minimus homo* (Charlotte is a *diminutive* of Carl, which originally meant man, or male). He then imagines the courtship as recapitulating the relation God had to Israel, since Charlotte is spiritually Jewish, that is, is publicly represented by the "church" and "state," the Assinghams. Adam is made to see Charlotte just as an earthly lover might—Densher, for example; Charlotte is a "portrait" (XXIII, 193) and an empty bowl (XXIII, 217). The finality of Adam's act in marrying Charlotte and its disinterestedness is indicated as it is in Milly Theale's case by the "pink glow" (XXIII, 221) of Adam's burning ships—pink standing for charity. (For Milly's "pink dawn of an apotheosis," see XIX, 220, and for other uses, 207–229 *passim*.)

of the law of greed and righteousness to reform its children, but the transgression must nonetheless be condemned. "Father, forgive them for they know not what they do" is the strongest plea we can make, but we must remember that in James, as in Plato, the distinction between knowledge and virtue is very hard to draw.

James offers then snatches away one set of balanced relations after another, so that we are variously engaged and interested in behalf of each party up to the point at which we reach his fullest sense of the world of the bowl. Beyond that point we need someone whose view is more inclusive. The first volume, "The Prince," is of course devoted to the world's view of Maggie and Adam, and Mrs. Assingham is its serene patroness. The second is, so to speak, God's view of the world, and something more, His experience of it—the first volume treats of man's experience, his puzzling and not quite assimilable experience, of the divine.

Maggie's situation is carefully canvassed by Mrs. Assingham at the end of the first volume, and to the reader her summary seems perfectly balanced, a kind of conclusion as to the sort of marital involvement the book has so far dealt with. There is a change in pitch and tone about the opening of the second volume, in which Maggie enters upon the consideration of the same questions. This is one of the signs of the novel's great accomplishment, which, most simply, is to make matters of feeling, belief, and thought undergo a change exquisitely commensurate with the change in point of view. To this accomplishment the tightness of James's situation contributes by making it perfectly clear that the very same group of elements, the very same storyteller's "case," figures for each character, and is nonetheless perfectly distinct. To this effect again the archetypal situation toward which James had been moving, in *The Ambassadors* and *The Wings of the Dove*, contributes by emphasizing the simplicity of the elements related with such a delicate and fitting fretwork of complications.

Maggie Verver, taking account (at the opening of the second volume) of the pagoda set in her garden, is beginning to be frightened. The strange tall structure obscurely threatens her yet seems to represent all the ostensible virtue of the marriages as a social device for at once keeping Adam and letting him go. But Maggie has the courage and the reserves Mrs. Assingham has glimpsed, as well as the faith in the power of love which only Adam knows in her. This Maggie is very like the reflective Henry James, pleased to find no tall assertive forms in Baltimore: ". . . I caught no glimpse of traffic, however mild, nor spied anything 'tall' at the end of any vista. This was in itself really a benediction, since I had nowhere, from the first, been infatuated with tallness; I was infatuated only with the question of manners, in their largest sense—to the finer essence of which tallness had already defined itself to me as positively abhorrent." [38]

It is with manners in this largest sense that Maggie must now begin to fight. The works of love take this form only, and the strangeness of the "tall tower" which Maggie imagines, the strangeness of the rite performed in it, the fearfulness of what stirs behind its door, is that this rite and this creature are naked self-assertion made manifest. And they are sharply contrasted with the figure the Prince makes for Adam, the figure of a Palladian church set down in the pleasant square of his life (XXIII, 135). That love acts in the world through manners, that the great writer can enforce this with style, is James's great moral contention. Maggie Verver is the person out of his whole array of persons who is given the most direct opportunity to illustrate this cherished belief. She has lived like a goddess in order that we may see her descend and work out this eminently human truth. Maggie is made to lie, to pretend,

[38] *The American Scene*, p. 305.

to manipulate the tricks and devices of the world in which she is embroiled; and it is in holding a balance between her "good faith" and her immersion in a worldly dilemma that James succeeds best. (XXIV, 52, 250).

From a worldly point of view, Maggie is completely unprepared to cope with adultery. The assumptions of "good faith" have been broad indeed. The Prince puts it this way: "What was supremely grotesque in fact was the essential opposition of theories—as if a galantuomo, as *he* at least constitutionally conceived of galantuomini, could do anything *but* blush to 'go about' at such a rate with such a person as Mrs. Verver in a state of childlike innocence, the state of our primitive parents before the Fall." (XXIII, 335) It is nonetheless with just such an assumption that Maggie sets out, and the reaction of the Prince and Charlotte is prompt. This is noted for us in the scene of the ball, at which the pair begin publicly to "go about" (XXIII, 266), much to Mrs. Assingham's discomfiture (she cares far more about public than about private behavior). A galantuomo would not remain one if he did not do something about such a view of him. "The grotesque theory, as he would have called it, was perhaps an odd one to resent with violence, and he did it—also as a man of the world—all merciful justice; but none the less assuredly there was but one way *really* to mark, and for his companion as much as for himself, the commiseration in which they held it." (XXIII, 335)

James could hardly say more plainly that Maggie's attitude is a threat to the Prince's very identity, which (quite in accord with the social arrangements of his world) has a sexual source. This is *not* a way of describing a bad man; it is, though, an implied reduction of sex to selfishness, and an implied elevation of Maggie's good faith. James is saying in effect: I will show you a man who derives his sense of himself from the responsiveness and submission of women, all of whose manners are quite delicately and

tastefully based on this power. I will show you moreover
how this actually subjects him to Charlotte, from whom he
gets his identity. And I will then proceed to indicate how
he may be subjected to Maggie's quite general love—provided that Maggie will see his problem and help him with
it, the problem, that is, of maintaining some sort of
individuality.

Maggie's realization of her situation leads first of all to
her simply going home at the time Charlotte and the
Prince are expected to return from Matcham, instead of remaining in her father's house. A struggle then begins in
which Amerigo exerts a strong tacit pressure to make
Maggie yield, as a wife yields before her husband's power
to shape and define situations. This pressure she resists.
Thereafter she resorts once more to the British Museum—
where Amerigo's family has an alcove of recorded history
all to itself—as if to try to understand what human history
is like. On her way home, she stops at the very curiosity
shop at which Amerigo and Charlotte had seen the bowl,
and she buys it for her father. Then, not long after, she
learns of the flaw from the dealer, who in the course of his
visit informs her of the identity of the lady for whom he
had been saving it. Maggie immediately summons Mrs.
Assingham.

This lady is afraid she will be brought to book. She does
not know how much Maggie knows, and can make nothing
of the bowl sitting on the mantelpiece. Maggie's charge,
though it involves her, is not leveled at her: "He knew her
before—before I had ever seen him." (XXIV, 160) Maggie
rather thinks the Prince, with his "beautiful cleverness"
(XXIV, 164) senses that something is up, and will not
come into the room where the bowl sits in its "rather
stupid elegance" (XXIV, 165). She hopes he will come in,
and Fanny, who fears a row, hopes he will not, hopes that
nothing at all will happen. Maggie's desire is phrased thus:
" 'I've wanted it to meet him,' she went on, 'and I've

wanted him to meet *it*, and to be myself present at the meeting.'" (XXIV, 164) Fanny is glad to have a side issue to pursue. She asks whether after the evening affair, to which they are to go with their husbands, Amerigo won't, in the natural course, come up with Maggie to this room and see the bowl. "On which Maggie gave her, after an instant's visible thought, the strangest of slow head-shakes. 'I don't know. Perhaps he'll never see it—if it only stands there waiting for him. He may never again,' said the Princess, 'come into this room.'" (XXIV, 165)

He may never come in, that is, since the issue is so grave for the marriage itself that it may end in rupture. He may never come in to meet "*it*" in Maggie's presence; he may never confront his other self in the presence of saving love.

Upon Maggie's saying that there is now too much to explain away (which in an earlier colloquy was what they had done), Fanny reflects that she "was there to explain away—of this she was duly conscious; for that at least had been true up to now. In the light of Maggie's demonstration, however, the quantity, even without her taking as yet a more exact measure, might well seem larger than ever. Besides which, with or without exactness, the effect of each successive minute in the place was to put her more in presence of what Maggie herself saw. Maggie saw the truth, and that was really while they remained there together enough for Mrs. Assingham's relation to it." (XXIV, 168) That the breaking of the bowl is an attempt to do away with Maggie's "truth" is pretty clear, but before this comes about, the two discuss for some pages the respective good intentions of the Prince, Charlotte, Fanny, and Adam himself. This discussion begins when Fanny gathers enough confidence to say that she has "tried to act for the best."

"I don't pretend to repudiate," she said after a little, "my own impressions of the different times I suppose you speak of; any more," she added, "than I can forget what difficulties

and, as it constantly seemed to me, what dangers, every
course of action—whatever I should decide upon—made for
me. I tried, I tried hard, to act for the best. And, you know,"
she next pursued while at the sound of her own statement a
slow courage and even a faint warmth of conviction came
back to her—"and, you know, I believe it's what I shall turn
out to have done."

This produced a minute during which their interchange,
though quickened and deepened, was that of silence only and
the long, charged look; all of which found virtual consecration
when Maggie at last spoke. "I'm sure you tried to act for
the best."

It kept Fanny Assingham again a minute in silence. "I never
thought, dearest, you weren't an angel."

Not however that this alone was much help! (XXIV,
168–169)

Though Maggie's being an angel isn't much help, since
it simply means being embodied charity, and what is here
required is something else, Mrs. Assingham proposes that
Adam should be left to handle the matter. "What he
undertook for you he'll do to the end. He didn't undertake it to break down; in what—quiet patient exquisite as
he is—did he *ever* break down? He had never in his life
proposed to himself to have failed, and he won't have done
it on this occasion." (XXIV, 175)

What Mrs. Assingham has earlier said of Adam is not
quite reassuring on this point of *his* adequacy to the situation of a man cuckolded by his son-in-law. To the Colonel
she has remarked that the chief thing about Adam is that
she won't *know* what he thinks. He is "beyond" her, "he
may be sublime" (XXIV, 135), but they will be cut off
from the knowledge. On the present occasion she is
curiously insistent on the efficacy of marital intercourse as
a substitute for coming to an understanding with the
guilty couple. Are not Adam and Charlotte "intimately together now?" And, "Aren't you and your husband—in
spite of everything?" (XXIV, 176)

Maggie's eyes still further if possible dilated. "It remains to be seen!"

"If you're not then where's your faith?" [39]

"In my husband—?"

Mrs. Assingham but for an instant hesitated. "In your father. It all comes back to that. Rest on it."

"On his ignorance?"

Fanny met it again. "On whatever he may offer you. *Take* that."

"Take it—?" Maggie stared.

Mrs. Assingham held up her head. "And be grateful." On which for a minute she let the Princess face her. "Do you see?"

"I see," said Maggie at last. (XXIV, 176)

This is "European" indeed! It has no possible relation to Maggie's sense of marriage, and it makes of her father a figure at once too exalted to be helped and wholly pitiable, for it assumes that he will bear the whole burden. Maggie turns away, moved, but not as Mrs. Assingham had hoped, toward acceptance. It is then that this merely intelligent woman fulfills her office. Handling the bowl, she finds it heavy, and assumes it is gold. [40] She says, "I don't believe in this, you know." (XXIV, 177) Maggie turns back to her and says, "You will when I tell you." But Mrs. Assing-

[39] Mrs. Assingham's eminently "European" view of Adam's responsibility is emblematically precise. Her use of the term "faith" at this crucial juncture, when she seeks to perpetuate the lie that these are really marriages—or proper ways to unite man to God—may be glossed with the following passage from *Secret* (p. 98): "And when this conflict becomes at last intolerable, that is to say, when the principle of authority in the church (faith) becomes so envenomed and insolent as actually to overbear the free principle (charity) instant equilibrium ensues in 'the world of spirits.' "

[40] When Fanny Assingham holds the bowl, she is emblematic of the whore of Babylon, "having a golden cup in her hand full of abominations and filthiness of her fornication . . ." (Revelation, 17:4). In addition to the passage on the cloacal church quoted at the beginning of Chapter IX, see *Remains*, p. 97; *Secret*, p. 50; and *Society*, p. 387.

ham won't be told. She is, however, told that the bowl is of crystal gilded—and that it has a crack. "A crack? Then your whole idea has a crack." She approaches the window, judges her margin of polished floor, and assures Maggie in almost the same breath that her husband has "never, never never—!" To which Maggie's response is, "Well, never what?" "Never," replies Fanny, "been half so interested in you as now. But don't you, my dear, really feel it?" (XXIV, 178)

Maggie took her time. "Oh I think what I've told you helps me to feel it. His having today given up even his forms; his keeping away from me; his not having come." And she shook her head as against all easy glosses. "It *is* because of that you know."

"Well, then if it's because of this—!" (XXIV, 178)

Fanny smashes the bowl on the floor, where it breaks into three parts.

After which, "Whatever you meant by it—and I don't want to know *now*—has ceased to exist," Mrs. Assingham said.

"And what in the world, my dear, did you mean by it?" (XXIV, 179)

This is the Prince, upon whose entrance, Mrs. Assingham, after a mute interchange, leaves, referring him to his wife for an answer to his question.

What Fanny, as distinguished from Maggie, means by *breaking* the bowl is, dramatically, to do away with evidence that the marriages she has "made" are failures. What the episode means emblematically is something more and something else. We have first to recall that Fanny is not so much a nature or detached human impulse as a power in the service of a nature. Her world is the world in which Adam or earth is given identity by Eve, indifferently self-ishness or righteousness. She is herself self-righteous, whereas Charlotte is exquisitely greedy, so they share the task of depicting the kind of scene which for all the Princes that have ever been, or for the *first* Adam, has been reality. As a power in the service of a nature, Fanny is worldly wisdom. The bowl is an appearance which must be destroyed in order that *other* appearances may be preserved—to wit the marriages. Fanny's commerce is always with appearances of this sort; they are all that self-righteous worldly wisdom can know.

The bowl, though, is not simply an appearance. It is like a work of art; indeed it is a work of art, which uses the shows of appearance to represent a truth. The bowl does depict the truth of the relationship between Charlotte and the Prince, and in fact between Charlotte, the Prince, Fanny, and the Colonel as well. (The Colonel's sheer materiality may be thought of as the delusion on which the cup rests, the foot.) Fanny, the stem, is the kind of thinking which holds the cup aloft, which relates mankind to a world materially conceived. On this stem stands the bowl itself, a vessel fit to hold all the ends and aims of self-righteousness and greed; to hold all factitious institutions, all social lies, incomplete (because rationalistic) truths, all the follies and evils of the Western past. Maggie has acquired the bowl—has taken on human nature if we follow the Christ parallel—by paying a high price to a Jew, who is representative of the merely illustrative or Jewish law (the law given us to show that we are incapable of living up to it). His scruple about her presenting a cracked object to a father is not simply a novelist's device. It is emblematic as well, since ritual cleanliness is precisely the mark of the Pharisaic world which distinguishes persons, saves some and damns others, and in general caters to our greed to be known as spiritually fatter than our fellows. Moreover, James has taken the liberty of using the Jew as a type of both swindling greed and self-righteousness. The cracked cup is an emblem of human nature as viewed under Old Testament law.

Yet, as we know, the cup is *providentially* cracked. It is

necessary for the Prince to be spurred by Charlotte to fill
the bowl with delusions, for otherwise he would not be
able to see the nullity of these delusions. Without Eve or
Charlotte mankind could not be saved. We have to perceive
God in a fashion "true to the experience of the creature."
We have to see the other self after a long train of greedy and
righteous errors in order to adopt Maggie or love as our
informing principle. When we do so, we may be emblematically shown in the form of "the bowl as it was to
have been," the bowl which Adam sees in describing the
Prince as "a pure and perfect crystal" (XXIII, 138–139).
This bowl is filled with the works of love and wisdom, and
to it Charlotte is condemned to sing hymns of praise in
American City. Again, as a final exfoliation of the meaning
of the bowl, the Prince is at once related to the bowl as it
was before being smashed, and to the bowl as it was to
have been. He has been compared by Adam to a Palladian
church, and we are reminded that the house of life is finally
"the chamber of the soul" (the novelist's phrase) and that
the elder James had said "man . . . is . . . destined to
house the creative infinitude within himself." It is the
divine-natural-humanity which is really exhibited at American City in the form of the works of "creative infinitude"
as contained within Amerigo, now the regenerate first
Adam, to whom divine wisdom really defers. *The Golden
Bowl* does not propose any religion other than the assertion of the wondrousness of man.

This explanation of the meanings of the bowl is necessary to an understanding of the scene of its breaking and
of Amerigo's self-confrontation. What Fanny Assingham
has done, defeats, by an ironic inversion, her actual purpose. She has the "good" worldly motive of smoothing over
the falsity of the situation. She asks Maggie to accept it on
whatever terms Adam proposes. But Adam cannot save the
Prince. Only Maggie's love can do that, and he has not
accepted it; he has not even known what to make of it,

since it seems to preclude his being "somebody," a Prince, a possessor, a man who gains his self-esteem from the Charlottes of the world. What Fanny proposes in breaking the bowl is really the perpetuation of a lie representative of all the lies of appearance, "good society," representative of the existing churches, which invert the real church, in which no distinction between "persons" is made. Fanny is defeated because she has made it possible for the Prince to see the self-limiting character of a life lived under the aegis of worldly wisdom and selfishness.

The Prince, at this moment, undergoes a death to selfhood. The bowl, separated into its elements, lies before him. Emblematically, he faces the other self in the presence of saving love. Something goes out of him that something else may come in. He stands for the first time in need of what Maggie alone can give. "It had operated within her now to the last intensity, her glimpse of the precious truth that by her helping him, helping him to help himself, as it were, she should help him to help *her*. Hadn't she fairly got into his labyrinth with him?—wasn't she indeed in the very act of placing herself there for him at its centre and core, whence, on that definite orientation and by an instinct all her own, she might securely guide him out of it?" (XXIV, 187) [41]

The position in which Maggie now finds herself is analogous to that of the heroine of *The Sense of the Past* or *The Jolly Corner*. The man whom she is to redeem has discovered that he has an "other" self; Maggie must supplant that other self, [42] must fight off its efforts to regain its position. She must in a measure act as it has acted, not

---

[41] Maggie will become the Prince's true selfhood—working from *within* the labyrinth of consciousness to help him create form without. Charlotte, the false selfhood, had confined him in an *external* form—the bowl. (*Lectures*, pp. 359, 393; and *Society*, p. 32.)

[42] See XXIV, 237. Maggie here imagines her encounter with evil in the world as an encounter with "a bad-faced stranger" in a "house of quiet. . . ."

with the impersonality of the Christ, but with the poetic and dramatic precision of a hero in the world. James's most carefully studied redeemer is a little American girl who has what may be compared to the taste of the poet—the imagination of love allied with the hardihood and courage to act.

What she endures is a kind of death to herself. She is forced, as Milly Theale is forced to endure the pains of identity. But neither her pain nor Milly's is attributable to the force of the temptation; it is rather the pain of denying oneself. Milly does not in the least want to marry Lord Mark; she is simply exposed to him and his view of her by the man she loves, Densher. Maggie has no interest in "society," but she is forced into it because it is the desert into which Amerigo has drifted. She goes in after him and finally is compelled by Charlotte to look at Charlotte's factitiously seemly but actually blasphemous version of the world—the people grouped around the card table at Fawns. In appearance this world is related by law and propriety; in fact it is related by adultery, greed, and lies. This is the emblematic meaning of Milly Theale's being led to look at the Bronzino by Lord Mark. These are Jamesian versions of Calvary. Both are forced to confront "the real thing" (here, the world as Charlotte sees it), and to bear the imputation that it is the standard to which they bow. "That was what she was learning to do, to fill out her appointed, her expected, her imposed character . . ." (XXIV, 71), James says of Maggie. This is to be a Princess rather than daughter and wife. Indeed, before she can be wife she must be Princess. She must make her inordinate concern for her father compatible with devotion to the Prince.

Here, of course, is one of the oddities of Maggie as redeemer. She is so bound up in her father that even having a child has not caught her up in the Prince's world, although she adores him. It is quite as if James meant to suggest that the Prince as a kind and masterful lover is a wonderful mystery to Maggie, just as the good faith and the mysterious capacity to ignore the immediate drama of human relationships, which characterizes the Ververs, are a mystery to the Prince. Maggie is really to marry, yet she must first, like Jane Eyre, wound the male pride before which she trembles and which she almost worships.

In the climax at Fawns, the final American, the little goddess, descends, becomes part of mankind. Fanny and the Colonel are house guests on this occasion. There is, moreover, a good deal of country house sociability which accords with Maggie's new role of the Princess really in the world—doing the "worldly" (XXIII, 318) as Charlotte had been doing it. Fanny and the Colonel go to Fawns with Fanny's rather anguished declaration as their motto. They've "work cut out" (XXIV, 123). They are to lie to everybody as a "social duty." Maggie has had in the meanwhile a good deal of talk with the Prince about the vendor of the bowl, his scruples, and his memory of the earlier pair of distinguished visitors who were on such intimate terms. It finally comes to her that the Prince has told Charlotte nothing, and that Charlotte, with her back to the wall, meditates an attack on Maggie—means to put her in a false position by upbraiding her for suspicions which she dare not announce to her father.

Charlotte had earlier wondered whether the Prince's "career" might be described as "a daily fighting matter on behalf of a good appearance" (XXIII, 290). His behavior at this time seems to justify the supposition that it had been just that. He surrenders appearances, goes to London alone, and glooms about in order to escape his consciousness of Charlotte. He also wants, Maggie believes, to be with her as he best can at this juncture, that is, to think of her alone.

She had hours of exaltation indeed when the meaning of all this pressed in upon her as a tacit vow from him to abide without question by whatever she should be able to achieve or think fit to prescribe. Then it was that even while holding her breath for the awe of it she truly felt almost able enough for anything. It was as if she had passed in a time incredibly short from being nothing for him to being all; it was as if, rightly noted, every turn of his head, every tone of his voice, in these days, *might* mean that there was but one way in which a proud man reduced to abjection could hold himself. During those of Maggie's vigils in which that view loomed largest the image of her husband thus presented to her gave out a beauty for the revelation of which she struck herself as paying, if anything, all too little. To make sure of it—to make sure of the beauty shining out of the humility and of the humility lurking in all the pride of his presence—she would have gone the length of paying more yet, of paying with difficulties and anxieties compared to which those actually before her might have been as superficial as headaches or rainy days. (XXIV, 228–229)

Her trouble, however, could not grow much worse without involving her father. Charlotte's, meanwhile, she can well imagine, since she is trapped, as Maggie had been, by ignorance. "Even the conviction that Charlotte was but awaiting some chance really to test her trouble upon her lover's wife left Maggie's sense meanwhile open as to the sight of gilt wires and bruised wings, the spacious but suspended cage, the home of eternal unrest, of pacings, beatings, shakings all so vain, into which the baffled consciousness helplessly resolved itself." (XXIV, 229)

It is through the bars that Charlotte "finally struck her as making a grim attempt." It is evening at Fawns. Adam and Mrs. Assingham are playing cards as partners against the Prince and Charlotte, while the Colonel sits writing letters and Maggie reads or seems to read, and feels with new force the anomalies the scene suggests. "Erect above all for her was the sharp-edged fact of the relation of the whole group, individually and collectively to herself—herself so speciously eliminated for the hour, but presumably more present to the attention of each than the next card

to be played." (XXIV, 230) They look all too settled and
sure: "The amount of enjoyed or at least achieved security
represented by so complete a conquest of appearances
was what acted on her nerves with a kind of provocative
force." (XXIV, 232).[43] She feels the temptation to break
in on the scene with denunciations. She rises and passes
behind the table, and each of the four silently recognizes
her, "yet the difference in these demonstrations made each
a separate passage–which was all the more wonderful,
since, with the secret behind every face, they had alike
tried to look at her *through* it and in denial of it" (XXIV,
234).

Maggie wanders off and finally makes her way out to
the terrace.

It all left her, as she wandered off, with the strangest of
impressions—the sense, forced upon her as never yet, of an
appeal, a positive confidence, from the four pairs of eyes, that
was deeper than any negation and that seemed to speak on the
part of each for some relation to be contrived by her, a
relation with herself, which would spare the individual the
danger, the actual present strain, of the relation with the
others. They thus tacitly put it upon her to be disposed of,
the whole complexity of their peril, and she promptly saw
why: because she was there, and there just *as* she was, to lift it
off them and take it; to charge herself with it as the scapegoat
of old, of whom she had once seen a terrible picture, had
been charged with the sins of the people and had gone forth
into the desert to sink under his burden and die. That indeed
wasn't *their* design and their interest, that she should sink
under hers; it wouldn't be their feeling that she should do
anything but live, live on somehow for their benefit, and
even as much as possible in their company, to keep proving to

[43] Once again we are in Gloriani's garden with Strether; or viewing
Milly's experience of "*appointed* felicity" at Matcham. This is perhaps the most interesting aspects of the trilogy I have called the
"divine novel," the play James makes throughout with *appearance*
and *reality*.

them that they had truly escaped and that she was still there to simplify. (XXIV, 234–235)

A moment later they look to her like characters, quite successful characters, in a play of her own composition, and once more *her* power to smash the bowl occurs to her. She walks further, and looks into the empty lighted drawing room. "Spacious and splendid, like a stage again awaiting a drama, it was a scene she might people, by the press of her spring, either with serenities and dignities and decencies, or with terrors and shames and ruins, things as ugly as those formless fragments of her golden bowl she was trying to pick up." (XXIV, 236) She wonders why she has not got "the straight vindictive view" (XXIV, 236) of her situation, a possibility as remote from her as its figured analogue, "a wild eastern caravan" (XXIV, 237).[44] Of course Maggie cannot afford the action which damns others, even to save herself and her husband. The bowl she is trying to rescue is after all made of the same elements as the one Fanny smashed: it is mankind that is to be saved, not persons. Out of these elements "the bowl as it was to have been" is made. After she has returned to glance in the window of the smoking room this comes to her. "The sight, from the window, of the group so constituted, *told* her why, told her how, named to her, as with hard lips, named straight *at* her, so that she must take it full in the face, that other possible relation to the whole fact which alone would bear upon her irresistibly. It was extraordinary: they positively brought home to her that to feel about them in any of the immediate, inevitable, assuaging ways, the ways usually open to innocence outraged and generosity betrayed, would have been to give them up, and that giving them up was, marvellously,

---

[44] In that "geography of the fundamental passions" (XXIV, 323), which is Maggie's world, the East is an emblem for *uncontrolled* passion. (See the Prince's figure, XXIII, 346, for the consummation of the adultery—it is like arrival at an oasis.)

not to be thought of. She had never, from the first hour of her acquired conviction, given them up so little as now. . . ." (XXIV, 237–238)

In the course of this reflection she comes into view of the drawing room once more, and sees Charlotte standing there. James's phrasing has an extraordinary effect in the context: ". . . Charlotte was in the room, launched and erect there in the middle and looking about her . . ." (XXIV, 238), a passage which makes Charlotte the most feral of all human creatures. That she has a momentous intention, in leaving the game and seeking Maggie out, is plain. Maggie, in her first agitation, flees along the terrace until she is once more opposite the smoking room. If Charlotte could persuade her father, on the ground of an intimacy and an alliance Maggie is ignorant of, that Maggie was simply wrong, "if so much as this was still firm ground between the elder pair, if the beauty of appearances had been so consistently preserved, it was only the golden bowl as Maggie herself knew it that had been broken. The breakage stood not for any wrought discomposure among the triumphant three—it stood merely for the dire deformity of her attitude toward them." (XXIV, 240) Maggie is indeed crowned with thorns when she can believe in Charlotte's power to get Adam to forsake her. A moment later her fear is realized; Charlotte has found her out. Yet even before she does so Maggie knows what she must do.

She finds herself being shown the quartette in the smoking room (the Colonel has taken Charlotte's place). "As she herself had hovered in sight of it a quarter of an hour before, it would have been a thing for her to show Charlotte—to show in righteous irony, in reproach too stern for anything but silence. But now it was she who was being shown it, and shown it by Charlotte, and she saw quickly enough that as Charlotte showed it so she must at present submissively seem to take it." (XXIV, 24)

This is the heart of the redeemer's task. She must accept humanity in all its wickedness, and to do so she must deny herself. Charlotte takes her to task in measured terms. She has been wanting, she says, to put a question to Maggie: "Have you any ground of complaint of me? Is there any wrong you consider I've done you? I feel at last that I've a right to ask you." (XXIV, 247) She presses hard and Maggie denies and denies and finally puts it flatly: "I accuse you—I accuse you of nothing." (XXIV, 250) She has helped Amerigo, and he is now helping her. He has lied. She is with him in lying to Charlotte. "He had given her something to conform to, and she hadn't unintelligently turned on him, 'gone back on' him, as he would have said, by not conforming. They were together thus, he and she, close, close together—whereas Charlotte, though rising there radiantly before her, was really off in some darkness of space that would steep her in solitude and harass her with care." (XXIV, 250) Maggie puts this clearly to herself: "*The right, the right—yes, it took this extraordinary form of humbugging, as she had called it, to the end. It was only a question of not by a hair's breadth deflecting into the truth.*" [45]

The awfulness of mere innocence backed by mere power has been qualified. This is what it is to be Amerigo's conscience, to supplant Charlotte in actuality. She has lied, not simply for her father, but for Amerigo as well. This is the climax, capped by the entry of the card-players, who find the two women embracing one another. It is a kind of cosmic change of guard. From here on, the book is busy, not with James's drama, but with his emblematic elaboration of its meaning.

And it is dominated by Adam. Think of the scene in which Maggie takes Charlotte the "right" volume of her novel

[45] Italics mine. Cf. Milly's assumption of Densher's identity—she lies to Mark for Densher's sake, convincing him that Densher loves her, Milly, and not Kate (XX, 381).

and suffers her accusations a second time—accusations which have the sting of worldly truth, for were Maggie and Adam not gods they might be called incestuous. This scene is but a development of the one I have just been quoting; the single important difference is that the decision to go to America, which Charlotte announces, is really the work of Adam, though Charlotte tries to make it appear her own device to have her husband to herself. The comparison which occurs to Maggie as she follows Charlotte in flight from her trouble has emblematic precision. Charlotte is Io, enduring the consequences of lying with a god (XXIV, 307).

This god, as he manifests himself, is not a very satisfying lover. He is "slightly stale" (XXIV, 169) at forty-six. Wisdom comes not so far into the world as charity. Adam's task is stern, and Charlotte feels the sternness. But the face he presents to Maggie is another matter. At the end of their second colloquy under the great oak, during which Maggie is on tenterhooks lest their easy relaxed hour, father and daughter together, become the occasion for confession of mutual fears and shames, Maggie suddenly realizes that Adam has found his solution. He and Charlotte are to go to American City. The conviction grows and spreads in her that he is a very great little man indeed. They have each been asserting, after their habit, that the sacrifices of the other have been excessive.

"I'll let you know, my dear, the day *I* feel you've begun to sacrifice me."

" 'Begun'?" she extravagantly echoed.

"Well, it will be for me the day you've ceased to believe in me."

With which, his glasses still fixed on her, his hands in his pockets, his hat pushed back, his legs a little apart, he seemed to plant or square himself for a kind of assurance it had occurred to him he might as well treat her to, in default of other things, before they changed their subject. It had the effect for her

of a reminder—a reminder of all he was, of all he had
done, of all, above and beyond his being her perfect little
father, she might take him as representing, take him as having
quite eminently, in the eyes of two hemispheres, been capable
of, and as therefore wishing, not—was it?—illegitimately, to
call her attention to. The "successful" beneficent person, the
beautiful bountiful original and dauntlessly wilful great citizen,
the consummate collector and infallible high authority he had
been and still was—these things struck her on the spot as
making up for him in a wonderful way a character she must
take into account in dealing with him either for pity or for
envy. . . . Before she knew it she was lifted aloft by the
consciousness that he was simply a great and deep and high
little man, and that to love him with tenderness was not to be
distinguished a whit from loving him with pride. It came to
her, all strangely, as a sudden, an immense relief. The sense
that he wasn't a failure, and could never be, purged their
predicament of every meanness—made it as if they had really
emerged, in their transmuted union, to smile almost without
pain. It was like a new confidence, and after another instant
she knew even still better why. Wasn't it because now also,
on his side, he was thinking of her as his daughter, was *trying*
her, during these mute seconds, as the child of his blood? Oh
then if she wasn't with her little conscious passion the child
of any weakness, what was she but strong enough too? It
swelled in her fairly; it raised her higher, higher: she wasn't
in that case a failure either—hadn't been, but the contrary;
his strength was her strength, her pride was his, and they
were decent and competent together. (XXIV, 272–275)

We need only a choir of angels to persuade us that this
dialogue under the tree ôf life is indeed taking place out of
time, and that God is hymning himself.

Maggie's sense of Charlotte as a desperate beast at large
recurs after this time with her father, and she begins to
voice pity for Charlotte under her breath, and to note
that he is frightening to Charlotte, who would hardly stop
suffering "so long as the little meditative man in the straw
hat kept coming into view with his indescribable air of

weaving his spell, weaving it off there by himself." Adam
has her in a silken halter, and sometimes, as she leads a
party of visitors through the great collection (she has begun to take a rather frantic interest in Adam's treasures),
her voice sounds "like the shriek of a soul in pain" (XXIV,
292).

On this score we get from Maggie an account which is
emblematically as well as dramatically lucid. The Ververs
are soon to leave, and Maggie and the Prince, seated in
Portland Place, are talking of her father's wife. " 'She's
wonderful and beautiful, and I feel somehow as if she
were dying. Not really, not physically,' Maggie went on
—'she's naturally so far, splendid as she is, from having
done with life. But dying for us—for you and me; and
making us feel it by the very fact of there being so much
of her left.' " (XXIV, 346)

The Prince admits that what is left will be for others,
but Maggie thinks they have not done with her: "It's as if
her unhappiness had been necessary to us—as if we had
needed her, at her own cost, to build us up and start us."
(XXIV, 346)

Hard is the apocalyptic fate of Eve, that wholly necessary incitement, that detour to salvation! She must marry
wisdom and be told what to love by her spouse. [46] None-

---

[46] See *Remains*, p. 251. The reclamation of the selfhood by Adam
may put a strain on the reader's imagination. However, the elder
James is categorical about this question: "The relation of creature
and creator between man and God, considered as a permanent one, is
a flagrant denial of God's spiritual humanity, which incessantly tends
to equalize creature with creator; and *a fortiori* therefore it defeats
the truth of God's *natural* humanity, which shows his highest glory
to lie in his spiritually vivifying the created nature, and making man's
lowest lusts eventually to praise him." See also *Secret*, p. 124.
At the end of *The Wings of the Dove*, Kate Croy says of Milly's
gift of her fortune to Densher: "She did it *for* us" (XX, 403). In
other words, the selfhood is forced to praise the divine love. At the
end of *The Golden Bowl*, Maggie Verver says of Charlotte Stant:
"It's as if her unhappiness had been necessary to us—as if we had
needed her, at her own cost, to build us up and start us." (XXIV, 346)

theless, what has governed man's desire may itself be prized and Maggie can cry out, "Father, father—Charlotte's great!" And to Maggie's "You know her best," Adam replies, "Oh but naturally!" (XXIV, 364) The little man is cocky; there is in his voice the accent of "possession and control." And Maggie is assured that Charlotte is not to be "wasted" (XXIV, 365); she is to be used; she is to be cicerone of the Museum. Now, when the Principino appears, even though Fanny's worldly wit and the Colonel's materialism are absent, humanity is complete. The final Americans have paired off with the final Europeans, and the Principino is the promise of a society which will not even know the cost—an abundant variety in "an achieved social fusion." [47]

Here the divine love asserts the indispensability of the selfhood to bring man to consciousness in order that he may know God. Such inversions are the very stuff of James's endless web.

[47] The question so often raised in the course of the novel as to how a balance or equilibrium is to be effected between the two couples (for example, see XXIV, 73) is answered in this final scene in the emblematic terms appropriate to the system of the elder James. For an account of creation as "an exquisitely balanced equation," see *Secret*, p. 129.

On the fact that this equation is emblematically a reconciliation of "Europe" (appearance) with "America" (reality), see *Substance*, pp. 529–537. For the novelist's figurative description of an eventual harmony between America and Great Britain, see *Essays in London*, p. 300.

Finally, on the fact that God is to appear within human consciousness, and not otherwise, see *Secret*, pp. 102–103.

XI *The Great Containing Vessel*

THIS IS NOT A CHAPTER OF CONCLUSIONS ABOUT HENRY
James, the novelist, because this book has not dealt directly with James as an artist, but with his convictions
about human beings and the universe they inhabit, a peculiar and characteristically American blend of morals and
metaphysics. [1] The intent of the preceding chapters may
be put in a sentence: Granted James's wonderfully fruitful
preoccupation with form, what is the nature of the human
energies that seek form? What is man as James saw him?
This question would long ago have been asked about a
thinker. It has been asked about James's great predecessors,
Hawthorne and Melville, because we have concluded that,
lacking a tradition they could take for granted in company with their readers, each of them deliberately appropriated certain elements of the larger tradition; and thus

---

[1] Recent discussions of James's ideas are listed in John Henry
Raleigh's article, "Henry James: The Poetics of Empiricism"
(PMLA, LXVI, March, 1951, pp. 107–123). See also Marius Bewley,
The Complex Fate, pp. 145–149. The best statement of the character
of James's interest in ideas, the "set" of his mind, is Dorothea Krook's
essay, "The Method of the Later Works of Henry James" (*The
London Magazine*, I, July, 1954, pp. 55–70).

they became conscious protagonists of aspects of the Western heritage, prophets as well as novelists. I have extended this familiar assertion to cover Henry James. My chief point has all along been apparent: To treat James's technique or his sensibility as finalities is to rob him of his historical setting as an American, and to deprive him of his title to be counted a contributor to our sense of the possibilities of experience. James must be viewed, like Hawthorne and Melville, as a poet of the human condition as well as an innovator in fiction.

One cannot reach this conclusion simply as the result of argument. I have asked the reader to experience James afresh, to cultivate a certain naïveté which might lead him to ask why a character is named "Fanny Assingham," or what lies behind James's curious use of Lionel Croy. My argument is addressed to readers who have been to this extent collaborators. A summary of the preceding chapters will be useful at this point. I began with an attempt to suggest how unashamedly and directly James spoke as a moralist, and tried to indicate the roots of his sense of the moral in his father's generation. Without his prophetic convictions he could not have sustained the assault of European sensation to which he responded so fully. In the following chapter I made a division in kind among James's works, many of which are strongly colored by the American moral passion, while others show hardly a trace of it. The third chapter introduced the thought of the elder Henry James through the novelist's account of it in his reminiscences. I attempted to show that a failure to apprehend the fundamental simplicity of "father's ideas" contributed to the belief that Henry James, the novelist, could hardly have understood or employed them, whereas he had in fact displayed a clearer sense of their usefulness as canons of moral judgment than William James. I proceeded to identify Gabriel Nash of *The Tragic Muse* with the elder James, and to demonstrate that this most didactic of James's novels affords the most direct presentation of the doctrine of the elder James.

The two chapters which follow give an account of two basic and parallel constellations of emblems in James: those which have to do with the portrait, and those which center about the house of life. These are shown to have been employed from 1870 onwards. The chapter which deals with *The Portrait of a Lady* and *The Princess Casamassima* interrupts my explication of the relation between father and son; it is concerned with the question of the effect of his father's notions on the mature novelist, who, in the eighties, displayed ambivalent feelings about his American heritage.

The three following chapters have to do with James's design for the divine novel. My treatment of *The Ambassadors*, *The Wings of the Dove*, and *The Golden Bowl* must be regarded as a preliminary essay. In the course of these chapters I introduced the third major emblematic paradigm, having to do with the bowl and its contents. Associated with the bowl and its division into cup, stem, and foot are the root, stem, flower, and sea, river, fountain paradigms. We may also recall the single most ambitious emblem of all, the turning screw. Adam Verver's "hill of difficulty," which is surmounted at the moment this modern Vertumnus is transformed, may stand as a detached example of the extraordinary involutions and ramifications which characterize the structure of *The Golden Bowl*.

If the reader is prepared to accept all these things, he must (together with this writer) confront two problems which this reading of James gives rise to. If Dante had been read by three generations of devoted and intelligent persons before it was learned that he had been influenced by Aquinas and Ptolemaic astronomy, his work would have been distorted in a manner analogous to the distortion in the current view of Henry James. This is the first problem. The second, no less interesting and urgent to

Americans, is this: How did James's ultimate humanism, so logical a development of the views of his father's generation, become unimaginable to us?

The answer to this second problem is in part at least the commonplace that we do not have the faith in our energies and our spontaneity which characterizes James. We think of such attitudes as appropriate to the period before the Civil War. And while it is true that James is usually called an American, the reasons offered for calling him one are hardly as categorical as those offered here. Much of James's work seems really to have been animated by the belief that the world can be saved by American good faith. James's critics have scouted the devout simple-mindedness which complements his complexity, and serves it as fuel.

Further, the fervor of James's American belief in the power of consciousness has often been read in the wrong context, as if the conscious man must forever be agonized by the terrible isolation of those who are conscious among the mass of the unaware. But when one has a truly religious sense of consciousness, truly believes that it makes all the differences that matter, one is immune to the social malaise of the artist in a mass society. James's moments of defeat and despair did not lead him (at least before his last visit to America) to question his original premises.

Not only is James misread when read in the context of alienation; he is also misread when read in that context afforded by the symbolist analysis of the function of language. His emblems are the icons of the unified consciousness, an account of being which is expressed in, but not created by, language. One cannot name a single emblem of importance which is not rigidly determined by an intention which must be called allegorical. No splatter of reference spills from the golden bowl. Finally, such ingenious and sensitive historical analyses as Stephen Spender's handling of *The Golden Bowl* are irrelevant. Adam

Verver is not indicative of a lapse of taste on the part of a writer aware of the burden of history. James had no such awareness; his divine novel was itself an epitome of all the history that mattered to him.

If these are the wrong modes in which to consider this American, what are the right ones? As I have suggested, a good many readers must consider James once again if he is to be read as our domestic Dante. But there are questions about the meaning of the body of his work, about its moral meaning, which may be specified here.

Many people have found it hard to preserve their own sense of the world of art, letters, history, and human relations when reading Henry James, because his attitudes toward our civilization are as detached as Emerson's. Rather more so, in fact, since the novelist is actively contemptuous of those who achieve fulfillment through sexual relationships, and this contempt is associated with a contempt for all human relationships not based on *"enjoyed communication and contact . . ."* [2] through writing or speaking. The act of communication, taking in through eye or ear, giving out through writing or talking, is the primary experience for him. His universal trope of the container and the thing contained has to do with his imaginative roots: "All life therefore comes back to the question of our speech, the medium through which we communicate with each other; for all life comes back to the question of our relations with each other." [3] In this son of the bootstrap myth we find a characteristically American hypostatization of the act of communication—it becomes so important in itself that the differences between the creatures who are to communicate with one another are denied partly because one wishes to establish the universal efficacy of the means. In this fundamental respect Henry James and John Dewey are akin.

[2] *Notes of a Son and Brother*, p. 225.
[3] *The Question of Our Speech*, p. 10.

But this denial of the differences established in nature may reach even further. The mind of Henry James was all-engrossing, imperial. He achieved a very nearly complete correspondence between the number and quality of things seen and the capacity to order them into an imaginative structure. His world is rendered wholly seamless and entire because it is quite literally the world which corresponds in every detail with the nature and the demands of the personality which apprehends it. The passages in *A Small Boy and Others* which emphasize James's concern with "others" as having a salience, an otherness that seemed much more satisfactory than simply being Henry James, suggest how fully the novelist entered into the world to grasp its every detail; but the consequence was that every alien detail underwent assimilation and transformation, so that James became the world, and the world became James. What his father predicted about the marriage of universality to particularity is an almost literal fact about the son's experience, and in the measure in which he succeeded as this sort of artist, it is a fact about his work as we experience it. One might make an anthology of observations about James which have this general purport. Many critics have said that James's characters approach the condition of impulses, natures, powers, symbolic constants, ideal limits of moral motion—to rehearse the terms used in the preceding chapters.

For James the whole middle ground of life which lies between the particulars observed and such universals as Maggie Verver's illimitable charity was swept bare for art. His father's taste for the unconditioned, which led to an explicit denial of the reality of sexuality and death, is present in the novelist, is, in fact, the very ground of his marvelous capacity for creating aesthetic order. As against the good European, delicately poised before the options of a complex culture, James is the good American, who succeeds in universalizing himself, finds the individual form which will contain totality. He became Constance Rourke's American Narcissus, intent on making a final image of the world as a reflection of consciousness, consciousness conceived as permeable throughout and rational through and through. In James the impulse of Emerson's generation to practice a Carthusian individualism came to artistic fulfillment.

But even in saying this much about the consequences of my thesis I am trenching on topics beyond this book. Nor is the explication of the poetics of this dreaming Narcissus my affair here. It must start, I believe, not with his notebooks or his prefaces, but with the metaphysical principle involved in the two ways of taking experience, the two loves, the two vessels—that which holds life in style, and that which constrains it through desire, convention, or force. The distinction, in James's own phrasing, is that between *"enjoyed* communication and contact," and that European "largeness of style" which is "the great containing vessel" of *"appointed* felicity" (XIX, 208–209). The apocalyptic democracy of the American myth unites the enjoyed with the appointed; where all men are conscious, constraint is banished. All flow into one final bowl; are ordered in one great house of life.

Starting at this point, a generation of scholars may—if they find the task inviting—proceed to work out the intricate pattern of figuration, allusion, and emblematic reflection spun by our American ancestor. Those who undertake this study will find themselves confronted by what is most American in us all—the bootstrap myth itself.

List of Works Cited

I BOOKS AND ARTICLES
BY THE ELDER HENRY JAMES.

Christianity: The Logic of Creation. London: Wm. White, 1857; New York: Appleton, 1857. (Library of the Union Theological Seminary)

The Church of Christ not an Ecclesiasticism: A Letter of Remonstrance to a Member of the Soi-Disant *New Church.* New York: Redfield, 1854. (Library of the Union Theological Seminary)

"Emerson," *Atlantic Monthly,* XCIV (1904), 740–745.

"Is Marriage Holy?" *Atlantic Monthly,* XXV (1870), 360–368.

Lectures and Miscellanies. New York: Redfield, 1852. (Columbia University Library)

The Literary Remains of the Late Henry James. Edited with an Introduction by William James. Boston: Houghton Mifflin Co., 1884.

Moralism and Christianity: or, Man's Experience and Destiny. New York: Redfield, 1850. (New York Society Library)

The Nature of Evil: Considered in a Letter to the Rev. Edward Beecher, D.D., Author of "The Conflict of Ages." New York: Appleton, 1855. (Library of the Union Theological Seminary)

Preface. Robert Sandeman. *Letters on Theron and Aspasio: Addressed to the Author.* New York: John S. Taylor; Boston: Weeks, Jordan and Co., 1838.

The Secret of Swedenborg: Being an Elucidation of His Doctrine of the Divine Natural Humanity. Boston: Fields, Osgood & Co., 1869.

The Social Significance of Our Institutions: An Oration Delivered by Request of the Citizens of Newport, R.I., July 4, 1861. Boston: Ticknor and Fields, 1861. (Reprinted in Joseph Blau's work cited below.)

Society: The Redeemed Form of Man, and the Earnest of God's Omnipotence in Human Nature: Affirmed in Letters to a Friend. Boston: Houghton, Osgood & Co., 1879.

"Some Personal Recollections of Carlyle." *Atlantic Monthly,* XLVII (1881), 593–609.

Substance and Shadow: or, Morality and Religion in Their Relation to Life: An Essay on the Physics of Creation. Boston: Ticknor and Fields, 1863.

"The Woman Thou Gavest with Me." *Atlantic Monthly,* XXV (1870), 66–72.

II WORKS BY HENRY JAMES, THE NOVELIST.

Collected Editions:

The Novels and Stories of Henry James. London: Macmillan & Co., 1921–1923.

The Novels and Tales of Henry James. New York: Charles Scribner's Sons, 1907–1909. 24 vols. Volumes XXV and XXVI, *The Ivory Tower* and *The Sense of the Past,* were added in 1917, and the whole was reprinted in 1922. This is known as the New York Edition.

Works Published Separately:

The American Scene. New York and London: Harper & Brothers, 1907.

Autobiography of Henry James. Ed. by F. W. Dupee. New York: Criterion, 1956.

Essays in London and Elsewhere. New York: Harper & Brothers, 1893.

The Finer Grain. New York: Charles Scribner's Sons, 1910.

French Poets and Novelists. London: Macmillan & Co., 1878.

Gabrielle de Bergerac. New York: Boni & Liveright, 1918.

Hawthorne. New York: Harper & Brothers, 1880.

"Is There a Life After Death?" *In After Days: Thoughts on the Future Life.* W. D. Howells, Henry James, et al. New York and London: Harper & Brothers, 1910.

The Letters of Henry James. Sel. and ed. by Percy Lubbock. New York: Charles Scribner's Sons, 1920. 2 vols.

The Middle Years. London: William Collins Sons & Co., 1917.

Notebooks. Ed. by F. O. Matthiessen and Kenneth B. Murdock. New York: Oxford University Press, 1947.

Notes of a Son and Brother. New York: Charles Scribner's Sons, 1914.

The Other House. New York: Macmillan Co., 1896.

Picture and Text. New York: Harper & Brothers, 1893.

Portraits of Places. New York: Lear Publishers, 1948.

The Question of Our Speech, The Lesson of Balzac: Two Lectures. Boston and New York: Houghton Mifflin Co., 1905.

"The Question of the Opportunities" (1898). Reprinted in *Literary Opinion in America.* Ed. by Morton Dauwen Zabel. Revised ed. New York: Harper & Brothers, 1951.

The Sacred Fount. New York: Charles Scribner's Sons, 1901.

A Small Boy and Others. New York: Charles Scribner's Sons, 1913.

The Tragic Muse. New York: Houghton Mifflin Co., 1890. 2 vols.

Travelling Companions. New York: Boni & Liveright, 1919.

Views and Reviews. Ed. by Leroy Phillips. Boston: Ball Publishing Co., 1908.

William Wetmore Story and His Friends. Boston: Houghton Mifflin Co., 1903. 2 vols.

Within the Rim and Other Essays, 1914–1915. London: William Collins Sons & Co., 1918.

III OTHER WORKS CITED.

Anderson, Quentin. "Henry James and the New Jerusalem." *Kenyon Review*, VIII (Autumn, 1946), 515–566.
——, ed. Introduction. *Henry James: Selected Short Stories.* New York: Rinehart & Co., 1950.
——. Review. F. O. Matthiessen. *The James Family. Modern Language Notes*, LXIV (February, 1949), 116–119.
——. "The Two Henry Jameses." *Scrutiny*, XIV (September, 1947), 242–251.
——. "Henry James, His Symbolism and His Critics." *Scrutiny*, XV (December, 1947), 12–19.
——. Review. Frederic Harold Young. *The Philosophy of Henry James, Sr. American Literature*, XXIV (January, 1953), 556–557.

Barzun, Jacques. "Henry James, Melodramatist." *The Question of Henry James, a Collection of Critical Essays.* Ed. by F. W. Dupee. New York: Henry Holt & Co., 1945, pp. 254–266.
Bewley, Marius. *The Complex Fate.* London: Chatto & Windus, 1952.
Blackmur, R. P. "Henry James." *The Literary History of the United States.* Ed. by Robert E. Spiller, et al. New York: Macmillan Co., 1948.
——. "In the Country of the Blue." *Kenyon Review*, V (Autumn, 1943), 595–617.
——. Introduction. *The Golden Bowl.* New York: Grove Press, 1952.
Blau, Joseph, ed. *American Philosophic Addresses, 1700–1900.* New York: Columbia University Press, 1946. (Includes *The Social Significance of Our Institutions*, by the elder Henry James, pp. 234–256.)
Bosanquet, Theodora. *Henry James at Work.* London: Printed and published by Leonard and Virgina Woolf at the Hogarth Press, 1924.

Burke, Kenneth. "Psychology and Form." *Literary Opinion in America.* Ed. by Morton Dauwen Zabel. Revised ed. New York: Harper & Brothers, 1951.

Coleridge, Samuel Taylor. *Aids to Reflection.* Ed. by Henry Nelson Coleridge. Preliminary Essay by The Rev. James Marsh. London: William Pickering, 1843.

Damon, S. Foster. *William Blake: His Philosophy and Symbols.* New York: Peter Smith, 1947.

Dupee, F. W. *Henry James.* New York: William Sloane Associates, 1951.

Edel, Leon, ed. Introductory Essay. *The Complete Plays of Henry James.* New York and Philadelphia: J. B. Lippincott & Co., 1949.

————. *Henry James: The Untried Years.* New York and Philadelphia: J. B. Lippincott & Co., 1953.

Emerson, Ralph Waldo. *The Complete Works of Ralph Waldo Emerson.* Ed. by Edward Waldo Emerson. Boston: Houghton Mifflin Co., 1903–1904. 12 vols.

Fergusson, Francis: "The Drama in *The Golden Bowl.*" *Hound and Horn.* VI (April–June, 1934), 407–413.

Gide, André. "Henry James." *The Question of Henry James, a Collection of Critical Essays.* Ed. by F. W. Dupee. New York: Henry Holt & Co., 1945.

Grattan, C. Hartley. *The Three Jameses.* London: Longmans, 1932.

James, William. Introduction. *The Literary Remains of the Late Henry James.* Boston: Houghton Mifflin Co., 1897.

Kelley, Cornelia Pulsifer. *The Early Development of Henry James. University of Illinois Studies in Language and Literature,* XV (May–February, 1930), n.s. 1–2.

Kenton, Edna, ed. Introduction. *Eight Uncollected Tales of Henry James.* New Brunswick, N. J.: Rutgers University Press, 1950.

Krook, Dorothea. "The Method of the Later Works of Henry James." *The London Magazine,* I, July, 1954, 55–70.

Larrabee, Harold A. "Henry James, Sr., '30, at Union." *Union Alumni Monthly,* XV (May, 1926), 236–247.

Leavis, F. R. *The Common Pursuit.* London: Chatto & Windus, 1952.

Leavis, F. R. *The Great Tradition.* New York: George W. Stewart, n.d.

——. "The Novel as Dramatic Poem (VII): *The Rainbow.*" *Scrutiny,* XIX (October, 1952), 15–30.

Matthiessen, F. O. *Henry James: The Major Phase.* New York: Oxford University Press, 1944.

——. *The James Family.* New York: Alfred A. Knopf, 1947.

——, ed. Introduction. *Stories of Writers and Artists,* by Henry James. New York: New Directions, n.d.

Miller, Perry. *Jonathan Edwards.* New York: William Sloane Associates, 1949.

Murdock, Kenneth B. *Increase Mather.* Cambridge, Mass.: Harvard University Press, 1925.

Niebuhr, Reinhold. *The Nature and Destiny of Man.* New York: Charles Scribner's Sons, 1941–1943. 2 vols.

Nuhn, Ferner. *The Wind Blew From the East.* New York: Harper & Brothers, 1942.

Perry, Ralph Barton. *The Thought and Character of William James.* Boston: Little, Brown & Co., 1935. 2 vols.

Raleigh, John Henry. "Henry James: The Poetics of Empiricism." *PMLA,* LXVI (March, 1951), 107–123.

Rosenzweig, Saul. "The Ghost of Henry James." *Partisan Review,* XI (Fall, 1944), 436–455.

Rourke, Constance. *American Humor.* New York: Harcourt, Brace & Co., 1931.

Sechrist, Alice Spiers. "James's Debt to Swedenborg." *The New Christianity,* XVIII (Winter, 1952), pp. 6–15.

Spender, Stephen. "The School of Experience in the Early Novels." *Hound and Horn,* VII (April–June, 1934), 417–433.

Trilling, Lionel. "An American View of Two Literatures." *Books.* No. 263 (August, 1951), 178–181.

——. *The Liberal Imagination.* New York: Viking Press, 1950.

Troy, William. "The Altar of Henry James." *The Question of Henry James: a Collection of Critical Essays.* Ed. by F. W. Dupee. New York: Henry Holt & Co., 1945.

Vivas, Eliseo. "Henry and William." *Kenyon Review,* V (Autumn, 1943), 580–594.

Warren, Austin. *The Elder Henry James.* New York: Macmillan Co., 1934.

———. "Myth and Dialectic in the Later Novels." *Kenyon Review,* V. (Autumn, 1943), 551–558.

Wharton, Edith. *A Backward Glance.* New York and London: D. Appleton Co., 1934.

Wilson, Edmund. "The Ambiguity of Henry James." *The Question of Henry James: a Collection of Critical Essays.* Ed. by F. W. Dupee. New York: Henry Holt & Co., 1945.

Wright, Charles H. H. *The Book of Koheleth, Commonly Called Ecclesiastes.* London: Hodder & Stoughton, 1883.

Young, Frederic Harold. *The Philosophy of Henry James, Sr.* New York: Bookman Associates, 1951.

Index